On the Third Hand

Caroline Postelle Clotfelter, a former Professor of Economics at Mercer University, is a graduate student of Birmingham-Southern College (B.A., 1940), Georgia State University (M.A., 1969), and The University of Alabama (Ph.D., 1973). She is currently a member of the Committee on the Status of Women in the Economics Profession (CSWEP), the American Economic Association (AEA), and the Southern Economic Association (SEA).

Royalties for *On the Third Hand* go to the James Hodson Clotfelter Scholarship at Birmingham-Southern College.

On the Third Hand

Humor in the Dismal Science,
an Anthology

Caroline Postelle Clotfelter

Ann Arbor

The University of Michigan Press

*A CIP catalog record for this book is available from the British
Library.*

Library of Congress Cataloging-in-Publication Data

On the third hand : humor in the dismal science, an anthology /
   Caroline Postelle Clotfelter.
      p.   cm.
   Includes index.
   ISBN 0-472-09529-3 (cloth). — ISBN 0-472-06529-7 (pbk.)
   1. Economics—Humor.   I. Clotfelter, Caroline Postelle.
PN6231.E295065   1996
330′.0207—dc20   96-41214
                                                       CIP

Contents

xi

Herbert Stein

Foreword

When the University of Michigan Press asked me to write a fore-word for Caroline Clotfelter's collection of economic humor, I, being an Economic Person (what we used to call Economic Man), totted up the likely costs and benefits. The cost would be having to read the manuscript. Although there are people who can write a foreword to a book they haven't read, I have not attained that degree of eminence. But I figured that reading the manuscript would not be a great burden. A book of economic humor could not be very long. Also, it would consist largely of writings by two of my favorite authors—Stephen Leacock and me. The benefits, however small, would outweigh the cost. The benefits would be mainly the pleasure of seeing my name in print and secondarily, probably, a free copy of the book.

Upon receiving the manuscript I was surprised to see how big it was, and what a range of authors was represented. It included, for example, writings by Adam Smith, Thomas Malthus, and George Stigler. (Don't think that I am going to name any of my living competitors!) But even though the manuscript was bigger than I had expected, reading it turned out to be even more fun than I had expected. In fact, many times I burst into audible laughter. Several people walking down the hall stuck their heads into my office with amazement. They didn't expect to hear laugh-ter in a "conservative" think tank, especially in its economics department. Because I didn't want them to know that I was read-ing a funny book on company time, I explained that I was laugh-ing at the idea of Bill Clinton being president of the United States.

You may wonder, as I did myself at first, how Adam Smith and Thomas Malthus get into a book of economic humor. The answer is that each discovered a paradox (or pair o' ducks, as Marx said) about the economy, and paradox is always funny. Smith discovered the optimistic paradox, which is that each person in pursuing his self-interest benefits others. Malthus discovered the pessimistic paradox, which is that the attempt to assist persons in misery increases the number of persons in misery.

The invitation from a university press to write a foreword to a book is a challenge to perform like a professor of literature and perpetrate some hermeneutics and semiotics. That is, it is a challenge to find something in the book that the ordinary reader, who is not a professor, will not find there—possibly because it is not there. I will give you a brief exposition of what I have found.

Humorous writing about economics has gone, so far, through four phases:

1. The classical period. This was when Smith and Malthus were writing about the economy—that is, about the process by which society is organized to create wealth.

2. Open season on economics. This was the period of transition from writing about the economy to writing about economics—that is, not about the economic system but about the professional analysis of the system. Humorous writing was about the pretentiousness, the opacity, and the impracticality of economics. This writing came less from economists than from noneconomists—Shaw, Mencken, Belloc, and such essayists.

3. Early narcissism. By this time—say, the 1930s—economics had become almost exclusively about economics. Also, economics had become so technical and sophisticated that only economists could understand it well enough to parody it. Economic humor became economists parodying other economists. Stigler on tail fins is a good example.

4. Higher-mathematical narcissism. In the next stage—certainly by the 1970s—economics had become an exercise in mathematics. Economic humor had become mathematical parodies of the tendency to express in complicated mathematical terms what might seem to be rather simple ideas. The number of mathematical articles was increasing with the passage of time but faster than the passage of time. The number of parodies of mathematical articles was increasing with the increase in the number of mathematical articles but faster than that. Therefore, the ratio of parodies to articles was rising. Or, to clarify,

If M is the number of mathematical articles, P is the number of parodies, and t is time, then

$$M = f(t), \quad dM/dt > 0, \quad \text{and} \quad dM'/dt > 0$$
$$P = g(M), \quad dP/dM > 0, \quad \text{and} \quad dP'/DM > 0$$

If we knew the functions f and g we would be able to calculate when the number of parodies would equal the number of mathematical articles, but we don't.

(That is not very fancy math, but I am not a fancy mathematician, which is why I write a foreword to a book of humor rather than an article in an academic journal.)

Where will economics, and economic humor, go next? One possibility is that we will dispense with the mathematical articles entirely and only write parodies, and parodies of the parodies. Perhaps economics will retrace its steps, and economists will return to writing about the economy, rather than about other economists. Who knows? But meanwhile, Dr. Clotfelter's collection is a true and, more important, amusing picture of where we are.

Preface and Acknowledgments

Economic satire is economics with a grain of salt, a rather uncommon mix. Inasmuch as the word "satire" is derived from the Latin *saturae*, meaning "miscellany," it is an apt description of the motley contents of this book. The selections, all previously published, include essays, allegories, verse, fables, cartoons, epigrams, parodies, and so forth. The authors, divided equally between economists and noneconomists, differ markedly in the way they denounce, deride, or mock a particular folly or vice. Methods range from gentle whimsy to savage wit. They have at least one thing in common, a penchant for ridicule. Otherwise, their literary styles and viewpoints are as diverse as their backgrounds.

Among the contributors, living and dead, are a Unitarian minister, a radio comedian, a publisher, an inventor, a member of the New York Stock Exchange, and a Greek slave. Mystery surrounds the death of one writer and the existence of another. There are at least two each of the following occupations: physician, broker, barrister, businessman, journalist, and U.S. Ambassador. In a manner of speaking, one female contributor became an economist more by marriage than by degree. More than one of the lot earned a Phi Beta Kappa key, a knighthood, or a Pulitzer Prize. Three were named Nobel Laureates—two accepted with alacrity, one without. For four authors whose satire displeased the pundits, penalties ranged from a jail term to rigor mortis. This may explain the occasional pseudonym.

Like tourists, readers of anthologies may choose the guided tour or they may strike out on their own. Some like a map, some don't. To entice readers who do, the material is divided into seven parts, each designed to shed light on its contents. One hopes that this arrangement, coupled with an index, might enhance the comprehension and enjoyment of readers unfamiliar with economics but curious about its content. For those quite at home with economics—corporate managers, students thirsting for knowledge, an occasional congressman, business customers, and economists—the chapter themes are standard fare for providing directions for a bit of levity.

The first two sections present views from within and without the profession of economics on the methods and other peculiar habits of those who profess it. Outsiders roast economists, the latter roast themselves. With diatribes outweighing accolades, the authors draw myriad and mirrored images of an esoteric science engaged in by people who speak in numbers and foreign tongues, never reach a consensus, and needlessly mislead the public with off-the-wall predictions of doom and gloom.

In the third section, the basic principles, premises, and issues of economics are the major topics. Among them, presented subtly or otherwise, are self-interest, opportunity cost, diminishing marginal utility, and the laws of supply and demand. The personification of insects, animals, fowl, and parts of the human anatomy in several selections lends support to the frequent criticism that economics is the study of the nonperson.

All Gaul was divided into three parts, economics into two: micro- and macroeconomics. The difference is in focus. Microeconomics, the theme of the fourth and fifth sections, concerns the bits and pieces of the economy. In macroeconomics, the subject of the last two sections, these bits and pieces are lumped together to form an amorphous and clumsy mass. What micro is to pebbles, macro is to boulders. From the micro perspective, markets for hamburger, trucks, cars, grapes, figs, clothes, and so forth, are objects of specific and identifiable interest. From the macro viewpoint, boats and burials, cars and trucks, grapes and figs are all thrown into the dumpster willy-nilly to emerge as part of a monster called Gross National Product. It can be frightening to the untrained observer.

Such key macroeconomic issues as money, national income, taxation, and deficits are objects of jest in the next-to-last section. These issues provide grist for the mill of the concluding chapter on policy, wherein are offered a variety of impractical schemes and bizarre recipes for curing poverty and unemployment, enhancing the government revenue, or whatever.

If one's hobby is collecting string and twisties, storage poses a problem. When the thing collected is economic humor, storage space is not at a premium, but reader consensus might be. Given the mysterious nature of a sense of humor, what turns one person on leaves another cold. This is to be expected, as are questions of why this piece was included, another not. With economic satire, what you see is what you get. Fortunately, an anthology is like a flea market, where persistent browsers nearly always find something to like. At any rate, it is comforting to think that this collection might possibly dispel the notion that economics and fun don't mix.

Grateful acknowledgment is made to the following authors, publishers, and journals for permission to reprint previously published materials.

Alfred A. Knopf, Inc. for excerpt from *Prejudices: Third Series* by H. L. Mencken, copyright 1922 and renewed 1950 by H. L. Mencken, reprinted by permission of Alfred A. Knopf, Inc.; and for excerpts from *After All* by Clarence Day, copyright 1936 and renewed 1964 by Katherine Briggs Day, reprinted by permission of Alfred A. Knopf, Inc.

American Economic Association for "Why Everything Takes 2.71828 . . . Times as Long as Expected," by Philip Musgrove, in *American Economic Review* 75, no. 1 (March 1985): 250–52. Copyright © American Economic Association. Reprinted with permission.

American Economic Association and Edward E. Leamer for excerpt from "Let's Take the Con Out of Econometrics," by Edward E. Leamer, in *American Economic Review* 73, no. 1 (March 1983): 31–43. Reprinted with permission.

The American Enterprise Institute for Public Policy Research, Washington, D.C., and Herbert Stein for "A Crypto-Liberal Takes the Cure," in *On the Other Hand . . .* by Herbert Stein (Washington, D.C.: AEI Press, 1995). Reprinted with permission.

A.P. Watt Ltd on behalf of Crystal Hale and Jocelyn Herbert for "The Negotiable Cow" and "The Tax on Virtue," in *Uncommon Law*, by A.P. Herbert. Reprinted with permission.

Atlanta Constitution for excerpt from a speech by Edward E. Yardeni, from a column by Nick Poulos, in *Atlanta Constitution* (February 24, 1983).

Augustus M. Kelley Publishers for excerpts from "The Jevonian Criticism of Marx," by George Bernard Shaw, in *Today* 3 (January 1885): 22–26, reprinted in *The Common Sense of Political Economy and Selected Papers and Reviews on Economic Theory,* vol. 2, by Philip H. Wicksteed (New York: Augustus M. Kelley Publishers, 1950); for excerpt from *Political Economy and Politics,* by Thomas de Quincey, edited by David Masson (London: A. and C. Black, Soho Square, 1897), reprinted 1970 by Augustus M. Kelley Publishers; and for excerpt from *The Alphabet of Economic Science,* by Philip H. Wicksteed (New York: Augustus M. Kelley Publishers, 1970). Reprinted with permission.

Peter L. Bernstein for "A Modest Proposal," by Linhart Stearns, in *Bernstein-Macaulay Bulletin,* September 1, 1958. Reprinted with permission.

Helen Bevington and Eva W. Lekachman for "Jeremy Bentham," by Helen Bevington, in *A History of Economic Ideas,* by Robert Lekachman (New York: McGraw-Hill Book Company, 1959). Copyright © 1959 by Robert Lekachman. Reprinted with permission.

Alan S. Blinder for "Christmas, Revisited," by Alan S. Blinder, in *Boston Globe,* January 11, 1983. Reprinted with permission.

Boston Globe for "Recovery, Recovery, Recovery, Now!" cartoon, by Larry Johnson, *Boston Globe,* January 11, 1983. Reprinted courtesy of *The Boston Globe.*

Kenneth E. Boulding for excerpt from "The Green Stamp Plan," in *Economics As a Science,* by Kenneth E. Boulding (New York: McGraw-Hill Book Company, 1970). Copyright © Kenneth E. Boulding. Reprinted with permission.

Cambridge University Press for excerpt from *Turgot on Progress, Sociology, and Economics,* edited by Ronald L. Meek (Cambridge: Cambridge University Press, 1973). Reprinted with permission.

Canadian Political Science Association and Barbara Nimmo for excerpt from "What Is Left of Adam Smith?" by Stephen B. Leacock, *Canadian Journal of Economics and Political Science* 1 (1935): 42–43. Reprinted with permission.

Harvard University Press for quote by Anne-Robert-Jacques Turgot, Baron de l'Aulne, from *The Prophets of Paris*, by Frank E. Manual (New York: Harper Torchbooks, 1965). Reprinted with permission.

Harvard University Press and Stephen M. Stigler for "Stigler's First Law of Sympathy" and "The Alarming Cost of Model Changes," by George J. Stigler. Reprinted by permission of the publishers from *The Intellectual and the Market Place* by George J. Stigler, Cambridge, Mass.: Harvard University Press, Copyright © 1963 by George J. Stigler; © 1984 by the President and Fellows of Harvard College.

Henry Holt and Company, Inc. for "The Secret Sits" and "The Hardship of Accounting," by Robert Frost, from *The Poetry of Robert Frost* edited by Edward Connery Lathem. Copyright 1936, 1942 by Robert Frost. Copyright © 1964, 1970 by Lesley Frost Ballantine. Copyright © 1969 by Holt, Rinehart and Winston. Reprinted by permission of Henry Holt and Company, Inc.

Houghton Mifflin Company for excerpt from *Almost Everyone's Guide to Economics*, by John Kenneth Galbraith and Nicole Salinger, copyright © 1978 by John Kenneth Galbraith; for excerpt from *Economics, Peace and Laughter*, by John Kenneth Galbraith, copyright © 1971 by John Kenneth Galbraith; and for excerpts from *A Life in Our Times*, by John Kenneth Galbraith, copyright © 1981 by John Kenneth Galbraith. Reprinted with permission.

Johnny Hart Studios for B.C. cartoon by Johnny Hart. Reprinted with permission.

Journal of Finance for "Biological Analogies for Money: A Crucial Breakthrough," by Alfred Martial, Unemployed, *Journal of Finance* 24, no. 1 (March 1969): 111–12. Reprinted with permission.

Irving Kristol for excerpt from "The Economic Common Sense of Pollution," by Larry E. Ruff, *Public Interest,* no. 19 (Spring 1970): 69. Copyright © National Affairs, Inc. Reprinted with permission.

Little, Brown and Company for "The Market Price," by Emily Dickinson, from *The Complete Poems of Emily Dickinson* edited by Thomas H. Johnson. Copyright 1929 by Martha Dickinson

Saturday Evening Post for excerpt from "Science vs. Humanities," by Jacques Barzun, *Saturday Evening* Post (1958), reprinted from *The Saturday Evening Post* © 1958; and for "Money" by Gertrude Stein, *Saturday Evening Post* (June 13, 1936); reprinted from *The Saturday Evening Post* © 1936. Reprinted with permission.

Vivian Shapiro for Bryan Sterling for excerpt from *The Best of Will Rogers,* edited by Bryan B. Sterling (New York: Crown Publishers, 1979), 95–96. Reprinted with permission.

Herbert Stein for "How To Introduce An Economist," by Herbert Stein, in *Fortune Magazine* (November 30, 1981): 134–35, reprinted in *Washington Bedtime Stories,* by Herbert Stein, The Free Press, 1984; and for "Verbal Windfall," by Herbert Stein, in *New York Times Magazine* (September 9, 1979), reprinted in *Washington Bedtime Stories,* by Herbert Stein, The Free Press, 1984. Reprinted with permission.

Stephen M. Stigler for excerpt from "A Dialogue in the Proper Economic Role of the State," by George J. Stigler, Selected Paper No. 7, Graduate School of Business, University of Chicago, 1963. Reprinted with permission.

Transaction Books for "The Stochastic Variable," "X Cantos," and "The Inflationary Spiral," in *Beasts, Ballads, and Bouldingisms,* by Kenneth E. Boulding (New Brunswick, N.J.: Transaction Books, 1980). Reprinted with permission.

John Trever for a cartoon, by Trever (after Escher), in *Albuquerque Journal,* 1982. Copyright © 1982 by John Trever. Reprinted with permission.

Tribune Media Services for a cartoon by Bill Schorr, *Los Angeles Herald,* 1982. Reprinted by permission: Tribune Media Services.

Universal Press Syndicate for cartoon by Tony Auth in *Philadelphia Inquirer,* 1979; and for cartoon by Pat Oliphant, copyright © 1974 *Denver Post.* Reprinted with permission.

University of Chicago Press for excerpt from "Proxies and Dummies," by Fritz Machlup, *Journal of Political Economy* 82, no. 4: 892; for "A First Lesson in Econometrics," by John J. Seigfried, *Journal of Political Economy* 78, no. 6: 1378–79; for "The Economics of the Afterlife," by Scott Gordon, *Journal of Political Economy* 88, no. 1: 213–14; for "The Economics of Brushing

Teeth," by Alan S. Blinder, *Journal of Political Economy* 82, no. 4: 887–91; for "A Note on the Opportunity Cost of Marriage," by Gary North, *Journal of Political Economy* 76, no. 2: 321–23; for "Marriage Customs and Opportunity Costs," by Madelyn L. Kafoglis, *Journal of Political Economy* 78, no. 2: 421–23; for "Toward a Deeper Economics of Sleeping," by T. C. Bergstrom, *Journal of Political Economy* 84, no. 2: 411–12; for "The Birth of Stagflation: A Fable," by Christopher U. Light, *Journal of Political Economy* 88, no. 6: 1255–59; and for "Twas a Night in the Sixties," by Martin S. Feldstein, *Journal of Political Economy* 89, no. 6: 1266–69. Reprinted with permission.

Wall Street Journal for "Rubik's Fiscal Policy," in *Wall Street Journal,* February 17, 1983: 30. Reprinted with permission.

W.H. Freeman and Company for excerpt from "From Malthus," from *Essay on the Principle of Population,* second edition, by Thomas R. Malthus, and for "On Malthus," by William Wordsworth, in *Population, Evolution and Birth Control: A Collage of Controversial Ideas,* assembled by Garrett Hardin (San Francisco: W.H. Freeman and Company, 1969). Reprinted with permission.

W. W. Norton & Company, Inc. for excerpt from *How to Lie with Statistics,* by Darrell Huff (New York: W. W. Norton Inc., 1954). Reprinted with permission.

Every effort has been made to trace the ownership of all copyrighted material in this book and to obtain permission for its use.

Part 1

Economists End-to-End—As Ithers See Them

Introduction

If you've driven U.S. highways in the Southeast, you soon become inured to giant outdoor advertising of anything from fast food restaurants to fireworks, textile outlets to motel accommodations, peaches to pecans. But imagine your surprise when going south on Interstate 85, near Spartanburg, South Carolina, to read this billboard:

> IF ALL ECONOMISTS WERE LAID END-TO-END . . .
> IT WOULD BE A GOOD THING.

Whether the sign was intended as a public service could not be determined—while end-to-end jokes about economists are virtually endless, it is not often that one is writ so large. Nonetheless, most economists take such joshing in stride, often joining in the fray with enthusiasm, as the pieces in this section illustrate.

Herbert Stein (1916–) is former chairman of the president's Council of Economic Advisers and, formerly, Professor of Economics at the University of Virginia. He is a senior fellow at the American Enterprise Institute and a regular contributor to the *Wall Street Journal*. He earned his Ph.D. at the University of Chicago. In "How to Introduce an Economist," written in 1981, Stein notes that a business meeting featuring an economist as speaker must be tax deductible—it is surely not for fun.

Professing himself a loyal advocate of the traditional tenets of private enterprise, H. L. Mencken (1880—1956) directs his caustic wit at the writings of economists who exhibit "the mental

timorousness and conformity which go . . . with school teaching."
The excerpt of "The Dismal Science" is taken from a collection of
Mencken's work in the period 1919–27. An authority on America's language and critic of its weaknesses, Mencken was a
founder of the *American Mercury* and a journalist for the *Baltimore Sun*.

In vivid contrast to Mencken's tone is the gentleness of
"Jeremy Bentham," a verse by Helen Bevington (1906–), an emeritus professor at Duke University. In his review of her book, *The
World and the Bo Tree,* in the *New York Times Book Review,* Tom
Sleigh called Bevington a "tireless tourist," noting her travels to
exotic places of the world between the ages 74 and 84. The verse,
published in the 1950s, teases Jeremy Bentham (1748–1832) for
his efforts to quantify happiness, alluding to what was called the
Felicific Calculus. Bevington does not refer to an unusual aspect of
Bentham's "after" life: following his instructions, his reconstructed skeleton and mummified head reside in a glass case at
University College, London.

Edmund Clerihew Bentley (1875–1956), British barrister, author, and journalist, is famous for an unusual verse form called
"clerihew," of which "John Stuart Mill" is an example.

According to Dwane Powell's cartoon, when economists take
over, even the local bar experiences chaos. The cartoon appeared
in 1980.

I am indebted to Dudley Dillard for the idea of including a
section of the most familiar economic jokes. Professor Dillard, the
respected University of Maryland economist, was familiar to
many graduate students as the author of a 1948 book on Keynesian economics that was rare indeed: it was understandable.
Dillard died in 1992.

In 1973, Martin Bronfenbrenner (1914–) presented a whimsical list of "an even dozen" petty and often contradictory failings
of economists and their trade. His concluding moral is that the
economist "had best 'do his own thing.'" Bronfenbrenner was
Kenan Professor of Economics at Duke University until his retirement in 1984. He is noted for his work on stagflation.

Myron E. Sharpe (1928–), president of M. E. Sharpe Inc., is
editor and publisher of *Challenge.* In the excerpt of "Why Economists Disagree," published in 1973, Sharpe paints a Brueghelian
image of the world of economics and its assorted practitioners.
That he, too, is a practitioner is supported by his claim that at one
time he had been "a publisher by day and an economist by night."

In his preface to *The Theory of the Leisure Class,* John Kenneth Galbraith said: "if Veblen is to be enjoyed, he must be read very carefully and slowly." To fully comprehend the brief passages quoted here, it also helps to be a botanist with a dictionary. Writing in 1898, Thorstein Veblen (1857–1929) had fun with words in his acid critique of economics and its shortcomings as an evolutionary science.

Almost twenty years ago, *Forbes Magazine* carried an article entitled, "But *Ceteribus* Are Never *Paribus,*" in which the writer attended a gathering of monetarists where "the economists were busy attacking each other's models . . . [and] . . . seemed to delight in confusing each other." The excerpt of "Bluffing the Value Theory," by George Bernard Shaw (1856–1950), is a good example of this mutual "jostling" of economists. The Shaw-Wicksteed debates began with the publication of "Das Kapital: A Criticism," by Philip H. Wicksteed, in 1884. Shaw published a rejoinder and the battle was engaged—the piece included here was written in 1889.

Shaw was a British (or, more accurately, Irish—he was born in Dublin) dramatist, essayist, vegetarian, and pamphleteer who slightly disliked capitalism. He was a friend of the Webbs and a founder of the London School of Economics and Political Science in 1895. When he was awarded the Nobel Prize for literature in 1925, he was reluctant to accept. One reason was his lifelong aversion to titles and honors. He had declined the Order of Merit; he had refused honorary university degrees because he thought them unfair to those who worked for such degrees. Furthermore, he was already wealthy, and only when he realized that he could put the 118,165 Swedish kronor to good use did he accept the award—he used the entire amount to finance a society for making Swedish literature available in English.

"Life among the Econ," written in 1973, is a parody of the clannishness of economists, their feeling of superiority to other social scientists, and the evolution of specialized areas within the profession. Unlike most economic articles, Axel Leijonhufvud's foray in "Econography" is written in a style with potential appeal even for those "outsiders" who are the objects of "tribal" mistrust. Professor Leijonhufvud is on the faculty of the Department of Economics at the University of California, Los Angeles.

How to Introduce an Economist

There are three lines to avoid, one joke worth considering, and a credible claim to be made.
                                                        —Herbert Stein

Summer is over, and the season of the business convention is upon us again. From White Sulphur Springs to Palm Springs, resorts will be filled with meetings of trade associations and corporations, each featuring a well-balanced program of golf and lectures. The presence of an economist on these programs is obligatory, because the Internal Revenue Service believes that a conference including a lecture by an economist cannot be for the purpose of pleasure and therefore must be a deductible expense.

As a result, hundreds of corporate executives and trade-association presidents are going to face the problem of introducing an economist. It is a good bet that over half of them will use one, two, or even three of the following lines:

1. "Economics is the dismal science." That was a favorite line of President Nixon's early in his Administration, perhaps because that was the only thing his speechwriter on economics, William Safire, knew about the subject. As time passed, both the President and his speechwriter learned more and gave up the cliché.

It is not an apt remark. Economics as a science is dismal only in the sense that it recognizes the existence of limits. But so do all sciences. Geometry is not called dismal because it says that the square of the hypotenuse cannot exceed the sum of the squares of the other two sides. Chemistry is not called dismal because two units of hydrogen have to be combined with one unit of oxygen to make water. No one goes around saying that these limits could be escaped by cutting marginal tax rates.

Now it is true that economists do not know where their limits are as well as other scientists know their limits. At times, economists have been too pessimistic in their judgments about the location of the limits. This was surely true of Malthus and his followers, who argued that laws of economics and nature destined man to live at the level of subsistence. But such pessimism is not an inherent feature of the science. In our time, the prevailing error has probably been to be excessively optimistic—to overestimate the productive capacity of the system—and that has led to inflationary policy.

2. "As President Truman said, 'I wish that I had a one-armed economist, so that he wouldn't say on the one hand and on the other hand.'" If that was what Mr. Truman wanted, he was wrong. Economics is an uncertain science. To all the questions difficult enough to reach the President, the answers are uncertain. If the answers could be given with 100% confidence, the decisions could be made by a lesser official. It is the President's role to decide what to do when no one "knows" what to do. It is the role of the President's economic advisers to tell him of his options and of the POSSIBLE consequences of his decision. It is their role to tell him that on the one hand this might happen and on the other hand that might happen. If the President isn't told that, he doesn't have the information he needs.

3. "Economists never agree." This is sometimes buttressed with a quotation attributed to George Bernard Shaw that if all economists were laid end to end, they would not reach a conclusion.

That is, in fact, not true. Economists agree on many things—probably on most things. It has been observed that if almost any economic subject is discussed in a group including economists and non-economists, the economists are likely to agree with each other and to disagree with the consensus of the non-economists. The contrary impression results in part from the fact that non-economists look to economists mainly for answers to the questions on which economics is most uncertain—notably the short-run forecast for the economy. Even on that subject there is usually not much disagreement. For example, in October's BLUE CHIP survey of economic forecasters, 30 out of 44 said that the real increase of the GNP between 1981 and 1982 would be between 1.2% and 2.9%. That is TOO MUCH agreement. The true range of probability is greater than that. On such matters the profession is divided into two groups. Most fall in the category of sheep, who cluster together to reduce the danger of an exceptional error. A few are contrarians, who exploit the sheepishness of the rest to distinguish themselves and hope for exceptional success.

If it is necessary to tell a joke in introducing an economist, the best one goes like this:

President Ford and Secretary Brezhnev were negotiating in the Kremlin. Throughout several days of discussion, Ford had on the table next to his place a bulging black briefcase, which he never opened. When the negotiations were satisfactorily concluded, Brezhnev asked Ford what was in the briefcase. Ford said that it was full of Colorado black beetles, and if the Russians had not agreed to his desires he would have released the beetles and they would have destroyed Soviet agriculture.

The following year negotiations were held in the White House. Brezhnev had alongside his chair a large wooden box, which he never opened. At the end of the talks, in similar circumstances, Brezhnev explained that if the outcome had not been satisfactory he would have opened the box and released its contents, a Hungarian economist, who would have destroyed the U.S. economy.

That story is, of course, most suitable for the introduction of a Hungarian economist, an occasion that arises only rarely in the U.S. Moreover, it is quite unfair, because the economists who have come to the U.S. from Hungary have been quite constructive.

In any case, there is no need to introduce an economist with a joke. It is done, presumably, to put the audience in a tolerant frame of mind, but that doesn't last. It only succeeds in irritating the economist, who then feels obliged to continue with other jokes. If the convention wants jokes, it should engage Art Buchwald. Economists should not be expected to tell jokes for one-fourth of Buchwald's fee.

A sufficient introduction of an economist might be the following:

We will now hear from Mr. ____, professor of economics at ____. He has spent his working life studying, teaching, and practicing economics. He is not a fortune-teller. He does not know when interest rates are going to go down. If he knew that, he would have already told the public and it would be too late for you to profit from the information. But he knows things about the future of interest rates that fortune-tellers do not know. He knows what seems to have made interest rates fluctuate in the past and what may influence them in the future. I use interest rates, of course, only as an example of the many aspects of the economic present and future with which we are concerned.

Professor ____ has in the past served as a government official. But he is not a political partisan, and we have invited him here not to present the views of any political party but to tell us what economics has to say, as well as he can. We have abandoned our past practice of inviting two economists, one Republican and one Democrat, with the thought that we could distill the truth from their competing statements. We found that this only gave us a cat-and-dog fight, which showed only who was the better debater—probably meaning the less honest.

Professor ____ has been a teacher and an adviser to government officials. We have asked him to take a similar role with us, and not to seek the role of salesman or entertainer.

Since many of you are already wearing your golf shoes, I may illustrate the role of the economist by comparison with the role of the teaching golf pro. He can instruct you in the rules of the game and he can explain to you what techniques tend to make for success and what do not. Where there are differences of opinion about that among qualified people, he can tell you what they are. But he cannot play the game for you. He cannot give you the physical equipment, the coordination, the judgment that make a good golfer. Some of you may become better golfers than the pro. Many of you will never break a 100. But you will all learn from him. So the economist cannot tell you what is going to happen or what you should do, but he can supply you with some of the information and ways of thinking that will be helpful to you in making up your own minds. He is worth listening to.

H. L. Mencken

The Dismal Science (excerpt)

Every man, as the Psalmist says, to his own poison, or poisons, as the case may be. One of mine, following hard after theology, is political economy. What! Political economy, that dismal science? Well, why not? Its dismalness is largely a delusion, due to the fact that its chief ornaments, at least in our own day, are university professors. The professor must be an obscurantist or he is nothing; he has a special and unmatchable talent for dullness; his central aim is not to expose the truth clearly, but to exhibit his profundity, his esotericity—in brief, to stagger sophomores and other professors. . . .

. . . [P]olitical economy continues to be swathed in dullness. As I say, however, that dullness is only superficial. There is no more engrossing book in the English language than Adam Smith's "The Wealth of Nations"; surely the eighteenth century produced nothing that can be read with greater ease to-day. Nor is there any inherent reason why even the most technical divisions of its subject should have gathered cobwebs with the passing of the years. Taxation, for example, is eternally lively; it concerns nine-tenths of us more directly than either smallpox or golf, and has just as much drama in it; moreover, it has been mellowed and made gay by as many gaudy, preposterous theories. As for foreign exchange, it is almost as romantic as young love, and quite as resistent to formulae. . . .

. . . [T]he amateur of such things must be content to wrestle with the professors, seeking the violet of human interest beneath the avalanche of their graceless parts of speech. A hard business, I daresay, to one not practiced, and to its hardness there is added the disquiet of a doubt. That doubt does not concern itself with the

8

doctrine preached, at least not directly. There may be in it nothing intrinsically dubious; on the contrary, it may appear as sound as the binomial theorem, as well supported as the dogma of infant damnation. But all the time a troubling question keeps afloat in the air, and that is briefly this: What would happen to the learned professors if they took the other side? In other words, to what extent is political economy, as professors expound and practice it, a free science, in the sense that mathematics and physiology are free sciences? At what place, if any, is speculation pulled up by a rule that beyond lies treason, anarchy and disaster? These questions, I hope I need not add, are not inspired by any heterodoxy in my own black heart. I am, in many fields, a flouter of the accepted revelation and hence immoral, but the field of economics is not one of them. Here, indeed, I know of no man who is more orthodox than I am. I believe that the present organization of society, as bad as it is, is better than any other that has ever been proposed. I reject all the sure cures in current agitation, from government ownership to the single tax. I am in favor of free competition in all human enterprises, and to the utmost limit. I admire successful scoundrels, and shrink from Socialists as I shrink from Methodists. But all the same the aforesaid doubt pursues me when I plow through the solemn disproofs and expositions of the learned professors of economics, and that doubt will not down. It is not logical or evidential, but purely psychological. And what it is grounded on is an unshakable belief that no man's opinion is worth a hoot, however well supported and maintained, so long as he is not absolutely free, if the spirit moves him, to support and maintain the exactly contrary opinion. In brief, human reason is a weak and paltry thing so long as it is not wholly free reason. The fact lies in its very nature, and is revealed by its entire history. A man may be perfectly honest in a contention, and he may be astute and persuasive in maintaining it, but the moment the slightest compulsion to maintain it is laid upon him, the moment the slightest external reward goes with his partisanship or the slightest penalty with its abandonment, then there appears a defect in his ratiocination that is more deep-seated than any error in fact and more destructive than any conscious and deliberate bias. He may seek the truth and the truth only, and bring up his highest talents and diligence to the business, but always there is a specter behind his chair, a warning in his ear. Always it is safer and more hygienic for him to think one way than to think another way, and in that bald fact there is excuse enough to hold his whole chain of syllogisms in suspicion. He may be earnest, he may be honest, but he is not free, and if he is not free, he is not anything.

Well, are the reverend professors of economics free? With the highest respect, I presume to question it. Their colleagues of archeology may be reasonably called free, and their colleagues of bacteriology, and those of Latin grammar and sidereal astronomy, and those of many another science and mystery, but when one comes to the faculty of political economy one finds that freedom as plainly conditioned, though perhaps not as openly, as in the faculty of theology. And for a plain reason. Political economy, so to speak, hits the employers of the professors where they live. It deals, not with ideas that affect those employers only occasionally or only indirectly or only as ideas, but with ideas that have an imminent and continuous influence upon their personal welfare and security, and that affect profoundly the very foundations of that social and economic structure upon which their whole existence is based. It is, in brief, the science of the ways and means whereby they have come to such estate, and maintain themselves in such estate, that they are able to hire and boss professors. It is the boat in which they sail down perilous waters—and they must needs yell, or be more or less than human, when it is rocked. . . .

Now consider the case of the professors of economics, near and far, who have *not* been thrown out.

Who, indeed, will give them full credit, even when they are right, so long as they are hamstrung, nose-ringed and tied up in gilded pens? It seems to me that these considerations are enough to cast a glow of suspicion over the whole of American political economy, at least in so far as it comes from college economists. And, in the main, it has that source, for, barring a few brilliant journalists, all our economists of any repute are professors. Many of them are able men, and most of them are undoubtedly honest men, as honesty goes in the world, but over practically every one of them there stands a board of trustees with its legs in the stock-market and its eyes on the established order, and that board is ever alert for heresy in the science of its being, and has ready means of punishing it, and a hearty enthusiasm for the business. Not every professor, perhaps, may be sent straight to the block, . . . but there are plenty of pillories and guardhouses on the way, and every last pedagogue must be well aware of it.

Political economy, in so far as it is a science at all, was not pumped up and embellished by any such academic clients and ticket-of-leave men. It was put on its legs by inquirers who were not only safe from all dousing in the campus pump, but who were also free from the mental timorousness and conformity which go inevitably with school-teaching—in brief, by men of the world, accustomed to its free air, its hospitality to originality and plain speaking. Adam Smith, true enough, was once a professor, but he threw up his chair to go to Paris, and there he met, not more professors, but all the current enemies of professors—the Nearings and Henry Georges and Karl Marxes of the time. And the book that he wrote was not orthodox, but revolutionary. Consider the others of that bulk and beam: Bentham, Ricardo, Mill and their like. Bentham held no post at the mercy of bankers and tripesellers; he was a man of independent means, a lawyer and politician, and a heretic in general practice. It is impossible to imagine such a man occupying a chair at Harvard or Princeton. He had a hand in too many pies: he was too rebellious and contumacious: he had too little respect for authority, either academic or worldly. Moreover, his mind was too wide for a professor; he could never remain safely in a groove; the whole field of social organization invited his inquiries and experiments. Ricardo? Another man of easy means and great worldly experience—by academic standards, not even educated. To-day, I daresay, such meager diplomas as he could show would not suffice to get him an instructor's berth in a freshman seminary in Iowa. As for Mill, he was so well grounded by his father that he knew more, at eighteen, than any of the universities could teach him, and his life thereafter was the exact antithesis of that of a cloistered pedagogue. Moreover, he was a heretic in religion and probably violated the Mann act of those days—an offense almost as heinous, in a college professor of economics, as giving three cheers for Prince Kropotkin.

I might lengthen the list, but humanely refrain. The point is that these early English economists were all perfectly free men, with complete liberty to tell the truth as they saw it, regardless of its orthodoxy or lack of orthodoxy. I do not say that the typical American economist of to-day is not honest, nor even that he is not as diligent and competent, but I do say that he is not free— that penalties would come upon him for stating ideas that Smith or Ricardo or Bentham or Mill, had he so desired, would have been free to state without damage. And in that menace there is an ineradicable criticism of the ideas that he does state, and it lingers even when they are plausible and are accepted.

Jeremy Bentham

A teapot he named Dick
And Dapple was his stick
He cherished pigs and mice
A fact which will suffice
To hint, from all we hear
He was a little queer.

They say he cherished men,
Their happiness, and then
Calmly assumed one could
Devise cures for their good,
Believing all men the same,
And happiness their aim.

He reckoned right and wrong
By felicity—lifelong—
And by such artless measure
As the quantity of pleasure.
For pain he had a plan,
Absurd old gentleman.

John Stuart Mill

John Stuart Mill,
By a mighty effort of will,

Overcame his natural bonhomie
And wrote *Principles of Political Economy.*

Dwane Powell

Jokes, Quips, and Definitions

An Economist Is "One Who"

1. knows more about money than people who have it.
2. takes a lot of unwarranted assumptions and reaches a foregone conclusion.
3. tells you what to do with your money after you have already done something with it.
4. knows the price of everything and the value of nothing (reverse for a Communist economist)
5. ". . . compensates for great uncertainty of knowledge with great certainty of statement."
   —John Kenneth Galbraith
6. ". . . will tell you what can happen under any given condition, and his guess is liable to be as good as anybody else's."
   —Will Rogers
7. [is] "an inhabitant of cloud-cuckoo land; one knowledgeable in an obsolete art; a harmless academic drudge whose theories and laws are but mere puffs of air in face of that anarchy of banditry, greed and corruption which holds sway in the pecuniary affairs of the real world."
   —*New Statesman*

Economics Is

1. the "dismal science."
   —Thomas Carlyle

15

2. "what economists do."

—Jacob Viner

3. "Art de compliquer les questions simple" ('Booktitle' in a false bookcase).

—Anne-Robert-Jacques Turgot, Baron de l'Aulne

4. "the riddle of the Sphinx."

—Stephen B. Leacock

End-to-End Economists

1. "If the economists of this world were laid end to end they wouldn't reach a conclusion."

—George Bernard Shaw

2. "If all economists were laid end-to-end . . . it would be a good thing."

—Billboard, Interstate 85, South Carolina

Chaos, Confusion, and Havoc

1. "The age of chivalry has gone. That of sophisters, economists, and calculators has succeeded, and the glory of Europe is extinguished forever."

—Edmund Burke

2. A physician, an engineer, and an economist were arguing about whose profession was oldest. "Healing is as old as man himself," said the physician. "That makes *mine* the oldest profession." "Not so," said the engineer. "God had to use engineering to create the world out of chaos and confusion." The economist said, "And who do you think created chaos and confusion?"

Assumptio Fantasia

A physicist, a chemist, and an economist are stranded on a deserted island with no tools and one can of food. The physicist and the chemist dream up ingenious schemes for opening the can. The economist says, "Assume a can-opener."

16

A Dozen Peccadilloes (excerpt)

During that "glorious third decade" when the heroes of Joseph Schumpeter's *History of Economic Analysis* were most creative, the peccadilloes of one obscure economics instructor (and present reviewer) included the collation of students', colleagues', and laymen's views on what was wrong with economics and economists. Their frequent mutual inconsistencies were marvelous to behold. An even dozen, recollected below, cancel themselves out fairly well, which is no proof that all was well with economics.

1. Economists are stooges of the capitalist class, who have sold their ideological birthrights to the Establishment for a mess of potage (with tenure).

2. Economists are secret revolutionists and/or bureaucrats, who will not let the system solve its own problems (which it could easily do if let alone).

3. Economists are destructive critics, who never have sound, practical, or constructive advice to offer.

4. Economists dodge the problems which they are paid to solve, and do irrelevant mathematical, statistical, or antiquarian puzzles instead.

5. Economists profess to tell us *How To Succeed in Business* (or on Wall Street) *Without Really Trying,* but none of them could run a peanut stand himself.

6. Economists (like other social "scientists") peddle what everyone knows, but in language nobody can understand.

7. Economists are asses in lion's skins or crows in peacock's feathers, copying the methods of true sciences like physics and astronomy where they do not apply.

8. Economists are worldly theologians, quoting one or another Great Man (or School) instead of doing their own thinking.

9. Economists are sheep, and follow the lead of their colleagues at Harvard.

10. Economists make judgments about historical situations without knowing history, about legal problems without knowing law, about political problems without knowing politics, about social problems without knowing anthropology or sociology, and about psychological problems without knowing psychology. (Such arrogance is allegedly unique to economists.)

11. Economists should limit themselves to inculcating and upholding proper social and ethical values in matters economic, leaving hard problems of analysis and experimentation to their betters in the natural sciences, engineering, and medicine.

12. Economists should stress the scientific as against the humanistic aspects of their discipline, and make economic science "hard" rather than "soft," as it has been. This means that theoretical work should become more rigorous and axiomatic, like contemporary mathematics. Empirical work should transcend historical "gossip" in favor of the quantitative testing of hypotheses quantitatively formulated. Policy problems involving art along with science should be left to politicians, lawyers, social workers, and preachers.

Every economist would plead *nolo contendere* to some charge on the list. Yet your obscure instructor saw (and sees) no reason to foul his own nest or to tar the majority of his seniors and superiors by any of the charges, singly or collectively. As for the methodological reforms (11 and 12), they run along lines so contradictory that not even a dialectical materialist could accept both at once. The moral of the entire list is the moral of Aesop's fable about the man, his son, and the ass—that one had best "do his own thing" without undue heed to the contradictory criticisms of the critics.

Myron E. Sharpe

Why Economists Disagree (excerpt)

Economics is like a Brueghel painting. All sorts of odd people are doing all sorts of odd things. Some are sawing wood and some are baking bread; some are hawking fish and some are just staring out windows; some are busy carousing while others are lying in the shade of a tree asleep; some are flying kites and others are washing dirty laundry in a brook. It's a disorderly, noisy scene. What can you expect from such a motley bunch? When they get together of an evening at the inn, you can hardly count on them to agree on much.

Let me explain at once that jostling, shoving and arguing are commonplace among economists, who engage in them with gusto. They are part of an honorable tradition that dates back to the beginnings of the science. This manner of behavior is quite in order. But at times the din reaches the proportions of Babel and the uninformed person may feel a slight sense of apprehension. . . . Is it not a strange science that has a hundred answers for every question? No, no. Quite normal. There are reasonable explanations for all these disagreements.

Thorstein Veblen

Why is Economics Not an Evolutionary Science?

In the hands of the later classical writers the science [of economics] lost much of its charm. . . . It was no longer a definition and authentication of the deliverances of current common sense as to what ought to come to pass; and it, therefore, in large measure lost the support of the people out of doors, who were unable to take an interest in what did not concern them; and it was also out of touch with that realistic or evolutionary habit of mind which got under way about the middle of the century in the natural sciences. It was neither vitally metaphysical nor matter-of-fact, and it found comfort with very few outside of its own ranks. Only for those who by the fortunate accident of birth or education have been able to conserve the taxonomic animus has the science during the last third of a century continued to be of absorbing interest.

But what does all this signify? If we are getting restless under the taxonomy of a monocotyledonous wage doctrine and a cryptogamic theory of interest, with involute, loculicidal, tomentous, and moniliform variants, what is the cytoplasm, centrosome, or karyokinetic process to which we may turn, and in which we may find surcease from the metaphysics of normality and controlling principles? What are we going to do about it?

Bluffing the Value Theory (excerpt)

The readers of *To-Day* must by this time be experts in the theory of value. First they had P. H. Wicksteed on the subject, then they had Shaw (me), then Wicksteed a second time, then Graham Wallas, then Hyndman, and now Shaw again. It began by Wicksteed saying that Marx was wrong and Jevons right, whereupon I contended that Marx was right and Wicksteed wrong, to which Wicksteed replied that I was wrong and Jevons right, Wallas coming in after a long interval with the suggestion that Marx and Jevons were equally right, and provoking Hyndman to declare that not only Wicksteed, myself and Wallas, but the whole of the English race save himself and two others are wrong. In revenge, I now propose to shew that Hyndman does not know what we were disputing about, or, to put it less curtly—for why should we not spare one another's feelings as much as possible?—that he does not, never did, and probably never will, understand either Marx's or Jevons's theory of value.

The fact is, this is a personal matter with me. When the controversy arose, I, a helpless novice in economics, was thrust upon the Jevonian bayonets with no better defense than my mother wit and such literary adroitness as I picked up professionally. I protested that I knew nothing about it, and that Hyndman, who was then at the head of the Socialist movement in London, was the proper person to undertake it. For he, professing himself an adept at the differential calculus, heaped scorn on Jevons' equations (which were perfectly unintelligible to me) and denounced him as a silly person who had announced the speedy exhaustion of our coal supply and referred commercial crises to the action of the sunspots. . . . I undertook to write "a comment" on Wicksteed's article on condition that he was to be offered fair space for a rejoinder if he survived to make one. All of which, including the survival of Wicksteed in robust health, came to pass in due course.

The controversy now passed from the pages of *To-Day* to the meetings of the Hampstead Historic Club, which was at first a Marxist reading party at the house of Arthur Wilson. A young Russian lady used to read out "Capital" in French to us until we began to quarrel, which usually occurred before she had gone on long enough to feel seriously fatigued. The first chapters in particular were of extraordinary efficacy in setting us by the ears. F.Y. Edgeworth as a Jevonian, and Sidney Webb as a Stuart Millite, fought the Marxian value theory tooth and nail; whilst Belfort Bax and I, in a spirit of transcendent Marxism, held the fort recklessly, and laughed at Mill and Jevons. The rest kept an open mind and skirmished on either side as they felt moved. In these wars, . . . I suffered many a bruise in defence of an untenable position. . . .

Jevons's "Theory of Political Economy" and his controversy with Cairnes, Wicksteed's article in *To-Day* for October, 1884 and his "Alphabet of Economic Science" (Macmillan, 1888), my review in the *National Reformer* and the Fabian Essay on the "Economic Aspect of Socialism" (*Our Corner*, December, 1888) are all extant and written in very choice English for the enlightenment of those who care to know the exact point under discussion, or to reassure themselves that Marx's indictment of individualism is independent of Marx's theory, right or wrong. However, I take the opportunity to throw out [a general remark].

1. I believe that Newton's theory of light was unsound. But I do not therefore affirm that the phenomena which he sought to explain by his theory do not exist, or that all his theories were fallacious and his statements false. For instance, I do not believe that a mixture of blue and yellow paint will be orange, or that if I jump out of a window I shall soar Baldwin-like to the skies. Nor— such is the perversity of the human intellect—do I even believe that Newton, generally speaking, was an ass, or that Young, who upset his theory of light, was a man of superior genius. In the same inconsistent way I believe that Marx's theory of value was unsound, and that Jevons upset it; and yet I do not, with Hyndman's powerful logic, proceed to infer that Marx was an idiot, "Das Kapital" a tissue of nonsense, Socialism an illusion, Jevons immensely Marx's superior, and commercial crises the direct out-

come of spots on the sun. I am quite willing to allow, in the handsomest manner, that Marx was the Aristotle of the nineteenth century. . . .

Let me in conclusion explain that I do not accuse Carl Marx of Marxism, and that I think he deserved something worthier from his pupils than idolatry.

—1889

Axel Leijonhufvud

Life among the Econ

The Econ tribe occupies a vast territory in the far North. Their land appears bleak and dismal to the outsider, and travelling through it makes for rough sledding; but the Econ, through a long period of adaptation, have learned to wrest a living of sorts from it. They are not without some genuine and sometimes even fierce attachment to their ancestral grounds, and their young are brought up to feel contempt for the softer living in the warmer lands of their neighbours, such as the Polscis and the Sociogs. Despite a common genetical heritage, relations with these tribes are strained—the distrust and contempt that the average Econ feels for these neighbours being heartily reciprocated by the latter—and social intercourse with them is inhibited by numerous taboos. The extreme clannishness, not to say xenophobia, of the Econ makes life among them difficult and perhaps even somewhat dangerous for the outsider. This probably accounts for the fact that the Econ have so far not been systematically studied. Information about their social structure and ways of life is fragmentary and not well validated. More research on this interesting tribe is badly needed.

Editor's Note: Since many of our younger readers are, with the idealism so charac-teristic of contemporary youth, planning to launch themselves on a career of good deeds by going to live and work among the Econ, the editor felt that it would be desirable to invite an Econologist of some experience to write an account of this little known tribe. Diligent inquiry eventually turned up the author of the present paper. Dr. Leijonhufvud was deemed an almost perfect candidate for the assign-ment, for he was exiled nearly a decade ago to one of the outlying Econ villages (Ucla) and since then has not only been continuously resident there but has even managed to get himself named an elder (under what pretenses—other than the growth of a grey beard—the editor has been unable to determine).

The information that we do have indicates that, for such a primitive people, the social structure is quite complex. The two main dimensions of their social structure are those of caste and status. The basic division of the tribe is seemingly into castes; within each caste, one finds an elaborate network of status relationships.

An extremely interesting aspect of status among the Econ, if it can be verified, is that status relationships do not seem to form a simple hierarchical "pecking-order," as one is used to expect. Thus, for example, one may find that A pecks B, B pecks C, and *then C pecks A!* This non-transitivity of status may account for the continual strife among the Econ which makes their social life seem so singularly insufferable to the visitor. Almost all of the travellers' reports that we have comment on the Econ as a "quarrelsome race" who "talk ill of their fellow behind his back," and so forth. Social cohesion is apparently maintained chiefly through shared distrust of outsiders. In societies with a transitive pecking-order, on the other hand, we find as a rule that an equilibrium develops in which little actual pecking ever takes place. The uncivilized anomaly that we find among the Econ poses a riddle the resolution of which must be given high priority in Econological research at this time.

What seems at first to be a further complication obstructing our understanding of the situation in the Econ tribe may, in the last analysis, contain the vital clue to this theoretical problem. Pecking between castes is traditionally not supposed to take place, but this rule is not without exceptions either. Members of high castes are not infrequently found to peck those of lower castes. While such behavior is regarded as in questionable taste, it carries no formal sanctions. A member of a low caste who attempts to peck someone in a higher caste runs more concrete risks—at the extreme, he may be ostracized and lose the privilege of being heard at the tribal midwinter councils.

In order to bring out the relevance of this observation, a few more things need to be said about caste and status in the tribe. The Econ word for caste is "field." Caste is extremely important to the self-image and sense of identity of the Econ, and the adult male meeting a stranger will always introduce himself with the phrase "Such-and-such is my field." The English root of this term is interesting because of the aversion that the Econ normally have to the use of plain English. The English words that have crept into their language are often used in senses that we would not recognize. Thus, in this case, the territorial connotation of "field" is entirely misleading for the castes do not live apart. The basic social unit is the village, or "dept." The depts of the Econ always comprise members of several "fields." In some cases, nearly every caste may be represented in a single dept.

A comparison of status relationships in the different "fields" shows a definite common pattern. The dominant feature, which makes status relations among the Econ of unique interest to the serious student, is the way that status is tied to the manufacture of certain types of implements, called "modls." The status of the adult male is determined by his skill at making the "modl" of his "field." The facts (a) that the Econ are highly status-motivated, (b) that status is only to be achieved by making "modls," and (c) that most of these "modls" seem to be of little or no practical use, probably accounts for the backwardness and abject cultural poverty of the tribe. Both the tight linkage between status in the tribe and modl-making and the trend toward making modls more for ceremonial than for practical purposes appear, moreover, to be fairly recent developments, something which has led many observers to express pessimism for the viability of the Econ culture.

Whatever may have been the case in earlier times, the "fields" of the Econ apparently do not now form a strong rank-ordering. This may be the clue to the problem of the non-transitivity of individual status. First, the ordering of two castes will sometimes be indeterminate. Thus, while the Micro assert their superiority over the Macro, so do the Macro theirs over the Micro, and third parties are found to have no very determined, or at least no unanimous, opinion on the matter. Thus the perceived prestige of one caste relative to another is a non-reflexive relation. In other instances, however, the ranking is quite clear. The priestly caste (the Math-Econ) for example, is a higher "field" than either Micro or Macro, while the Devlops just as definitely rank lower. Second, we know that these caste-rankings (where they can be made) are not permanent but may change over time. There is evidence, for example, that both the high rank assigned to the Math-Econ and the low rank of the Devlops are, historically speaking, rather recent phenomena. The rise of the Math-Econ seems to be associated with the previously noted trend among all the Econ towards more ornate, ceremonial modls, while the low rank of the Devlops is due to the fact that this caste, in recent times, has not strictly enforced the taboos against association with the Polscis, Sociogs, and other tribes. Other Econ look upon this with considerable apprehension as endangering the moral fiber of the tribe and suspect the Devlops even of relinquishing modl-making.

If the non-transitivity of Econ status seems at first anomalous, here at least we have a phenomenon with known parallels.[1] It may be that what we are observing among the Econ is simply the decay of a once orderly social structure that possessed a strong ranking of castes and, within each caste, a perfectly unambiguous transitive status ordering.

Grads, Adults, and Elders

The young Econ, or "grad," is not admitted to adulthood until he has made a "modl" exhibiting a degree of workmanship acceptable to the elders of the "dept" in which he serves his apprenticeship. Adulthood is conferred in an intricate ceremony the particulars of which vary from village to village. In the more important villages, furthermore, (the practice in some outlying villages is unclear) the young adult must continue to demonstrate his ability at manufacturing these artifacts. If he fails to do so, he is turned out of the "dept" to perish in the wilderness.

This practice may seem heartless, but the Econ regard it as a manhood rite sanctioned by tradition and defend it as vital to the strength and welfare of the dept. If life is hard on the young, the Econ show their compassion in the way that they take care of the elderly. Once elected an elder, the member need do nothing and will still be well taken care of.

Totems and Social Structure

While in origin the word "modl" is simply a term for a concrete implement, looking at it only in these terms will blind the student to key aspects of Econ social structure. "Modl" has evolved into an abstract concept which dominates the Econ's perception of virtually all social relationships—whether these be relations to other tribes, to other castes, or status relations within his caste.

---

1. Cf., e.g., the observations concerning the Indian *jajmani*-system in Manning Nash, *Primitive and Peasant Economic Systems,* Scranton, Pa., 1966, pp. 93 ff, esp. p. 94: "For example, goldsmiths give polluting services to potters, and the potters receive pollution from herders, who in turn give polluting services to goldsmiths. In this exchange of ritually crucial interaction the goldsmiths see themselves above the potters and below the herders, but the herders are below the potters, yet above the goldsmith caste." Precisely.

Thus, in explaining to a stranger, for example, why he holds the Sociogs or the Polscis in such low regard, the Econ will say that "they do not make modls" and leave it at that.

The dominant role of "modl" is perhaps best illustrated by the (unfortunately very incomplete) accounts we have of relationships between the two largest of the Econ castes, the "Micro" and the "Macro." Each caste has a basic modl of simple pattern and the modls made by individual members will be variations on the theme set by the basic modl of the caste. Again, one finds that the Econ define the social relationship, in this instance between two castes, in terms of the respective modl. Thus if a Micro-Econ is asked why the Micro do not intermarry with the Macro, he will answer: "They make a different modl," or "They do not know the Micro modl." (In this, moreover, he would be perfectly correct, but then neither, of course, would he know the Macro modl.)

Several observers have commented on the seeming impossibility of eliciting from the member of a "field" a coherent and intelligible account of what distinguishes his caste from another caste which does not, in the final analysis, reduce to the mere assertion that the modls are different. Although more research on this question is certainly needed, this would seem to lend considerable support to those who refer to the basic modl as the *totem* of the caste. It should be noted that the difficulty of settling this controversial question does not arise from any taboo against discussing caste with strangers. Far from being reticent, the Econ will as a rule be quite voluble on the subject. The problem is that what they have to say consists almost entirely of expressions of caste-prejudices of the most elemental sort.[2]

To the untrained eye, the totems of major castes will often look well-nigh identical. It is the great social significance attached to these minor differences by the Econ themselves that have made Econography (the study of Econ arts and handicrafts) the central field of modern Econology. As an illustration, consider the totems of the Micro and the Macro. Both could be roughly described as formed by two carved sticks joined together in the middle somewhat in the form of a pair of scissors (cf. Figure 1).

Certain ceremonies connected with these totems are of great interest to us because of the indications that they give about the

---

2. This observation is far from new. One finds it recorded, for example, in Machlyup's *Voyages* in the account of "The Voyage of H.M.S. Semantick to the Coast of Econland."

origin of modl-making among the Econ. Unfortunately, we have only fragmentary accounts by various travellers of these ceremonies and the interpretations of what they have seen that these untrained observers essay are often in conflict. Here, a systematic study is very much needed.

The following sketchy account of the "prospecting"-ceremony among the Macro brings out several of the riddles that currently perplex Econologists working in this area:

Figure 1-A. Totem of the Micro   Figure 1-B. Totem of the Macro

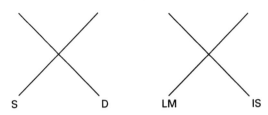

The elder grasps the LM with his left hand and the IS with his right and, holding the totem out in front of himself with elbows slightly bent, proceeds in a straight line—'gazing neither left nor right' in the words of their ritual[3]—out over the chosen terrain. The grads of the village skip gaily around him at first, falling silent as the trek grows longer and more wearisome. On this occasion, it was long indeed and the terrain difficult . . . the grads were strung out in a long, morose and bedraggled chain behind their leader who, sweat pearling his brow, face cast in grim determination, stumbled onward over the obstacles in his path . . . At long last, the totem vibrates, then oscillates more and more; finally, it points, quivering, straight down. The elder waits for the grads to gather round and then pronounces, with great solemnity: "Behold, the Truth and Power of the Macro."

It is surely evident from an account such as this why such a major controversy has sprung up around the main thesis of the 'Implementarist' School. This influential Econographic School ar-

3. The same wording appears in the corresponding Micro-ritual. It is reported that the Macro belittle the prospecting of the Micro among themselves saying that the Micro "can't keep from gazing right." The Micro, on their side, claim the Macro "gaze left." No one has offered a sensible hypothesis to account for this particular piece of liturgical controversy. Chances are that far-fetched explanations are out of place and that this should simply be accepted as just another humdrum example of the continual bickering among the Econ.

gues that the art of modl-carving has its historical origin in the making of tools and useful "implements," and that ceremonies such as the one described above reflect, in ritual form, the actual uses to which these implements were at one time put.

Fanciful as the 'Implementarist' hypothesis may seem, it would be injudicious to dismiss it out of hand. Whether the Macro-modl can be regarded as originally a "useful implement" would seem to hinge in the first place on whether the type of "prospecting" ritualized in the described ceremony produces actual results. The Macro themselves maintain that they strike gold this way. Some travellers and investigators support the contention, others dismiss it as mere folklore. The issues are much the same as those connected with attempts to appraise the divining-rod method of finding water. Numerous people argue that it works—but no scientific explanation of why it would has ever been advanced.

We do have some, apparently reliable, eyewitness' reports of gold actually being struck by the Macro. While not disputing the veracity of all such reports, skeptical critics argue that they must be heavily discounted. It is said, for example, that the Econ word for "gold" refers to any yellowish mineral however worthless. Some Econologists maintain, moreover, that the prospecting ceremony is seldom, if ever, conducted over unknown ground and that what the eyewitnesses have reported, therefore, is only the "discovery" of veins that have been known to the Macro for generations.

One might ask how the practice manages to survive if there is nothing to it. The answer is simple and will not be unexpected to those acquainted with earlier studies of the belief-systems of primitive peoples. Instances are known when the ceremony has not produced any concrete results. When this happens, the Macro will take either of two positions. Either he will accuse the member performing the ceremony of having failed to follow ritual in some detail or other, or else defend the man's claim that the gold is there by arguing that the digging for it has not gone deep enough.[4]

---

4. The latter rationalization is the more palatable since it puts the blame on a different caste, namely the O'Maitres or O'Metrs (transcriptions vary) who do the digging work of both the Macro and the Micro.

The "diggers" caste is of special interest to those concerned with the underdevelopment of the Econ. Traditionally the lowest Econ caste, the O'Metrs, were allowed to perform only the dirtiest manual tasks and—more significant in Econ eyes—lacked a totem of their own. In more recent times, however, it is through this

It is clear enough that, whichever position is taken, the "phenomena are saved" in the sense that the role of the totem in the belief-system of the caste remains unassailed.

Myths and Modls

In recent years, interest in controversies about whether certain Econ modls "work" or not (or in what sense they may be said to "work") has dwindled. This is certainly not because the issue has been settled—it is fair to say that we are today less certain than ever of what the answers to the questions raised by the Implementarists would be. It is rather that our methodological perspective has changed so that the Implementarist issue is no longer seen as productive of "good" questions. The "New Econology," as it is known, stresses *Verstehen* and, correspondingly, rejects attempts to appraise Econ belief-systems according to rationalistic criteria purloined from modern natural science.[5]

It has become increasingly clear that the Econ associate certain, to them significant, beliefs with every modl, whether or not they also claim that modl to be a "useful tool." That taking "usefulness" as the point of departure in seeking to understand the totemic culture of this people leads us into a blind alley is particularly clear when we consider the Math-Econ caste.

The Math-Econ are in many ways the most fascinating, and certainly the most colorful, of Econ castes. There is today considerable uncertainty whether the "priest" label is really appropriate for this caste, but it is at least easy to understand why the early travellers came to regard them in this way. In addition to the deeply respectful attitude evidenced by the average Econ towards them, the Math-Econ themselves show many cultural patterns that we are wont to associate with religious orders or sects among other peoples. Thus they affect a poverty that is abject even by Econ standards, and it seems clear that this is by choice rather than necessity. It is told that, to harden themselves, they periodically

---

caste that industrialization has begun to make some inroads among the Econ. Free from the prejudices instilled through an education concentrating on modl-carving and the associated totemic beliefs, the O'Metrs take willingly to modern machinery and have become quite proficient for example, at handling power shovels and power mills. The attitude of the rest of the tribe towards these erstwhile untouchables taking the lead in industrialization is, as one would expect, one of mingled scorn and envy.

5. C. Levi-Strauss, *The Savage Mind* should be mentioned here as essential reading for anyone with a serious interest in the belief-systems of the Econ.

venture stark naked out into the chill winds of abstraction that prevail in those parts. Among the rest of the Econ, who ordinarily perambulate thickly bundled in wooly clothing, they are much admired for this practice. Furthermore, glossolalia—the ability to say the same thing in several different tongues[6]—is a highly esteemed talent among them.

The Math-Econ make exquisite modls finely carved from bones of walras. Specimens made by their best masters[7] are judged unequalled in both workmanship and raw material by a unanimous Econographic opinion. If some of these are "useful"—and even Econ testimony is divided on this point—it is clear that this is purely coincidental in the motivation for their manufacture.

There has been a great deal of debate in recent years over whether certain Econ modls and the associated belief-systems are best to be regarded as religious, folklore and mythology, philosophical and "scientific," or as sports and games. Each category has its vocal proponents among Econologists of repute but very little headway has been made in the debate. The ceremonial use of modls (see above) and the richness of the general Econ culture in rituals has long been taken as evidence for the religious interpretation. But, as one commentator puts it, "If these beliefs are religious, it is a religion seemingly without faith." This interpretation seems to have stranded on this contradiction in terms and presently is not much in favor. More interesting are the arguments of those who have come to view certain Econ belief-systems as a form of quasi-scientific cosmological speculation. As an illustration, Mrs. Robinson's description of what she terms the "Doctrine of K," which is found prevalent among the members of the powerful Charles River villages, inevitably brings to mind the debates of the ancient Ionian philosophers over whether water, air, or fire was the "basic stuff" of the universe. The Doctrine of K bears, in fact, striking resemblances to the teachings of Anaximander.[8] It is

---

6. I.e., in several Math tongues—the Indo-European languages, for example, do not count.

7. The budding collector of Econographica should know that most of the work found on the market today is imitative and done by apprentices. Much of it is nonetheless aesthetically superior to, say, the crudely carved totems of the Macro and certainly to the outsized, machine-made modls nowadays exported by the O'Metrs who have no artistic tradition to fall back on.

8. Arthur Koestler, *The Sleepwalkers*, New York 1968, pp. 22–23, aptly summarizes Anaximander's teachings: "The raw material (of the universe) is none of the familiar forms of matter, but a substance without definite properties except for being indestructible and everlasting. Out of this stuff all things are developed,

known, moreover, that in some other depts a "Doctrine of M" is taught but we do not as yet have an understandable account of it and know, in fact, little about it except that it is spurned (as heresy?) by the Charles River Econ. Spokesmen for the cosmology view buttress their arguments by pointing out the similarities between the Math-Econ and the Pythagorean brotherhood. Whether the Math-Econ know it or not, they point out, they do obey the ancient Pythagorean principle that "philosophy must be pursued in such a way that its inner secrets are reserved for learned men, trained in Math."

The sports and games interpretation has gained a certain currency due to accounts of the modl-ceremonies of the Intern caste.[9] But even here it is found that, though the ceremony has all the outward manifestations of a game, it has to the participants something of the character of a morality play which in essential respects shapes their basic perception of the world.

The Econ and the Future

It would be to fail in one's responsibility to the Econ people to end this brief sketch of life in their society without a few words about their future. The prospect for the Econ is bleak. Their social structure and culture should be studied now before it is gone forever. Even a superficial account of their immediate and most pressing problems reads like a veritable catalogue of the woes of primitive peoples in the present day and age.

They are poor—except for a tiny minority, miserably poor. Their population growth rate is among the highest in the world. Their land is fairly rich, but much of the natural resources that are their birth-right has been sold off to foreign interests for little more than a mess of pottage. Many of their young are turning to pot and message. In their poverty, they are not even saved from the problems of richer nations—travellers tell of villages half-buried in the refuse of unchecked modl-making and of the eye-sores left on the once pastoral landscape by the random strip-mining of the

---

and into it they return; before this our world, infinite multitudes of other universes have already existed, and been dissolved again into the amorphous mass."

If one were to dignify this primitive doctrine with modern terminology, one would have to put Anaximander in the "putty-putty, bang-bang" category.

9. One observer casts his account of this ceremony explicitly in parlour-game terms: "Each player gets 2 countries, 2 goods, 2 factors, and a so-called Bowley Box . . ." etc., etc., and also compares the Intern game, in terms of intellectual difficulty, with checkers.

O'Metrs. It is said that even their famous Well Springs of Inspiration are now polluted.

In the midst of their troubles, the Econ remain as of old a proud and warlike race. But they seem entirely incapable of "creative response" to their problems. It is plain to see what is in store for them if they do not receive outside aid.

One may feel some optimism that the poverty problems *can* be solved. While population growth may slow down in time, one can have little hope that the ongoing disintegration of Econ culture will be halted or could be reversed. Here the sad and familiar story of a primitive people's encounter with "modern times" is repeating itself once again. The list of symptoms is long and we will touch only on a few.

Econ political organization is weakening. The basic political unit remains the dept and the political power in the dept is lodged in the council of elders. The foundations of this power of the elders has been eroding for some time, however. Respect for one's elders is no more the fashion among the young Econ than among young people anywhere else. Authority based on age and experience has weakened as recognized status has come increasingly to be tied to cleverness in modl-making. (As noted before, many elders will be inactive as modl-makers.) Although dept establishments have responded to these developments by cooptation of often very young modl-makers as "elders," the legitimacy of the political structure in the eyes of the Econ people is obviously threatened—and the chances of a constructive political response to the tribe's problems correspondingly lessened.

The Econ adult used to regard himself as a life-long member of his dept. This is no longer true—migration between depts is nowadays exceedingly common and not even elders of a village necessarily regard themselves as permanent members. While this mobility may help them to cope with the poverty problem, it obviously tends further to weaken political organization. Urbanization should be noted as a related problem—many villages are today three or four times as large as only a generation or two ago. Big conurbations, with large transient populations, and weak and ineffective political machinery—we are all familiar with the social ills that this combination breeds.

Under circumstances such as these, we expect alienation, disorientation, and a general loss of spiritual values. And this is what we find. A typical phenomenon indicative of the break-up of a culture is the loss of a sense of history and growing disrespect for tradition. Contrary to the normal case in primitive societies, the Econ priesthood does not maintain and teach the history of the tribe. In some Econ villages, one can still find the occasional elder who takes care of the modls made by some long-gone hero of the tribe and is eager to tell the legends associated with each. But few of the adults or grads, noting what they regard as the crude workmanship of these dusty old relics, care to listen to such rambling fairytales. Among the younger generations, it is now rare to find an individual with any conception of the history of the Econ. Having lost their past, the Econ are without confidence in the present and without purpose and direction for the future.

Some Econographers disagree with the bleak picture of cultural disintegration just given, pointing to the present as the greatest age of Econ Art. It is true that virtually all Econographers agree that present modl-making has reached aesthetic heights not heretofore attained. But it is doubtful that this gives cause for much optimism. It is not unusual to find some particular art form flowering in the midst of the decay of a culture. It may be that such decay of society induces this kind of cultural "displacement activity" among talented members who despair of coping with the decline of their civilization. The present burst of sophisticated modl-carving among the Econ should probably be regarded in this light.

Part 2

The Language and Methods of Economics

Introduction

If all critics of economics were laid end to end, some would point to its dismalness, others to its language. Is economics dull, esoteric, arcane, as its detractors claim? Ask the average sophomore in Econ 101. Most, if not all, are taking the course because it is a requirement, and many will develop a severe case of somnia before the term ends.

Consider the first selection in Part 2, a 1970s cartoon from *Mad Magazine.* An economics teacher pays a young man $20 to listen to his lecture—and still puts him to sleep. If the hapless teacher had done his homework he would recall that listening, like everything else, has its opportunity cost. Adjusting for inflation, the bribe would exceed $67 in 1990. Little pity can be shown an econ instructor with such money to waste and stupidity to match.

Apparently, the problem of listener lethargy is not new to economics. John Fred Bell related an anecdote about Abbe Ferdinando Galiani (1728–87) in *A History of Economic Thought.* It seems that Galiani, an Italian economist, "was a very witty writer who saw in physiocratic writings nothing but absurdity. He proposed that his own monument bear a Latin inscription stating that he had 'wiped out the economists, who were sending the nation to sleep.'"[1]

---

1. John Fred Bell, *A History of Economic Thought,* 2d ed. (New York: The Ronald Press Co., 1967), 121n.

The second selection, an advertisement of an economic "lecture series," is taken from the first (and only) issue, volume CLXXVI, of the *Gall Street Journal,* a facetious facsimile of one of the nation's leading newspapers. The spoof features, among other things, "special emphasis on big words."

Big words are only part of the problem noneconomists encounter with the language of economics. A. R. J. Turgot (1727–1781), the French statesman and Physiocrat, must have had a sense of humor, for he had a false bookcase. One of the fake book titles was *Art de compliquer les questions simple.* If Turgot was referring to economic methods as well as language, little did he know how bad it could get.

If current trends continue, economics will be so mathematized by 2000 A.D. that only a few economists, and no noneconomists, will be able to comprehend the literature. Most of the contributors to this section are economists, yet their offerings include as much criticism as apologia.

Stephen B. Leacock (1869–1944) is the only economist represented here who achieved greater fame as a humorist. He himself claimed that he was neither—to humorists he was an economist, to economists he was a humorist. He received his Ph.D. degree in political economy from the University of Chicago, and headed the department of economics at McGill University for 28 years. Jacob Viner was his student. Although Leacock wrote numerous serious articles and books on economic topics, he is ignored by most economists. A pity. Leacock's first piece, an excerpt from a 1940 writing, reflects his growing bitterness with the methods and language of his profession.

John Kenneth Galbraith (1908–) is usually described in contradictory superlatives: the best-known gadfly, "the first hippie economist,"[2] the most outstanding economist, the worst economist, and always the tallest economist. At 6 feet 8 inches, he fits the last description. If he and Paul Volcker, the former Federal Reserve chairman, were placed end to end, they would reach more than 13 feet. Galbraith is known in the economic trade as a "popularizer," which does not make him very popular with his colleagues. Yet he was elected president of the American Economic Association in 1970, a signal honor in economics. His ability to write eloquently in a profession not exactly noted for its spritely

---

2. Al Capp, "The Hippie Economics," *Nation's Business,* September 1967, 64.

writing may have prompted Paul Samuelson to describe him as the "noneconomist's economist." Galbraith was U.S. ambassador to India 1961–63, head of the Office of Price Administration, 1941–43, and Paul M. Warburg Professor Emeritus at Harvard. In "The Language of Economics," Galbraith offers an apologia and a put-down of economic literature.

Readers reap a "Verbal Windfall" when Herbert Stein defines words and terms that economists are constantly torturing audiences with. Just as everyone suspected all along, Keynesian is worse than a four-letter word—it's an "all-purpose pejorative"!

Alfred Marshall (1842–1924) is considered the founder of neoclassical economics. His *Principles,* published in 1890, appeared in many editions and was the leading U.S. textbook for many years. The textbook generally relegates graphs and diagrams to footnotes, a reflection of the attitude Marshall displays in "Burn the Mathematics." Marshall was so influential that one need go no further to find the culprit for the dusty prose of economic literature. In an 1896 letter, he rebuked F. Y. Edgeworth for his "dry & caustic humour . . . ," saying, "I dislike jokes in an Economic Journal."[3]

In an article published in 1936, *Through a Glass Darkly,* Stephen B. Leacock offers an artful putdown of mathematical economics. He claims that it is designed to get rid of readers.

The brief excerpt by Oliver Wendell Holmes (1809–94) takes a literary view that we need to "learn to think in letters instead of figures." Holmes was a physician, a poet, and the father of the U.S. Supreme Court justice named after him. He was professor of anatomy at Cambridge, Massachusetts. The excerpt is from the *Autocrat of the Breakfast Table,* which was first published in the *Atlantic Monthly* in 1857–58 in a continuing and unacknowledged series.

Holmes is followed by another example of George Bernard Shaw's wit, his story of the "plausible boy."

Kenneth E. Boulding (1910–93) was born in Liverpool and came to the United States after graduating from Oxford. He studied under Frank Knight at Chicago and under Schumpeter at Harvard. It is rumored that he wrote verses while he was in committee meetings. Perhaps "The Stochastic Variable" and "X Cantos" came "out of committee," in a manner of speaking.

---

3. Alfred Marshall to Francis Y. Edgeworth, Balliol Croft, Cambridge, England, 10. vi. 96.

Dennis H. Robertson's "Lament" is a bit of whimsy on non-mathematical lines. Robertson (1890–1963) held the chair of political economy at Cambridge until his retirement in 1957. He received honorary degrees from several universities, including Harvard (1936), and was knighted in 1953.

Edward E. Leamer's expertise in econometrics gives special weight to his spoof of the specialty. A professor of economics at UCLA, Leamer has published articles in *Econometrica* and the *Journal of the American Statistical Association*.

In "Lies, Damn Lies . . ." (as Disraeli is reputed to have characterized statistics), forecasting takes the stage as the butt of public abuse. Ditto for the Tony Auth cartoon.

At the 53rd annual awards dinner of the Overseas Press club of America, in May 1992, Tony Auth was the winner for best cartoon on foreign affairs. He is with the *Philadelphia Inquirer.* In Auth's cartoon here, the head of the Council of Economic Advisers is dressed as Merlin the Magician.

MIT's Paul A. Samuelson (1915–) was the 1970 Nobel laureate in economic science. He is the author of a best-selling textbook first published in 1948. The excerpt, "On Economic Forecasting," is whimsy with a message: there are inevitable errors in economic forecasting—if the only alternatives are prophets and soothsayers, economists are still the best things on the block.

The cartoon that follows seems to cast doubt on Samuelson's trust in economists. Could it be the crystal ball?

One way to forecast is to "extrapolate," to project a current or past trend into the future. The problem is, as Darrell Huff (1913–) suggests, that trends can change. Variety may be the spice of life, but it plays havoc with prediction. The excerpt is from Huff's classic, *How to Lie with Statistics.* Huff was a Phi Beta Kappa at Iowa State University, where he earned undergraduate and graduate degrees.

"The Fable of the Cat," an allegorical tale (no double entendre intended) appeared in 1970 in an in-house *Survey* of Morgan Guaranty Trust Company. The company was the result of the 1959 merger of two century-old firms, J. P. Morgan and Company and Guaranty Trust Company of New York. The general moral of the fable is clear: A recessionary feline can't be predicted.

Mark Twain (Samuel Langhorne Clemens, 1835–1910) may be the most widely read, most often quoted, and best-loved of American humorists. In the piece taken from *Life on the Mississippi,* Mark Twain uses extrapolation to predict that the Lower

Mississippi will shrink to only a mile and three quarters in 742 years. Mississippians need not worry. The piece was written in 1874, so shrinkage will not be complete until the year 2616 A.D., when people reading this anthology will either be dead or in extremely poor health.

Robert Frost (1874–1963), unofficial poet laureate of the United States, was winner of four Pulitzer Prizes. Although he never graduated from college, he was poet-in-residence at Amherst, Harvard, the University of Michigan, and Dartmouth. One secret of Frost's "The Secret Sits" is that the message is bigger than the verse.

Part 2 of this book ends with John J. Siegfried's "A First Lesson in Econometrics," truly an example of Turgot's "Art de compliquer les questions simple." Siegfried's final equation, simplifying 1 + 1 = 2, makes him a kind of Rube Goldberg (see part 4) of the econometric art. Siegfried (1945–) received his Ph.D. at the University of Wisconsin and is currently professor of economics at Vanderbilt University.

The Soporiferous Economics Teacher

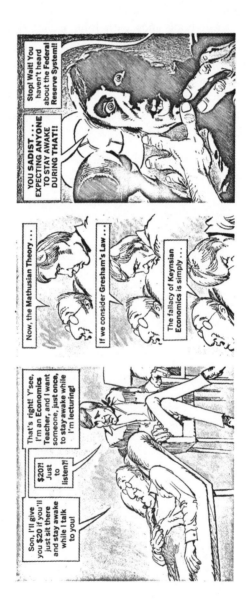

43

Stephen B. Leacock

Sliced History and Green Geography (excerpt)

Perhaps the best index of what has happened to the science of economics is what has happened to the teaching of it in our colleges. The colleges have a system for meeting such difficulties.

When opinion gets confused—living opinion—the colleges can always fall back on the opinion of the dead. If living men can't think, let's have a catalogue of all that dead men ever thought, and the students can learn that. In fact, economics can be all dosed up with history, as doctors dose a patient with iron. And statistics. If we don't understand the industrial world, at least let us have statistics. The continental area of the United States is 3,026,789 square miles and the number of spindles in Lowell, Mass., is 201,608 (or is it?). That's the stuff. Make a four-year course and give a degree in it—a D.F.

And with that, of course, goes the familiar therapeutics of putting in "qualifications," what is called the "relative" view— that a thing is partly so and partly isn't so. Any book of what is called "general economics," after indicating the continental area of the United States and the number of spindles in Lowell, Mass., proceeds to a series of propositions as to why wages partly rise and partly don't, why prices may fall, or perhaps leap up, proving that black is in a sense white, except that where it is white it is partly black. This course is called Economics I. From it you get to first base.

And, most of all, if we can't understand it, let's at least see that outsiders don't. Let us dress economics up in esoteric language, give it a jargon of its own, and break away from plain terms like labour and profit and money and poverty. Let's talk of "categories" and "increments" and "margins" and "series." Let's call our appetite for breakfast our consumer's marginal demand. That will fool them. And if I buy one cigar but won't buy two, call that my submarginal saturation point for nicotine.

Above all, let us call in the help of the psychologist. He's the fellow with the technique. Turn him onto the theory of value, and grandfather Adam Smith won't know his own offspring.

Accordingly, the theorist of today, following in the tracks of the dead scholasticism, the lost Babylonian and the Egyptian dozing in the dust of the pyramids, runs his economics to finer and finer distinctions that have lost all meaning for everyday life. He can no longer talk of our wants; he must have marginal wants, degrees of wants, increments of satisfaction, curves of desire meeting in an equilibrium. The difference as between plain language and this jargon is as between digestion and a stomach-ache. To the college economist a boy standing in front of a pastry shop represents a submarginal increment of satisfaction. Give him ten cents and he comes out with a consumer's surplus in him. You can see it sticking out. . . .

Take enough of that mystification and muddle, combine it with the continental area of the United States, buttress it up on the side with the history of dead opinion and dress it, as the chefs say, with sliced history and green geography, and out of it you can make a doctor's degree in economics. I have one myself.

John Kenneth Galbraith

The Language of Economics (excerpt)

Among the social sciences, and indeed among all reputable fields of learning, economics occupies a special place for the reproach that is inspired by its language. . . . Other scholars emerge from the eccentricities of their own terminology to condemn the economist for a special commitment to obscurity. . . .

. . . That economics has a considerable conceptual apparatus with an appropriate terminology cannot be a serious ground for complaint. Economic phenomena, ideas and instruments of analysis exist. They require names. . . .

. . . It is sometimes said that the economist has a special obligation to make himself understood because his subject is of such great . . . importance. By this rule the nuclear physicist would have to speak in monosyllables.

A physician, at least in the United States, does not tell you that a patient is dying. He says that the prognosis as of this time is without significant areas of encouragement. The dead man becomes . . . to his lawyer . . . the decedent . . . Economists have similar vanities of expression . . . an accomplished practitioner can often get the words parameter, stochastic and aggregation into a single sentence. But it would be hard to prove that the working terminology of the subject is more pretentious or otherwise oppressive than that of jurisprudence, gynecology or advanced poultry husbandry.

. . . [W]hether clear and unambiguous statement is the best medium for persuasion in economics . . . one may have doubts.

Had the Bible been in clear, straightforward language, had the ambiguities and contradictions been edited out and . . . the language been constantly modernized to accord with contemporary taste, it would almost certainly have been, or have become, a work of lesser influence. The archaic constructions and terminology put some special strain on the reader. Accordingly, by the time he has worked his way through, say, Leviticus, he has a vested interest in what he has to read. . . .

. . . The contradictions of the Old Testament also mean that with a little effort anyone can find a faith that accords with his preferences and a moral code that is agreeable to his tastes, even if fairly depraved. In consequence, dissidents are not extruded from the faith; they are retained and accommodated in a different chapter.

Finally, the ambiguities of the Scripture allow of infinite debate over what is meant. This is most important for attracting belief. . . .

Difficulty, contradiction and ambiguity have rendered precisely similar service in economics . . . .

. . . [C]onsider the complex language and the difficult mathematics . . . What is involved . . . is less the language of economics than its sociology. . . .

Professional economists, like members of city gangs, religious organizations, aboriginal tribes, British regiments, craft unions, fashionable clubs, learned disciplines, holders of diplomatic passports and, one is told, followers of the intellectually more demanding criminal pursuits, have the natural desire of all such groups to delineate and safeguard the boundary between those who belong and those who do not. This has variously been called the tribal, gang, club, guild, union or aristocratic instinct . . . everything within depends on the exclusion of what is without.

Verbal Windfall

Reporting of economics in the press has greatly increased in volume and sophistication, but the economic literacy of readers, even of the *New York Times,* has not kept pace. Therefore the public may not be getting the full benefit of the economic wisdom being spread before it. As a contribution to remedying this situation, I present here definitions of some words and terms most commonly encountered in current discussions.

Balanced Budget Amendment: An amendment to the Constitution proposed by politicians who have never balanced the budget, requiring their successors to achieve and maintain equality between two undefined conditions for undefined periods subject to undefined penalties, unless they decide to do otherwise.

Consumer: A person who is capable of choosing a president but incapable of choosing a bicycle without help from a government agency.

Consumerism: A policy of imposing regulatory burdens on production which hold down the incomes of workers, thereby keeping them from buying things they want that aren't good for them.

Demand Management: A ritual practice of governments, after 1936, in which they sought, by manipulating taxes, government spending, and money supply, to propitiate the gods and achieve full employment, efficiency, and economic growth. This last came to be regarded as a twentieth-century superstition.

"Verbal Windfall," by Herbert Stein, in the *New York Times Magazine,* September 9, 1979. Reprinted in *Washington Bedtime Stories,* by Herbert Stein, pp. 65–68.

Deregulation: A process of restoring free markets by eliminating the old, small regulations we are used to, as in the case of airline fares, and imposing big new regulations—as in the case of who can use how much energy of what kind for what purpose—with the result that the total number of regulations becomes larger and stranger.

Energy Program: A plan under which low-cost energy will be taxed and high-cost energy will be subsidized, thus discouraging production of low cost energy and encouraging production of high-cost energy, and assuring that energy is produced at unnecessarily high cost. A variant of this is known as "The Nation's First Comprehensive Energy Program," which means the president's latest rendition of an oft-told story.

Eurodollar: A word used to indicate that economic discussion has reached its most rarefied level and amateurs should now leave the room.

Keynesian: An all-purpose pejorative used by editorial writers and politicians for economic policies they don't like. The origins of the term are obscure, but it probably derives from a British economist, John Maynard Keynes, whose economic writing is no longer read and who is best known as a member of the Bloomsbury set, a friend of Virginia Woolf, and husband of Lydia Lopokova, a famous ballerina.

Monetarism: The theory that there is a stable and predictable relation between the price level as effect and the supply of money as cause. This theory has firm empirical support if the definition of the money supply is allowed to vary in an unstable and unpredictable way.

Neo-conservatism: Old wine drunk by new winos, who have discovered the philosophy of Lady Marchmain: "I realize that it is possible for the rich to sin by coveting the privileges of the poor. The poor have always been the favorites of God and His saints, but I believe that it is one of the special achievements of Grace to sanctify the whole of life, riches included."

Obscene: A word formerly applied to books but now obsolete in that context and routinely applied to profits. This has given rise to a revision of Jimmy Walker's statement that he never knew a girl to be ruined by a book—to the effect that many, however, have been ruined by profits.

Quick Fix: Always used in the sentence "There is no quick fix." That should be interpreted to mean that the speaker is doubtful whether there is a long-run solution to the problem in question.

Rational Expectations: This is the hottest thing in economics in 1979. It seems that people cannot rationally expect the success of a policy whose success depends on the people's not understanding the policy. The lady in the box cannot be fooled by the illusionist who pretends to saw her in half.

Rationing by Price: A system in which economic goods go to the people who are most willing to pay for them. This is the normal way of distributing goods in capitalist countries, and is increasingly used in Communist countries. Economists generally consider it an efficient system, but some politicians consider it immoral and prefer a system of rationing by political pull.

Recession: Formerly a term of scientific analysis, this has now lost all meaning. It was briefly revived in 1979 by Alfred Kahn, an economist who was appointed President Carter's chief inflation fighter and after a few months of notoriety was never heard from again. When the White House staff complained that Kahn was tarnishing the president's image by constantly saying, "Yes, we have no bananas," Kahn cleverly substituted the word "recession" for "banana."

Supply Side: A theory which became popular in the late 1970s and which held that big effects could be produced by small actions. For example, a tax cut of $1 billion would raise the national income by $5 billion, increase the government revenue by $2 billion, reduce unemployment, and restrain inflation. This theorem was discovered written on the back of a napkin in a McDonald's restaurant. That gave rise to the axiom "There ain't no such thing as a free lunch, but there is a cheap one."

Underlying Inflation Rate: This is the inflation rate that would exist in the absence of special factors and to which the inflation rate will tend to return when the special factors have disappeared. These special factors include everything having to do with the prices of energy, food, housing, and medical care. The underlying rate of inflation is always below this year's actual rate and above last year's actual rate.

Wage-Price Guidelines: (Also known as guideposts or standards.) Wage-price controls imposed by a president who says that he will never impose wage-price controls. The repeated use of wage-price guidelines as a way of trying to control inflation is the leading example in economic policy of the triumph of hope over experience.

Windfall Profits: Profits earned by people who invested their money in developing a resource, such as oil, which later turns out to be of great value to other people who were not sufficiently foresighted or venturesome to invest their own money. For example, the grasshopper said to the ant, "What big windfall profits you have there, friend!"

Alfred Marshall

Burn the Mathematics (excerpt)

I had a growing feeling in the later years of my work at the subject that a good mathematical theorem dealing with economic hypotheses was very unlikely to be good economics: and I went more and more on the rules—(1) Use mathematics as a shorthand language, rather than an engine of inquiry. (2) Keep to them until you have done. (3) Translate into English. (4) Then illustrate by examples that are important in real life. (5) Burn the mathematics. (6) If you can't succeed in 4, burn 3. This last I did often.

Stephen B. Leacock

Through a Glass Darkly

It is to be feared that many readers of this magazine will pass this article by—the modest as too learned, the learned as too ignorant; the light as too heavy, and the heavy as too light. All will be mistaken. What is here said is very real truth—even if softened now and again with an attempt to alleviate it by what is very real fun—and represents a very real and important issue.

The clergy, in their similar despairing call for attention at the opening of a sermon, take a text. Let me, therefore, as the prelude to this essay, take mine from the pages of one of the most eminent and conspicuous works in economics that have appeared in the past few years. The writer of it is the holder of one of the most respected chairs in England, in a university of which I dare not breathe the name. If I did, I should be crushed flat at once under the deadweight of prestige and authority. In any case it would seem invidious and personal to say that in my opinion the particular book of a particular author is tommyrot, when what I really mean is that a hundred recent books by a hundred recent authors are tommyrot.

The author in this case before us is undertaking a discussion of what he calls the 'size of real incomes.' That is about as near to a plain intelligible phrase as a trained economist can get. An ordinary person would prefer to say 'what people get for their money,' but that would be just a little too easy to understand. The writer goes on to say that if, conceivably, all people used and consumed one and the same thing, and only one, then we could compare what each got with what every other got by the mere quantity or number. But in reality people consume all kinds of different things with all kinds of preferences.

So far the sky is clear. There has been no warning of mathematics. The readers are as unsuspecting as the crowd in the Paris streets before Napoleon Bonaparte turned on the grape shots of Vendemiaire.

Now comes the volley: —

It may perhaps be thought that the difficulty can be overcome by comparing real incomes, not in themselves, but in respect of their values. It is, of course, always possible, with a pricing system, to value each of two real incomes in terms of any commodity that we choose, and to set the values so reached over against one another. This is frequently done in terms of money. Unfortunately, however, the two valuations will, in general, be related to one another in different ways according to what commodity is taken as the measure of value. Thus, suppose that we have two incomes each comprising items of three sorts—A,B,C; that in the first income the quantities of these items are a,b,c, with money prices p_a, p_b, p_c; and in the second α, β, γ, with money prices π_α, π_β, π_γ. The money value of the first income divided by that of the second is then $(ap_a + bp_b + cp_c)/(\alpha\pi_\alpha + \beta\pi_\beta + \gamma\pi_\gamma)$. Call this m. The value of the first income divided by that of the second in terms of commodity A is π_α/p_a m; in terms of commodity B, π_β/p_b m; in terms of commodity C, π_γ/p m. These quantities are obviously, in general, different. There is nothing to prevent one of them being greater, while another is less, than unity. Thus the result of comparisons depends on the choice we make of the commodity in terms of which valuations are to be made; and this is purely arbitrary. Nothing useful, therefore, can be accomplished on this plan.

As the last echo of the paragraph dies away, the readers are seen to lie as thickly mown down as the casualties of Vendemiaire. The volley has done its work. There will be no further resistance to the argument on the part of the general public. Theirs not to reason why, theirs but to do and die. They will learn to surrender their economic thought to the dictation of the elite. They are not to question where they do not understand.

The last sentence of the paragraph, the final shot, is not without humor. 'Nothing useful,' it says, 'can be accomplished on this plan.' No, indeed, nothing much, except getting rid of the readers. For the whole of the 'plan' and its pretentious mathematics, when interpreted into plain talk, amounts to something so insignificant and so self-evident that it is within reach of the simplest peasant who ever lived in Boeotia, or failed at Cambridge. It only means that different people with the same money would buy different things; one might buy roses, one cigars, and another concert tickets; and you couldn't very well compare them because the weight wouldn't mean anything, and the color wouldn't, nor the number. As to what you pay for them *in money* and why you paid—well, that is the very thing we want to find out.

Or shall I state the same thing like this: 'It is hard to compare Janie's doll with Johnny's dog.' Or let us put it into rural York-shire: 'There's a mowt of folks i' country; happen one loike this aw t'other chap that; dang me if I know 'oo gets best on it. Or in Cree Indian (Fort Chipewyan, H.B. Post, Athabaska Lake): 'Hole-in-the-Sky take four guns, two blanket; squaw take one looking glass, one hymnbook.'

What the problem means is that he can't really compare what Hole-in-the-Sky got and what the squaw got. That's all.

II

What has been just said is not meant as fun: it is meant in earnest. If the mathematical statement helped the thought,—either in presentation or in power of deduction,—it would be worth while. But it doesn't. It impedes it. It merely helps to turn economics into an esoteric science, known only to the few. The mathematician is beckoning economics toward the seclusion of the dusty chamber of death, in the pyramid of scholasticism. He stands at the door that he has opened, his keys in his hand. It is dark within and silent. In the darkness lie the mummified bodies of the learnings that were, that perished one by one in the dead mephitic air of scholasticism; of learning that had turned to formalism and lost its meaning, to body and lost its soul, to formula and lost its living force. Here lie, centuries old, the Schol-arship of China, the Learning of Heliopolis, the Medicine that the Middle Ages killed, and the Reason that fell asleep as Formal Logic.

All are wrapped in a sanctity that still imposes. They sleep in all the symbols of honor, with a whisper of legend still about them. But the work they would not do, the task they could not ful-fill, is left still to the fresh bright ignorance of an inquiring world.

Put without prolixity: Any well-established dignified branch of knowledge, finding its problems still unsolved, turns to formalism, authority, symbolism, the inner system of a set of devotees, excluding the world; philosophy becomes scholasticism, science turns to thaumaturgy, religion to dogma, language to rhetoric, and art to symbolism.

Modern economics and philosophy and psychology have so far utterly failed to solve their main problems. So they are beginning to 'dig in' as scholasticism. For economics, mathematical symbolism is the means adopted.

III

So few people are accustomed to use mathematical symbols that it is hard to discuss them in an essay of this sort without incurring the very danger here denounced and 'sidetracking' the reader. But something of their nature everybody knows. Very often a mathematical symbol or expression does convey an idea very quickly and clearly. Thus the simple and self-evident little charts and graphs used in newspapers to show the rise and fall of production and trade, the elementary index numbers used to show the movement of prices—these things are immensely useful. But they are only a method of presentation of what is known, not a method of finding out what is not known.

Very often we use simple mathematical expressions as a vehicle of common language, as when we say 'fifty-fifty,' or 'a hundred per cent American,' or 'half-soused,' or 'three-quarters silly.' We could go further if we liked, and instead of saying 'more and more' we could say $A + n + n$. . . . we could express a lot of our ordinary dialogue in mathematical form. Thus:—

'How is your grandmother's health?' 'Oh, it depends a good deal on the weather and her digestion, but I am afraid she always fusses about herself: to-day she's about fifty-fifty.'

Mathematically this is a function of two variables and a constant, and reads:—

$$f(\text{W.D.} + \text{fuss}) = 1/2$$

The result is, in all seriousness, just as illuminating and just as valuable as the mathematics quoted above.

We could even go further and express a lot of our best poetry in mathematical form:—

56

Tennyson's 'Light Brigade'

Half a league, half a league,
   Half a league onward . . .
Then they rode back, but not,
   Not the six hundred.

The mathematician would prefer:—

$$\frac{1/2 + 1/2 + 1/2}{600} = 600 - N$$

Or, try this as an improvement on Byron:—

Childe Harold's Pilgrimage

Did ye not hear it?—No; 't was but the wind,
   Or the car rattling o'er the stony street;
      On with the dance!

$$d + d + d + d \ldots d(n)$$

Let joy be unconfined;

$$j + j + j + \ldots \text{infinity}$$

No sleep till morn, when Youth and Pleasure meet.

$$M - S = Y + P$$

Or, to quote a verse of 'Lord Ullin's Daughter' (done as mathematics), in which I once depicted the desperate efforts of the highland boatman:—

The angry water gains apace
Both of his sides and half his base,
   Till as he sits he seems to lose
   The square of his hypotenuse.

Or, to go a little deeper, by venturing into Descartes's brilliant method of indicating space and motion by means of two or more coordinates as a frame of reference, we can make the opening of Gray's 'Elegy' a little more exact.

The lowing herd winds slowly o'er the lea.

We can indicate the exact path by a series of points at successive moments of time $(p - p_1 - p_2 - p_3 \ldots p_n)$, and by dropping perpendiculars from each of these to the coordinates we can indicate the area swept by the lowing herd, or rather the area which it ought to sweep but doesn't.

IV

Let me explain here that in this essay I do not wish in any way to deny the marvelous effectiveness of mathematical symbols in their proper field. I have for mathematics that lowly respect and that infinite admiration felt by those of us who never could get beyond such trifles as plane trigonometry and logarithms, and were stopped by a *nolle prosequi* from the penetration of its higher mysteries. Mathematical symbols permit of calculation otherwise beyond our powers and of quantitative expression that otherwise would require an infinity of time. It is no exaggeration to say that mathematical symbols are second only to the alphabet as an instrument of human progress. Think what is entailed by the lack of them. Imagine a Roman trying to multiply LXXVI by CLX. The Roman, indeed, could make use of an abacus,—the beads on wires of the Chinese, the familiar nursery toy,—but multiplication with beads only, and without written symbols on a decimal or ascending place-plan, is a poor and limited matter. See who will in this connection the mediaeval work called *Accomptung by Counters*—A.D. 1510. Contrast with these feeble expedients the power of expression and computation that symbols give us! The Hebrew psalmist used to ask with awe who could number the sands of the sea! Well, I can! Put them, let us say, at $(100)^{100}$ and we've only used six figures and two crooked lines! And if that is not enough use three more figures:—

$$100$$
$$100$$
$$100$$

Where are the sands of the sea now? Gone to mud! Light moves fast and space is large, but symbols can shoot past them at a walk. Take the symbol for a 'light-year' and cube it! You can see it all there in half a dozen strokes, and its meaning is as exact as the change out of a dollar.

Consider this. There is a famous old Persian story, known to everybody, of the grateful king who asked the physician who had saved his life to name his own reward. The physician merely asked that a penny—or an obol or something—be placed on the first square of a chessboard, two on the next, and then four, and so on, till all the sixty-four spaces were filled! The shah protested at the man's modesty and said he must at least take a horse as well. Then they counted the money, and presumably the shah fell back dead! The mathematical formula that killed him was the series $(1 + 2 + 4 \ldots N)$, where $N = 64$: the sum of a geometrical progression—and, at that, the simplest and slowest one known to whole numbers.

As a matter of fact, if the king and the physician had started counting out the pennies at the rate of five thousand an hour and had kept it up for a seven-hour day, with Sundays off, it would have taken them a month to count a million. At the end of a year they'd be only on square No. 20 out of the sixty-four; granting that the king and the physician were each sixty-two years old (they'd have to be that to have got so far in politics), their expectation of life would be fifteen years, and they'd both be dead before they got to the thirtieth square; and the last square alone would call for 10,000,000,000,000,000,000 pennies. In other words, they are both alive now and counting.[1]

V

But all of this wonder and power and mystery is of no aid in calculating the incalculable. You cannot express the warmth of emotions in calories, the pressure on the market in horsepower, and the buoyancy of credit in specific gravity! Yet this is exactly what the pseudo-mathematicians try to do when they invade the social sciences. The conceptions dealt with in politics and economics and psychology—the ideas of valuation, preference, willingness and unwillingness, antipathy, desire, and so forth—cannot be put into quantitative terms.

It would not so much matter if this vast and ill-placed mess of mathematical symbolism could be set aside and left to itself while the real work of economics went on. Thus, for example, is left

---

1. If any reader doubts these calculations I refer him to my colleague, Professor Charles Sullivan of McGill University, and if he doubts Professor Sullivan I refer him so far that he will never get back.

—Author

aside by the real modern physicists, such as Rutherford and Soddy, the whole mass of the Einstein geometry—which from their point of view is neither here nor there. (Many people don't know that.) But in the case of economic theory these practitioners undertake to draw deductions; to dive into a cloud of mathematics and come out again holding a theory, a precept, an *order*, as it were, in regard to the why of the depression, or a remedy for unemployment, or an explanation of the nature of saving and investment. They are like—or want to be like—a physician prescribing a dose for the docile and confiding patient. He writes on a piece of paper, '$\partial \Delta \rho \%$,' and says, 'Take that.' Thus one of the latest and otherwise most deservedly famous of the mathematical economists advises us in a new book, heralded as the book of the year, that our salvation lies in the proper adjustment of investment and demand. Once get this right and all the rest is easy. As a first aid the great economist undertakes to explain the relation of investment and demand in a preliminary, simple fashion as follows:—

More generally the proportionate change in total demand to the proportionate change in investment equals

$$\frac{\Delta Y}{Y} \bigg/ \frac{\Delta I}{I} = \frac{\Delta Y}{Y} \cdot \frac{Y - C}{\Delta Y - \Delta C} = \frac{1 - \dfrac{c}{y}}{1 - \dfrac{dc}{dy}}$$

To 99.9 per cent of the world's readers this spells good-bye. If economics can only be made intelligible in that form, then it moves into the class of atomic physics. The great mass of us are outside of it. We can judge it only by its accomplishments; and, as economics so far has accomplished nothing, the outlook is dark.

Now I do not know what all that Delta and Y stuff just quoted means, but I am certain that if I did I could write it out just as plainly and simply as the wonderful theorem up above about different people spending their money on different things. In other words, mathematical economics is what is called in criminal circles 'a racket.'

Letters Yes, Figures No (excerpt)

All economical and practical wisdom is an extension or variation of the following arithmetical formula: 2 + 2 = 4. Every philosophical proposition has the more general character of the expression a + b = c. We are mere operatives, empirics, and egotists, until we learn to think in letters instead of figures.

George Bernard Shaw

A Plausible Boy (excerpt)

I somewhat mistrust mathematical symbols. I remember at school a plausible boy who used to prove to me by algebra that one equals two. He always began by saying, "Let x equal a." I saw no great harm in admitting that; and the proof followed with rigorous exactness. The effect was not to make me proceed habitually on the assumption that one equals two, but to impress upon me that there was a screw loose somewhere in the algebraic art, and a chance for me to set it right some day when I had time to look into the subject. And I feel bound to make the perhaps puerile confession that when I read Jevons's *Theory of Political Economy,* I no sooner glanced at the words "let x signify the quantity of commodity," than I thought of the plausible boy, and prepared myself for a theory of value based on algebraic proof that two and two makes five. But as it turned out, Mr. Jevons, less ingenious or more ingenuous than my schoolfellow, arrived at no more remarkable conclusion than that if x equalled y, y equalled x, which I should have granted freely without the aid of algebra.

The Stochastic Variable

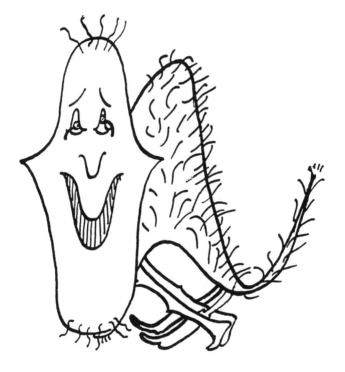

The wild Stochastic Variable
Is loose, and vague, and quite unstable.
He's so imperfectly located
It's quite a job to get him mated.

X Cantos

On Learning the Mathematics of Linear Programming

Canto I.

How pleasant it can be to sit
And contemplate the infinite!
The more so, when we recognize
It's only zero in disguise.

Canto II.

The integers march by in fine
Unending, but still counted, line
And in between them march the class
Of fractions in a solid mass.
Then in the rules that don't exist,
Between the fractions, we must list
Uncountable irrational hosts
Of infinitely slender ghosts,
While somewhere in the endless sky
Imaginary Numbers fly
Illumined by the ethereal sun
Of the square root of minus one.

Canto III.

Now, climbing up the mental stairs,
Numbers go by in ordered pairs,
Or, (having no bisexual scruples)
In threes or fours, or in n-tuples.
And so we see (in words director)

That *marriage* is a kind of *vector*
(Though here some varying views prevail
On which sex forms the head, or tail).
Vectors have length and pure direction
And multiply by sheer erection.
They add themselves, like pulling horses,
In parallelograms of forces.

Canto IV.

Between two points lie lots of stations
Called convex linear combinations,
Like intermediate stops that lie
Between two railroad termini
(With three points, now, the combination
Defines a neat triangulation)
And generalizing this, we get
The notion of a convex set.

Canto V.

The extreme point, like young Jack Horner,
Sits lonely in a kind of corner,
And therefore has no points as brothers
That sit with it between two others.

Canto VI.

Take any set, or thing, or crowd,
And wrap it in a kind of shroud.
Then when the shroud is tight and full
We see it as a *Convex Hull.*

Canto VII.

If S and T are convex sets
Their *intersection* then begets
Another set of convex kind.
(Not so, their union, we find
For unions, strangely, may beget
A wholly unparental set.)

Canto VIII.

These theorems are neat and true,
But do they have an end in view?
They do indeed, so let us sing
The Praise of Linear Programming!

Canto IX.

There is a field a point is on
Surrounded by a polygon,
The sides of which, he plainly sees,
Are linear inequalities.
For these expressions (more or less)
Are fences that he can't transgress.
Within the polygon we get
The *feasible* (well-corralled) set.
The problem now, if not the moral,
Is *where,* within the fence, or corral,
A roving point (or wandering beast)
Can get the furthest north-northeast.

Canto X.

I do not want to spend my days
In writing out the i's and j's,
Yet i's and j's are an enigma
When squashed into a double sigma.

Dennis H. Robertson

The Non-econometrician's Lament

As soon as I could safely toddle
My parents handed me a Model.
My brisk and energetic pater
Provided the accelerator.
My mother, with her kindly gumption,
The function guiding my consumption;
And every week I had from her
A lovely new parameter,
With lots of little leads and lags
In pretty parabolic bags.

With optimistic expectations
I started on my explorations,
And swore to move without a swerve
Along my sinusoidal curve.
Alas! I knew how it would end:
I've mixed the cycle and the trend,
And fear that, growing daily skinnier,
I have at length become non-linear.
I wander glumly round the house
As though I were exogenous,
And hardly capable of feeling
The difference 'tween floor and ceiling.
I scarcely now, a pallid ghost,
Can tell *ex-ante* from *ex-post:*
My thoughts are sadly inelastic,
My acts incurably stochastic.

Edward E. Leamer

Let's Take the Con Out of Econometrics (excerpt)

The applied econometrician is like a farmer who notices that the yield is somewhat higher under trees where birds roost, and he uses this as evidence that bird droppings increase yields. However, when he presents this finding at the annual meeting of the American Ecological Association, another farmer in the audience objects that he used the same data but came up with the conclusion that moderate amounts of shade increase yields. A bright chap in the back of the room then observes that these two hypotheses are indistinguishable, given the available data. He mentions the phrase "identification problem," which, though no one knows quite what he means, is said with such authority that it is totally convincing. The meeting reconvenes in the halls and in the bars, with heated discussion whether this is the kind of work that merits promotion from Associate to Full Farmer; the Luminists strongly opposed to promotion and the Aviophiles equally strong in favor. . . .

The images I have drawn are deliberately prejudicial. First, we had the experimental scientist with hair neatly combed, wide eyes peering out of horn-rimmed glasses, a white coat, and an electronic calculator for generating the random assignment of fertilizer treatment to plots of land. This seems to contrast sharply with the nonexperimental farmer with overalls, unkempt hair, and bird droppings on his boots. Another image, drawn by Orcutt, is even more damaging: "Doing econometrics is like trying to learn the laws of electricity by playing the radio." . . .

. . . The econometric art as it is practiced at the computer terminal involves fitting many, perhaps thousands, of statistical models. One or several that the researcher finds pleasing are selected for reporting purposes. This searching for a model is often well intentioned, but there can be no doubt that such a specification search invalidates the traditional theories of inference. The concepts of unbiasedness, consistency, efficiency, maximum-likelihood estimation, in fact, all the concepts of traditional theory, utterly lose their meaning by the time an applied researcher pulls from the bramble of computer output the one thorn of a model he likes best, the one he chooses to portray as a rose. The consuming public is hardly fooled by this chicanery. The econometrician's shabby art is humorously and disparagingly labelled "data mining," "fishing," "grubbing," "number crunching." A joke evokes the Inquisition: "If you torture the data long enough, Nature will confess" (Coase). Another suggests methodological fickleness: "Econometricians, like artists, tend to fall in love with their models" (wag unknown). Or how about: "There are two things you are better off not watching in the making: sausages and econometric estimates." . . .

This rhetoric is understandably tiring. Methodology, like sex, is better demonstrated than discussed, though often better anticipated than experienced.

Lies, Damn Lies, and Crystal Balls

DIVINATION, *n*. The art of nosing out the occult. Divination is of as many kinds as there are fruit-bearing varieties of the flowering dunce and the early fool.

—Ambrose Bierce

Suppositions which are arrived at on the basis of a small number of poorly understood facts yield to suppositions which are less absurd, although no more true.

—Anne Robert Jacques Turgot, Baron d'Aulne

Error Dynamics

Economics humbles its practitioners both in their optimism and in their doubts.

The experience of being disastrously wrong is salutory; no economist should be denied it, and not many are.

—John Kenneth Galbraith

The "staying-alive rule": the rule on staying alive as a forecaster is to give 'em a *number* or give 'em a *date*, but *never give 'em both at once.*

—Jane Bryant Quinn

Proxies and Dummies

Let us remember the unfortunate econometrician who, in one of the major functions of his system, had to use a proxy for risk and a dummy for sex.

—Fritz Machlup

Forecasting Made Easier

It's very easy to be an economist these days. Back in the 1960s, an economist who made a wrong prediction on the start of a recession had to wait years to be proved right. Nowadays, if you miss a call, all you have to do is wait six months.

—Edward E. Yardeni

Six Eskimos in a Bed

Economic forecasters are like six eskimos in one bed; the only thing you can be sure of is that they are all going to turn over together.

—Roy Blough

Tony Auth

Paul A. Samuelson

On Economic Forecasting (excerpt)

If prediction is the ultimate aim of all science, then we forecasters ought to award ourselves the palm for accomplishment, bravery, or rashness. We are the end-product of Darwinian evolution and the payoff for all scientific study of economics. Around the country, students are grinding out doctoral theses by the use of history, statistics, and theory—merely to enable us to reduce the error in our next year's forecast of GNP from $10 billion down to $9 billion.

Just as ancient kings had their soothsayers and astrologists, modern tycoons and prime ministers have their economic forecasters. Eastern sorcerers wore that peaked hat which in modern times we regard as a dunce's cap; and I suppose if the head fits, we can put it in. . . .

How well can economists forecast? The question is an indefinite one, and reminds us of the man who was asked what he thought about his wife, and had to reply, "Compared to what?" . . .

. . . [B]ad as we economists are, we are better than anything else in heaven and earth at forecasting aggregate business trends—better than gypsy tea-leaf readers, Wall Street soothsayers and chartist technicians, hunch-playing heads of mail order chains, or all-powerful heads of state.

Pepper . . . and Salt

"Don't laugh -- she's called the last five
Dow Jones turnarounds right on the nose."

Darrell Huff

On Extrapolation (excerpt)

Extrapolations are useful, particularly in that form of soothsaying called forecasting trends. But in looking at the figures or the charts made from them, it is necessary to remember one thing constantly: The trend-to-now may be a fact, but the future trend represents no more than an educated guess. Implicit in it is "everything else being equal" and "present trends continuing." And somehow everything else refuses to remain equal, else life would be dull indeed.

The Fable of the Cat

The meeting in Mouseville was uncommonly well attended. Every seat in the hall was taken. In the crowd were a sizable number of mice who were alarmed by recent events. Others at the meeting were quite calm, not at all concerned. And the rest—the vast majority—seemed bewildered. They simply wanted to be told what *really* was happening in their community.

The chairman, a no-nonsense type, quickly set forth the reason for the meeting. An old problem, it seemed, had returned to make life difficult for Mouseville and its inhabitants. After nine years of peace and quiet a cat was reported to be moving into the neighborhood.

When the squeaks of dismay died down, the chairman hastened to explain that reports of a cat were no more than that. No positive identification had yet been made. And there was considerable difference of opinion among knowledgeable members of the community as to whether such a cat even existed.

"I say there is too much loose talk about a cat," spoke up one member of the group who, owing to his position, could exert a powerful influence over the entire community.

"I heartily agree," was the comment uttered by another respected leader, who ranked high in the councils of government. He went on to say: "Even if something were to threaten us for two consecutive quarters I still would not jump to the conclusion that it was a cat, necessarily." An even more reassuring statement was made by a mouse who the audience knew held learned degrees in political economy—even though his statements sometimes lacked a sense of total commitment to proper English usage. With his cigar stabbing the air for emphasis, he stated: "There ain't gonna be no cat!" The flat prediction brought a chorus of approval and much pawclapping from a small group of mice who concerned themselves with Mouseville's political process. Their leader spoke out: "It is absolutely unacceptable to have a cat—especially in an election year."

Squeakers of Gloom

Despite such attempts to allay the community's fears, not all the members seemed convinced. Some of the mice suspected that there might be a cat in the neighborhood. There *was* a certain smell in the air. Others were certain of it. The latter group, one by one, stood up to speak out against complacency:

From a builder of snug three and four bedroom nests: "I know a cat when I see one. This is a huge cat that is threatening my very life."

The gunslinging manager of the Trap-Free Growth Fund complained: "There is no doubt of it. It's a cat in bear's clothing."

Said the plump proprietor of Honest Sam's Auto Emporium, concerned about slumping sales of the new compact Rodent: "Consumers are not buying. They're worried about the cat."

There was no doubt in the mind of a workmouse, recently let go from his job: "To me it's a whole family of cats—a real disaster."

The tide of concern in the meeting clearly was rising. There seemed no end to those who were jumping to their feet to warn of impending danger. Even those mice who were merely visiting Mouseville felt constrained to speak up. One of these, a variety of Friedmouse hailing from the midwest, said: "We are bound to have a ferocious cat because the cheese supply has been flat for nine months."

A big-city mousebanker, worried about sinking prestige, credit-card backlash, and depreciated bond accounts, added: "Maybe we can now hope that our lords and masters will parcel out a slightly bigger ration of cheese. An extra sliver a day could keep the cat away."

A short, gnome-like mouse—obviously a foreign visitor— applauded that comment and advised: "You U.S. mice must do something about the cat. Every time you get a cat we have a lion in Europe." That comment led the mouse seated nearby, sad of face with whiskers that drooped forlornly, to warn in lugubrious tones: "The cat is the least of our worries. Pollution is going to kill us all."

Up to that point in the meeting the issue had been rather clean-cut. Some thought that there was no cat to worry about; others thought to the contrary. Then things began to get fuzzy.

One mouse insisted that what he had seen was a tiny kitten, not a cat. He called it a "mini-cat"—and drew some delighted squeaks from the audience for his originality. Another member of the community, an industry economouse cautious by nature although not always really careful, allowed that he had detected something but that he needed more time to decide what it was he had seen. "Maybe if I had a little longer to analyze the reports I have been getting I could be more certain," he added, a bit lamely.

By this time the audience was getting restive. A meeting called to eliminate confusion was merely adding to it.

"Words, words, figures, figures," cried one mouse, his tail twitching with impatience. "I hear descriptions, none of which is on the same base, that vary from a small furry animal, of unspecified origin, to a huge alley cat that will turn out to be worse than anything we have had to face since the Great Cat of the early 1930's. Is there a cat or isn't there?" The comment brought a chorus of agreement, much stamping of feet and lashing of tails. The meeting was threatening to get out of hand.

Defining a Feline

Then the chairman displayed his storied wisdom. *The Institute*, staffed by economice with formidable powers of analysis, would decide whether there was a cat or not. Who would dispute the findings of *The Institute*? After all, was it not *The Institute* that had always made the determination? It could be counted on to make a calm, scholarly, dispassionate judgment, going in great depth into the size of the cat, when it arrived, and how long it had been around.

It was a masterstroke. The audience was delighted. Now they would know whether they should worry about a cat or go on munching their cheese free of worry.

Alas, one mouse was not quite satisfied. He raised his paw for attention—a timid gesture, almost as if he hoped the chairman would not notice. But the chairman did notice. The question came tumbling out: "When can we expect to get the news—whether there is a cat or not?"

The chairman had hoped no one would ask. But now the query had been made. He replied, as briskly as possible: "The last time *The Institute* was called upon to make a judgment about a cat was in 1960–61. It took the better part of a year to decide that there had been a cat. But, as a matter of general practice, *The Institute* does not announce that there is a cat until the cat has left the neighborhood."

As the chairman had feared, his reply led inevitably to further comments and queries. "That's a long time to wait to find out about the cat," shouted one mouse. Another asked: "What shall we do in the meantime?"

The chairman huffed and puffed but no answer came to mind. To his immense relief he saw the venerable elder of the community slowly rise from his chair and beckon for attention. The chairman was happy to oblige. All eyes shifted to the slightly stooped figure with white whiskers. He spoke:

"Fellow citizens, do not be excessively concerned about the various descriptions of the cat that you have been hearing. The mini-cat, the two-quarter cat, and so on. You can get caught in semantic quicksand.

"If there is a cat it will not be long now before we will all know. Any cat worthy of the name will not stay hidden indefinitely, I promise you. Meantime, do not panic and take rash action over a cat that may or may not materialize."

The quiet, measured tones of the oldtimer calmed the assembled mice. They liked his pragmatic approach—of crossing *that* bridge when they came to it. Besides, it put off to another day the dreary and difficult business of deciding what to do about a cat, if in fact there was one.

The mice filed out of the hall. The chairman silently congratulated himself on his adroit handling of the meeting. But in truth it must be said that the amount of bewilderment in Mouseville had not been reduced by as much as a cat's whisker.

Mark Twain

Extrapolating: The Lower Mississippi in 742 Years (excerpt)

. . . [D]ry details are of importance in one particular. They give me an opportunity of introducing one of the Mississippi's oddest peculiarities,—that of shortening its length from time to time. If you will throw a long, pliant apple-paring over your shoulder, it will pretty fairly shape itself into an average section of the Mississippi River; that is, the nine or ten hundred miles stretching from Cairo, Illinois, southward to New Orleans, the same being wonderfully crooked, with a brief straight bit here and there at wide intervals. The two-hundred-mile stretch from Cairo northward to St. Louis is by no means so crooked, that being a rocky country which the river cannot cut much. . . .

. . . [T]he Mississippi between Cairo and New Orleans was twelve hundred and fifteen miles long one hundred and seventy-six years ago. It was eleven hundred and eighty after the cut-off of 1722. It was one thousand and forty after the American Bend cut-off. It has lost sixty-seven miles since. Consequently its length is only nine hundred and seventy-three miles at present.

Now, if I wanted to be one of those ponderous scientific people, and 'let on' to prove what had occurred in the remote past by what had occurred in a given time in the recent past, or what will occur in the far future by what has occurred in late years, what an opportunity is here! Geology never had such a chance, nor such exact data to argue from! Nor 'development of species,' either! Glacial epochs are great things, but they are vague—vague. Please observe:—

In the space of one hundred and seventy-six years the Lower

Mississippi has shortened itself two hundred and forty-two miles. That is an average of a trifle over one mile and a third per year. Therefore, any calm person, who is not blind or idiotic, can see that in the Old Oölitic Silurian Period, just a million years ago next November, the Lower Mississippi River was upwards of one million three hundred thousand miles long, and stuck out over the Gulf of Mexico like a fishing-rod. And by the same token any person can see that seven hundred and forty-two years from now the Lower Mississippi will be only a mile and three-quarters long, and Cairo and New Orleans will have joined their streets together, and be plodding comfortably along under a single mayor and a mutual board of aldermen. There is something fascinating about science. One gets such wholesome returns of conjecture out of such a trifling investment of fact.

Robert Frost

The Secret Sits

We dance round in a ring and suppose,
But the Secret sits in the middle and knows.

John J. Siegfried

A First Lesson in Econometrics

Every budding econometrician must learn early that it is never in good taste to express the sum of two quantities in the form:

$$1 + 1 = 2. \tag{1}$$

Any graduate student of economics is aware that

$$1 = \ln e, \tag{2}$$

and further that

$$1 = \sin^2 q + \cos^2 q. \tag{3}$$

In addition, it is obvious to the casual reader that

$$2 = \sum_{n=0}^{\infty} \frac{1}{2^n}. \tag{4}$$

Therefore equation (1) can be rewritten more scientifically as

$$\ln e + (\sin^2 q + \cos^2 q) = \sum_{n=0}^{\infty} \frac{1}{2^n}. \tag{5}$$

It is readily confirmed that

The work on this paper was supported by no one. The author would like to credit an unknown but astute source for the original seeds for the analysis.

$$1 = \cosh p \sqrt{1 - \tanh^2 p}, \tag{6}$$

and since

$$e = \lim_{\delta \to \infty} \left(1 + \frac{1}{\delta}\right)^{\delta}, \tag{7}$$

equation (5) can be further simplified to read:

$$\ln \left[\lim_{\delta \to \infty} \left(1 + \frac{1}{\delta}\right)^{\delta} \right] + (\sin^2 q + \cos^2 q)$$
$$= \sum_{n=0}^{\infty} \frac{\cosh p \sqrt{1 - \tanh^2 p}}{2^n}. \tag{8}$$

If we note that

$$0! = 1, \tag{9}$$

and recall that the inverse of the transpose is the transpose of the inverse, we can unburden ourselves of the restriction to one-dimensional space by introducing the vector X, where

$$(X')^{-1} - (X^{-1})' = 0. \tag{10}$$

Combining equation (9) with equation (10) gives

$$[(X')^{-1} - (X^{-1})']! = 1, \tag{11}$$

which, when inserted into equation (8) reduces our expression to

$$\ln \left\{ \lim_{\delta \to \infty} \left\{ [(X')^{-1} - (X^{-1})'] + \frac{1}{\delta} \right\} \right\} + (\sin^2 q + \cos^2 q)$$
$$= \sum_{n=0}^{\infty} \frac{\cosh p \sqrt{1 - \tanh^2 p}}{2^n}. \tag{12}$$

At this point it should be obvious that equation (12) is much clearer and more easily understood than equation (1). Other methods of a similar nature could be used to simplify equation (1), but these will become obvious once the young econometrician grasps the underlying principles.

Part 3
Economics 101—
The Invisible Hand

Introduction

Adam Smith (1723–90) held the chair of moral philosophy at Glasgow, is the father of academic economics, and had a lot of fatherly influence on his descendants. Economists occasionally disagree (see the preceding articles), but there is almost universal consensus on the assumption that self-interest motivates human behavior. Smith did not invent the notion, but he articulated it well. In 1759, Smith wrote *The Theory of Moral Sentiments,* from which the excerpt on "self-admiration" is taken. The quotations that follow, from *The Wealth of Nations,* illustrate Smith's concept of the "invisible hand," an idea as easy to understand as to draw. In short, when individual self-interest is pursued unrestrained, society benefits. To put it mildly, there is some dissent on this.

When the University of Chicago's George J. Stigler (1911–91) won the Nobel Prize in economics in 1982, the columnist George Will remarked that he deserved the "Nobel Prize in Wit." In its February 1992 issue, the *Journal of Political Economy,* which he edited for 19 years, honored him in a memorial that referred to his "good humor." As described in Stigler's essay, "Stigler's First Law of Sympathy," published in 1963, Professor Sidney Siegel offers unimpeachable "proof" that "sympathy is always at a maximum."

People who yearn for a simpler life would find it more appealing if doing without were not part of the deal. Oliver Wendell Holmes satirizes this view in "Contentment," written in 1858. A few changes here and there and the verse would fit the 1990s. "The Rich Man," a Franklin P. Adams verse written in 1911, carries a similar strain of thought.

The conversation between a Man and a Goose in the allegorical verse by Ambrose Bierce (1842–1914?) includes more than one basic economic idea. One is that human wants are insatiable. The other is that you can't have your goose and eat it too.

Ambrose Bierce was a journalist, printer's devil, fabulist, and satirist. Among the many pseudonyms he adopted are Dod Grile, J. Milton Sloluck, William Herman, and Mrs. J. Milton Bowers. He is often compared to Jonathan Swift and George Bernard Shaw because of his mordant wit, and his satires provoked more than one challenge to a duel. While his life was legendary, his death remains a mystery. He disappeared after going to Mexico and was never heard from again. Stories of his death range from suicide to survival in some South American country.

The role of the "wasteful spender" has been a source of controversy in the history of economic thought. In the early nineteenth century, David Ricardo displayed a little-known wit on the topic. Criticizing the claim of Thomas Malthus that a large body of "unproductive consumers" is necessary to maintain effective demand, Ricardo scoffed, "as necessary as a fire." The next three selections, written before the Malthus–Ricardo exchange, support the role of the free spender.

As possibly the earliest precursor of the invisible hand, Aesop (ca. 620–560 B.C.) has been sadly neglected. In "The Belly and the Other Members," Aesop personifies parts of the body in a departure from his customary "beast fable." The moral of the short piece is that the "useless" belly contributes to the "common good." Sound familiar?

The problem with acknowledging Aesop as the first invisible hand advocate is the unanswerable question of his existence (scholars who deny there was an Aesop probably want to make sure that Adam Smith gets all the credit). Besides, if Aesop lived, there are also unanswered questions about how he died, not whether. Aesop, who was known as Ysopets (perhaps by those who couldn't pronounce Aesop), was the only Greek slave among the contributors to this collection. He is supposed to have died a violent death at the hands of the inhabitants of Delphi, and, although the cause is not known, there is speculation among scholars (presumably those who don't deny his existence) that his insulting sarcasms were to blame. To make amends or whatever, there is a marble statue of Aesop in Rome's Villa Albani—the sculptor depicted him as ugly and deformed. Apparently, Aesop just couldn't win.

Bernard de Mandeville (1670–1733), a Dutch physician, spent much of his life in England. He was admired by Benjamin Franklin, criticized sharply by Adam Smith, and rarely made house calls. His satire, *The Grumbling Hive, or Knaves Turnd Honest,* was published in 1705, then again in 1714. The expanded 1723 version, *Fable of the Bees; or Private Vices, Publick Benefits,* was indicted as a public nuisance by a Middlesex grand jury. Adam Smith criticized the *Fable* as a "great fallacy," grudgingly conceding its author's "lively and humorous . . . eloquence," and admitting that its thesis "bordered on the truth."[1]

De Mandeville's theme, that wasteful spending is the "wheel that turn'd the trade," is restated in Alexander Pope's satirical 1732 poem on the advantages of "well-dispers'd [riches] to quench a Country's thirst." As they say, if you have it, spend it. Pope (1688–1744) was an English poet and friend of Jonathan Swift and John Arbuthnot, with whom he waged a battle against bad literature in the Scriblerus Club.

The B.C. cartoon parodies the "diamond-water" paradox of value that puzzled Adam Smith and his followers until the marginal revolution "cleared" things up. The cartoon was drawn by Johnny (John Lewis) Hart, an American cartoonist born in 1931. In addition to drawing B.C., Hart was the creator of the Wizard of Id.

In "Three Observations on Desire," Jacques Barzun, Thomas de Quincey, and Philip H. Wicksteed reflect on the properties of a motley assortment of potentially desirable objects. Barzun (1907–) was dean and provost of Columbia University, where he earned his A.B., M.A., and Ph.D. and became a member of Phi Beta Kappa. The Barzun quotation came from a 1958 magazine article. Thomas de Quincey (1785–1859) demonstrates the relative nature of the origin of desire. Philip H. Wicksteed (1844–1927) was a Unitarian minister in London. He made a considerable contribution to the economic literature of marginal utility—the excerpt in this section is an example—and is represented below in this collection.

Only seven of Emily Dickinson's poems were published in her

---

1. "The Theory of Moral Sentiments," in *Adam Smith's Moral and Political Philosophy,* ed. Herbert W. Schneider (New York: Harper & Row, 1948), 43, 49.

lifetime. Dickinson (1830–86) is considered the greatest American woman poet. Her verse, "The Market Price," mixes metaphor with whimsy and pathos.

There is none of Dickinson's gentility in Terry Southern's Babbittlike billionaire, August Guy Grand. As "the last of the big spenders," Grand has a flair for "making it hot" for others, testing the adage that "every man has his price." Southern (1926–95) wrote the screenplay for Dr. Strangelove and was a contributor to *Esquire* and other magazines.

Robert Frost's epigram on the burden of record keeping is carried to absurdity in Colonel Stoopnagle's comic exaggeration, "The Farm Budget," which follows.

Colonel Stoopnagle (1897–1950) was a pseudonym for Frederick Chase Taylor. Stoopnagle is supposed to have said that he started life as an infant and turned into a radio comedian, unlike infants who turn into people. He entered radio as a sideline to the brokerage business, teaming up with Budd Hulick in the comedy team, "Colonel Stoopnagle and Budd." In "The Farm Budget," Stoopnagle advises those who would profit from farming on the importance of having an "observant wife."

The man whom Stephen Leacock called "the apostle of the empty cradle" uses an allegorical "feast" in a sardonic portrayal of how scarcity arises from plenty. While Thomas Malthus (1766–1834) was known as a practical joker in private life, his book on population provoked Thomas Carlyle's "dismal science" epithet. The excerpt is taken from Malthus's second edition of the *Essay on Population*, 1803. The first edition, in 1798, was published anonymously.

William Wordsworth (1770–1850) was poet laureate of Great Britain in the period 1843–50. A contemporary of Malthus, he outlived him by 16 years. Wordsworth, who fathered six children, one out of wedlock, laments "getting and begetting" in the apparent belief that the misguided "flags of good intentions" only apply to others (preempting the "not in my back yard" syndrome).

Economics concerns earthly scarcities, so it is understandable that so few economists are interested in a world where there are none (of course, there may be other reasons for this lack of interest). Christopher Morley once said, "Heaven is not for pallid saints but raging and risible men." Scott Gordon must be a risible man. In "The Economics of the Afterlife," Gordon demonstrates that a different dimension of time is necessary to validate the assumption that there is no scarcity in heaven. After all, he notes, one cannot "play the harp and go swimming simultaneously."

Time is also a factor in the heavenly media. Philip H. Wicksteed, man of the cloth and the world, applies the notion of diminishing marginal utility to the act of praying. Written in 1910, the Wicksteed essay shows that in prayer and in goods there is increasing opportunity cost—the more one has of one thing, the more one values additional units of an alternative. When choosing between more prayer and more self-defense, "we give up the cant of the absolute."

A study by Staffan B. Linder gives Wicksteed's analysis more than theoretical significance. According to Linder, "the average length of sermons seems to have declined . . . the priest has shortened the liturgy." In Sweden, writes Linder, churches advertise "sermons of reasonable length . . . adapted to the modern individual."[2]

The section on "Posthumous Humor . . ." includes light, but significant, remarks on the afterlife. Summarized, the comments suggest that if problems are deferred long enough they will solve themselves, small comfort to those whose mortality is a matter of record.

The closing entry in part 3 is a verse Stephen Leacock wrote in 1936, in the midst of world depression. The length and depth of the depression subjected free market theory to its severest test. Thus, Leacock pleads with Adam Smith to "come up and apologize." But dead men tell no tales.

2. *The Harried Leisure Class* (New York: Columbia University Press, 1970), 108.

Adam Smith

Success and Self-Admiration (excerpt)

Great success in the world, great authority over the sentiments and opinions of mankind, have very seldom been acquired without some degree of . . . excessive self-admiration. The most splendid characters, . . . men who have performed the most illustrious actions, . . . brought about the greatest revolutions, both in the situations and opinions of mankind; the most successful warriors, the greatest statesmen and legislators, the eloquent founders and leaders of the most numerous and most successful sects and parties, have, many of them, been not more distinguished for their very great merit than for a degree of presumption and self-admiration altogether disproportioned even to that very great merit. This presumption was, perhaps, necessary, not only to prompt them to undertakings which a more sober mind would never have thought of, but to command the submission and obedience of their followers to support them in such undertakings. When crowned with success, accordingly, this presumption has often betrayed them into a vanity that approached almost to insanity and folly. Alexander the Great appears not only to have wished that other people should think him a god, but to have been at least very well disposed to fancy himself such. Upon his deathbed, the most ungodly of all situations, he requested of his friends that to the respectable list of deities into which he himself had long before been inserted, his old mother Olympia might likewise have the honour of being added.

A Certain Propensity in Human Nature (excerpt)

This division of labour, from which so many advantages are derived . . . is the necessary . . . consequence of a certain propensity in human nature . . . ; the propensity to truck, barter, and exchange one thing for another . . . [I]t is common to all men, and to be found in no other race of animals. . . . Nobody ever saw a dog make a fair and deliberate exchange of one bone for another with another dog. Nobody ever saw one animal by its gestures and natural cries signify to another, this is mine, that yours. . . .

Invisible Hand (excerpt)

. . . [E]very individual necessarily labours to render the annual revenue of the society as great as he can. He generally, indeed, neither intends to promote the public interest, nor knows how much he is promoting it . . . he intends only his own gain, and he is in this . . . led by an invisible hand to promote an end which was no part of his intention. . . .

George J. Stigler

Stigler's First Law of Sympathy

The Previous Literature

The heroic figure in the scientific analysis of sympathy, before the appearance of the present essay, was Freud. Writing with incandescent intuition and a command of the literature that is fortunately uncommon, he addressed himself squarely to the central problem of this paper: the construction of a law of sympathy which describes precisely the relationship between the quantity of sympathy and the object of the sympathy.

This problem became, indeed, a fixation: Freud recurred to it in literally a score of his lesser known essays, seeking by an immensely resourceful panoply of methodologies to demonstrate the existence of such a law. We must attach the heaviest significance to his final, definitive, and lugubrious assessment of the prospects for finding such a law: *Es ist ganz unmöglich.*[1]

The famous intradisciplinary research team, known as Arroh-Friedmon-Reader-Soloh, has recently renewed the attack upon this problem, employing the most powerful techniques of modern mathematical economics, including ridicule, only to reach

---

This paper was written at the Center for Advanced Study in the Behavioral Sciences in 1958, where it received the Award of the Interdisciplinary Knot. Its characters have been thinly disguised for publication, except for my lamented friend Sidney Siegel. He would, I am sure, rather have one facet of a remarkable personality caricatured than be given flimsy anonymity.

I wish to express my debt to T .... P .... for performing on his abacus the tedious statistical calculations, and to John Thukey for challenging their accuracy.

1. "Schrecklichkeit Noch Einmal," *Gesammelte Schriften,* xiv, 27.

the same conclusion as Sam Freud. Their results culminated in what they termed the AFRS Theorem:

If S is sympathy, and RS is any regularity in the behavior of S, then RS is topologically indifferent.

But the team, as its last joint act, has since repudiated this theorem,[2] and now three much weaker propositions have been offered in its stead, each an individual effort:

PROPOSITION A: *If S is sympathy, S belongs to A.*

PROPOSITION F: *Scientific laws are provided at minimum cost in optimum quantity by a well organized price system.*

PROPOSITION S: *Sympathy is not a durable commodity.*

Only Proposition F calls for brief, and cavalier, comment. Friedmon offers (without price) three arguments in defense of the proposition that the offer of an adequate sum for a law of sympathy would have called forth such a law, if one existed. His first proof is that potato chips are supplied in this manner; this proof fails because potato chips are different from sympathy. His second proof is that the Russians, who do not have a well organized price system, have no law of sympathy; this proof fails because he cannot read Russian. His final proof, if such it may be called, is that competition always works well, and scholars are competitive; but he forgets—although for him this must have been especially difficult—that not all scholars work.

The most recent work in this tradition has been done by the experimentalist, Sidney Siegel, Ph.D.[3] Siegel produced suitable objects of sympathy under laboratory conditions and then measured the amount of sympathy they elicited. The objects of sympathy were a set of students who were subjected to tortures ranging from a hot foot to what the experimentalist describes as "scenes difficult to view with composure even before the next of kin arrived." As the measure of sympathy, each observer was asked to draw a coin from one of three buckets. These buckets contained

---

2. One member, who prefers to remain anonymous writes: "My . . . colleagues have slopped again, and I would appreciate it if you would refer, not to the AFRS Theorem, but to the AFS Fallacy."

3. In *The Uses of Stanford Graduate Students.*

pennies, nickels, and $20 gold pieces, and the observer was asked to withdraw a coin proportional to the sympathy he felt for the student in the iron cage. Siegel found that sympathy is always at a maximum: whether the observer was laughing callously or sobbing in utter misery, he or she always withdrew a $20 gold piece, which under the conditions of the experiment he or she was entitled to keep.

Siegel's demonstration that sympathy is always at a maximum is structured, and therefore well worth the $13 million in $20 gold pieces his study cost the Ford Foundation. But this usually careful experimentalist had one crucial flaw in his design, which vitiates the results: the bucket with the $20 gold pieces had better illumination. One may also raise a question, or at least an eyebrow, at his collection of observers for the experiments: it is surely remarkable that under random sampling with replacement the observers were: Henry Siegel (100 times), Horace Siegel (50 times), Hortense Siegel (700 times), and Mrs. Sidney Siegel (remainder of times).[4]

Genesis of My First Law[5]

I customarily begin the day at a sedentary pace. After an ice cold shower for twenty minutes, I get out of bed and read one of the New York *Times* Hundred Neediest Cases to maintain a sense of well-being. I then eat a light breakfast and compose a stanza of my romantic epic, *Science is a Boy's Best Friend*.

But things were very different on April 11, 1946. For one thing I had not gotten to bed the previous night, and so did not have to arise. For another, I was in a railroad station. And for still another, I was feeling sorry for myself—a fugitive sentiment due to acute financial distress, a sick child, a threatening letter from my wife in Reno, and a grand jury indictment. And then it happened, a characteristic instance of serendipity. My sympathy for myself, I carelessly calculated, was at the rate of 127 units per minute, and the vagrant thought flitted through my mind: how sorry was I for other people? I was about to dismiss the query with an off-hand "enough," when it occurred to me that my sympathy

---

4. In a recent letter from the French Riviera, Siegel's secretary writes: "M. Siegel now believes his table of random numbers contained misprints."

5. I describe the discovery only as a contribution to the sociology of science. Hasty readers may prefer to skip this section, and careful readers to go back to the first section. I am indebted to Kenneth Burke for writing between the lines.

for a person fell off, the more distant he was. And he could be far away not only in a geographical sense, but also socially. Would it not be possible to construct a vast social law corresponding to Newton's law for physical bodies, but naturally superior because distance was a more complex concept in social relations?

I kept putting this line of thought out of mind, but finally the handsome young lady on the bench facing me got her stocking straightened and I recurred to it. Its plausibility mounted, and I vowed to dedicate my time and talents to its development.

For several years I worked with a zeal, tenacity, and resourcefulness that modesty will not allow me to describe. And to no avail. The shrewdest hypothesis was contradicted by evidence; the most brilliant conjecture crashed upon the shoal of inconsistency. I grew sorrier for myself, and at one point my self-sympathy attained the rate of 197 units per minute.

In the fall of 1950 the outlook was so bleak that I contemplated abandonment of the scholarly life for that of the concert violinist. A chance encounter with a Frank Reach did much to end this sterile period. We met in a Sausalito bar, and I eagerly poured my tale of woe into his receptive ear. His initially cheerful, not to say flushed, countenance turned somber and finally despondent, and he suggested that we both consult a psychiatrist. He had heard of a Dr. Samage, unusual among his craft in possessing a two-person couch. I remember little of the session—the damp weather had forced Frank and me to take preventive ministrations against pneumonia—except that Dr. Samage's second question (his first concerned financial resources) was directed to Frank, and asked for a recounting of the occasions on which the subject of sex had entered his head. In all candor, Frank appeared to have a one-track mind.

The next day I was the subject of analysis, and as I recall, the conversation went as follows:

Dr.: What's eating you, chum?
I: Misfortune is my mistress.

[To be continued, perhaps, in a future year.]

95

Oliver Wendell Holmes

Contentment

Little I ask; my wants are few;
   I only wish a hut of stone
(A *very plain* brown stone will do)
   That I may call my own;
And close at hand is such a one,
In yonder street that fronts the sun.

Plain food is quite enough for me;
   Three courses are as good as ten;
If Nature can subsist on three,
   Thank Heaven for three. Amen!
I always thought cold victual nice—
My *choice* would be vanilla-ice.

I care not much for gold or land;
   Give me a mortgage here and there—
Some good bank-stock—some note of hand,
   Or trifling railroad share—
I only ask that Fortune send
A *little* more than I shall spend.

Honors are silly toys, I know,
   And titles are but empty names;
I would, *perhaps,* be Plenipo—
   But only near St. James;
I'm very sure I should not care
To fill our Gubernator's chair.

Jewels are baubles; 'tis a sin
    To care for such unfruitful things;
One good-sized diamond in a pin—
    Some, *not so large,* in rings—
A ruby, and a pearl, or so,
Will do for me—I laugh at show.

My dame should dress in cheap attire
    (Good, heavy silks are never dear);
I own perhaps I *might* desire
    Some shawls of true cashmere,
Some marrowy crapes of China silk,
Like wrinkled skins on scalded milk.

I would not have the horse I drive
    So fast that folks must stop and stare;
An easy gait—two, forty-five—
    Suits me; I do not care—
Perhaps for just a single *spurt,*
Some seconds less would do no hurt.

Of pictures, I should like to own
    Titians and Raphaels three or four—
I love so much their style and tone—
    One Turner, and no more
(A landscape—foreground golden dirt—
The sunshine painted with a squirt).

Of books but few—some fifty score
    For daily use, and bound for wear;
The rest upon an upper floor;
    Some *little* luxury *there*
Of red morocco's gilded gleam,
And vellum rich as country cream.

Busts, cameos, gems—such things as these,
    Which others often show for pride,
I value for their power to please,
    And selfish churls deride;
One Stradivarius, I confess,
Two Meerschaums, I would fain possess.

97

Wealth's wasteful tricks I will not learn,
    Nor ape the glittering upstart fool;
Shall not carved tables serve my turn,
    But *all* must be buhl?
Give grasping pomp its double share—
I ask but *one* recumbent chair.

Thus humble let me live and die,
    Nor long for Midas' golden touch;
If Heaven more generous gifts deny,
    I shall not miss them *much*—
Too grateful for the blessing lent
Of simple tastes and mind content.

Franklin P. Adams

The Rich Man

The rich man has his motor-car,
    His country and his town estate.
He smokes a fifty-cent cigar
    And jeers at Fate.

He frivols through the livelong day,
    He knows not Poverty, her pinch.
His lot seems light, his heart seems gay;
    He has a cinch.

Yet though my lamp burns low and dim,
    Though I must slave for livelihood—
Think you that I would change with him?
    You bet I would!

Ambrose Bierce

Political Economy

"I beg you to note," said a Man to a Goose,
As he plucked from her bosom the plumage all loose,
"That pillows and cushions of feathers, and beds
As warm as maids' hearts and as soft as their heads,
Increase of life's comforts the general sum—
Which raises the standard of living." "Come, come,"
The Goose said impatiently, "tell me or cease,
How that is of any advantage to geese."
"What, what!" said the man—"you are very obtuse!
Consumption no profit to those who produce?
No good to accrue to Supply from a grand
Progressive expansion, all around, of Demand?
Luxurious habits no benefit bring
To those who purvey the luxurious thing?
Consider, I pray you, my friend, how the growth
Of luxury promises—" "Promises," quoth
The sufferer, "what?—to what course is it pledged?
To pay me for being so often defledged?"
"Accustomed"—this notion the plucker expressed
As he ripped out a handful of down from her breast—
"To one kind of luxury, people soon yearn
For others and ever for others in turn.
The man who to-night on your feathers will rest,
His mutton or bacon or beef to digest,
His hunger to-morrow will wish to assuage
With goose and a dressing of onions and sage."

The Belly and the Other Members

It is said that in former times the various members of the human body did not work together as amicably as they do now. On one occasion the members began to be critical of the belly for spending an idle life of luxury while they had to spend all their time laboring for its support and ministering to its wants and pleasures.

The members went so far as to decide to cut off the belly's supplies for the future. The hands were no longer to carry food to the mouth, nor the mouth to receive, nor the teeth to chew it.

But, lo and behold, it was only a short time after they had agreed upon this course of starving the belly into subjection when they all began, one by one, to fail and flop and the whole body to waste away. In the end the members became convinced that the belly also, cumbersome and useless as it seemed, had an important function of its own, and that they could no more exist without it than it could do without them.

Application: As in the body, so in the state, each member in his proper sphere must work for the common good.

Bernard de Mandeville

The Fable of the Bees (excerpt)

The worst of all the multitude
Did something for the common good.
   This was the state's craft, that maintain'd
The whole, of which each part complain'd:
This, as in musick harmony,
Made jarrings in the main agree;
Parties directly opposite,
Assist each oth'r, as 'twere for spight;
And temp'rance with sobriety
Serve drunkenness and gluttony.
   The root of evil, avarice,
That damn'd ill-natur'd baneful vice,
Was slave to prodigality,
That noble sin; whilst luxury
Employ'd a million of the poor,
And odious pride a million more:
Envy itself and vanity
Were ministers of industry;
Their darling folly, fickleness
In diet, furniture, and dress,
That strange ridic'lous vice, was made
The very wheel that turn'd the trade.
Their laws and cloaths were equally
Objects of mutability;
For what was well done for a time,
In half a year became a crime;
Yet whilst they altered thus their laws,
Still finding and correcting flaws,

They mended by inconstancy
Faults which no prudence could foresee.

   Thus vice nursed ingenuity,
Which join'd with time and industry,
Had carry'd life's conveniences,
Its real pleasures, comforts, ease,
To such a height, the very poor
Lived better than the rich before;
And nothing could be added more.

. . . .

No Honour now could be content,
To live and owe for what was spent,
Liv'ries in Broker's shops are hung;
They part with Coaches for a song;
Sell stately Horses by whole sets;
And Country-Houses to pay debts.
Vain cost is shunn'd as moral Fraud;
They have no Forces kept Abroad;
Laugh at th' Esteem of Foreigners,
And empty Glory got by Wars;
They fight, but for their Country's sake,
When Right or Liberty's at Stake.
The haughty Chloe
Contracts th' expensive Bill of Fare,
And wears her strong Suit a whole Year.

Now mind the glorious Hive, and see
How Honesty and Trade agree:
The Shew is gone, it thins apace;
And looks with quite another Face,
For 'twas not only they that went,
By whom vast sums were yearly spent;
But Multitudes that lived on them,
Were daily forc'd to do the same.
In vain to other Trades they'd fly;
All were o'er-stocked accordingly.
The price of Land and Houses falls;
Mirac'lous Palaces whose Walls,
Like those of Thebes, were raise'd by Play,
Are to be let . . .
The Building Trade is quite destroy'd,
Artificers are not employ'd;

No limner for his Art is fam'd,
Stone-cutters, Carvers are not nam'd.

Bare Virtue can't make Nations live
In Splendour. They that would revive.
A Golden Age, must be as free,
For Acorns as for Honesty.

Alexander Pope

Poor Avarice: The Blessings of Prodigality

Riches, like insects, when conceal'd they lie,
Wait but for wings, and in their season, fly.
Who sees pale Mammon pine amidst his store,
Sees but a backward steward for the Poor;
This year a Reservoir, to keep and spare,
The next a Fountain, spouting thro' his Heir,
In lavish streams to quench a Country's thirst,
And men and dogs shall drink him 'till they burst.

· · · · · · · · · · · · · · · · ·

The Sense to value Riches, with the Art
T'enjoy them, and the Virtue to impart,
Not meanly, nor ambitiously pursu'd,
Not sunk by sloth, nor rais'd by servitude;
To balance Fortune by a just expence,
Join with Oeconomy, Magnificence;
With Splendor, Charity; with Plenty, Health;
Oh teach us, BATHURST! yet unspoil'd by wealth!
That secret rare, between th' extremes to move
Of mad Good-nature, and of mean Self-love.
To Want or Worth well-weigh'd, be Bounty giv'n,
And ease, or emulate, the care of Heav'n.
Whose measure full o'erflows on human race
Mend Fortune's fault, and justify her grace.
Wealth in the gross is death, but life diffus'd,
As Poison heals, in just proportion us'd:
In heaps, like Ambergrise, a stink it lies,
But well-dispers'd, is Incense to the Skies.

Three Observations on Desire

A Fifth (excerpt)

[T]rade depends on people's desire for products they could easily live without. The desire, the taste, establishes the utility of all man-made things, a fifth of whiskey or a Fifth of Beethoven.

Some men are so selfish that they read a book or go to a concert for their own sinister pleasure, instead of doing it to improve social conditions, as the good citizen does when drinking cocktails or playing bridge.

—Jacques Barzun

Hay (excerpt)

. . . [I]t might be alleged that hay meets no human desire, but only a bestial desire. True . . . the hay may be nothing to the man who buys it; but his horse . . . is a connoisseur in hay, . . . and that which in some proportion is essential to the desires of his horse becomes secondarily a purpose to the man.

—Thomas de Quincey

Bibles (excerpt)

It is interesting to note that there are considerable manufactures of things the direct desire for which seldom or never asserts itself at all. There are immense tracts and Bibles produced, for instance, which are paid for by persons who do not desire to use them but to give them away to other persons whose desire for them is not in any way an effective factor in the proceeding. And there are numbers of expensive things made expressly to be bought for "presents," and which no sane person is ever expected to buy for himself.

—Rev. Philip H. Wicksteed

The Market Price

I took one draught of Life,
I'll tell you what I paid—
Precisely an existence—
The market price, they said.

They weighed me, dust by dust,
They balanced film with film,
Then handed me my being's worth—
A single dram of Heaven.

Terry Southern

Does Every Man Have a Price?

Out of the gray granite morass of Wall Street rises one building like a heron of fire, soaring up in blue-white astonishment— *Number 18 Wall*—a rocket of glass and blinding copper. It is the *Grand Investment Building*, perhaps the most contemporary business structure in our country, known in circles of high finance simply as *Grand's*.

Offices of *Grand's* are occupied by companies which deal in *mutual funds*—giant and fantastic corporations whose policies define the shape of nations.

August Guy Grand himself was a billionaire. He had 180 millions cash deposit in New York banks, and this ready capital was of course but a part of his gross holdings.

In the beginning, Grand's associates, wealthy men themselves, saw nothing extraordinary about him; a reticent man of simple tastes, they thought, a man who had inherited most of his money and had preserved it through large safe investments in steel, rubber, and oil. What his associates managed to see in Grand was usually a reflection of their own dullness: a club member, a dinner guest, a possibility, a threat—a man whose holdings represented a prospect and a danger. But this was to do injustice to Grand's private life, because his private life was atypical. For one thing, he was the last of the big spenders; and for another, he had a very unusual attitude towards *people*—he spent about ten million a year in, as he expressed it himself, *"making it hot for them."*

At fifty-three, Grand had a thick trunk and a large balding bullet-head; his face was quite pink, so that in certain half-lights he looked like a fat radish-man—though not displeasingly so, for he always sported well-cut clothes and, near the throat, a diamond the size of a nickel . . . a diamond now that caught the late afternoon sun in a soft spangle of burning color when Guy stepped through the soundless doors of *Grand's* and into the blue haze of the almost empty street, past the huge doorman appearing larger than life in gigantic livery, he who touched his cap with quick but easy reverence.

"Cab, Mr. Grand?"

"Thank you no, Jason," said Guy, "I have the car today." And with a pleasant smile for the man, he turned adroitly on his heel, north towards Worth Street.

Guy Grand's gait was brisk indeed—small sharp steps, rising on the toes. It was the gait of a man who appears to be snapping his fingers as he walks.

Half a block on he reached the car, though he seemed to have a momentary difficulty in recognizing it; beneath the windshield wiper lay a big parking ticket, which Grand slowly withdrew, regarding it curiously.

"Looks like you've got a *ticket,* bub!" said a voice somewhere behind him.

Out of the corner of his eye Grand perceived the man, in a dark summer suit, leaning idly against the side of the building nearest the car. There was something terse and smug in the tone of his remark, a sort of nasal piousness.

"Yes, so it seems," mused Grand, without looking up, continuing to study the ticket in his hand. "How much will you eat it for?" he asked then, raising a piercing smile at the man.

"How's that, mister?" demanded the latter with a nasty frown, pushing himself forward a bit from the building.

Grand cleared his throat and slowly took out his wallet—a long slender wallet of such fine leather it would have been limp as silk, had it not been so chock-full of thousands.

"I asked what would you take to *eat* it? You know . . ." Wide-eyed, he made a great chewing motion with his mouth, holding the ticket up near it.

The man, glaring, took a tentative step forward.

"Say, I don't *get* you, mister!"

"Well," drawled Grand, chuckling down at his fat wallet, browsing about in it, "simple enough really . . ." And he took out a few thousand. "*I* have this ticket, as you know, and I was just wondering if you would care to *eat* it, for, say"—a quick glance to ascertain—"six thousand dollars?"

"What do you mean, '*eat it*'?" demanded the dark-suited man in a kind of a snarl. "Say, what're you anyway, bub, a *wise-guy*?"

"'*Wise*-guy' or '*grand* guy'—call me anything you like . . . as long as you don't call me '*late-for-chow!*' Eh? Ho-ho." Grand rounded it off with a jolly chortle, but was quick to add, unsmiling, "How 'bout it, pal—got a taste for the easy green?"

The man, who now appeared to be openly angry, took another step forward.

"*Listen,* mister . . ." he began in a threatening tone, half clenching his fists.

"I think I should warn you," said Grand quietly, raising one hand to his breast, "that I am armed."

"*Huh?*" The man seemed momentarily dumfounded, staring down in dull rage at the six bills in Grand's hand; then he partially recovered, and cocking his head to one side, regarded Grand narrowly, in an attempt at shrewd skepticism, still heavily flavored with indignation.

"Just who do you think you *are,* Mister! Just what is your *game?*"

"Grand's the name, easy-green's the game," said Guy with a twinkle. "Play along?" He brusquely flicked the corners of the six crisp bills, and they crackled with a brittle, compelling sound.

"*Listen* . . ." muttered the man, tight-lipped, flexing his fingers and exhaling several times in angry exasperation, " . . . are *you* trying . . . are you trying to tell ME that you'll give *six thousand dollars* . . . to EAT that"—he pointed stiffly at the ticket in Guy's hand—"to *eat* that TICKET?!?"

"That's about the size of it," said Grand; he glanced at his watch. "It's what you might call a 'limited offer'—expiring in, let's say, *one minute.*"

"Listen, mister," said the man between clenched teeth, "if this is a gag, *so help me* . . ." He shook his head to show how serious he was.

"No threats," Guy cautioned, "or I'll shoot you in the temple—well, what say? Forty-eight seconds remaining."

"Let's *see* that money!" exclaimed the man, quite beside himself now, grabbing at the bills.

Grand allowed him to examine them as he continued to regard his watch. "Thirty-nine seconds remaining," he announced solemnly. "Shall I start the *big count down?*"

Without waiting for the latter's reply, he stepped back and, cupping his hands like a megaphone, began dramatically intoning, *"Twenty-eight . . . twenty-seven . . . twenty-six . . ."* while the man made several wildly gesticulated and incoherent remarks before seizing the ticket, ripping off a quarter of it with his teeth and beginning to chew, eyes blazing.

"Stout fellow!" cried Grand warmly, breaking off the count down to step forward and give the chap a hearty clap on the shoulder and hand him the six thousand.

"You needn't actually eat the ticket," he explained. "I was just curious to see if you had your price." He gave a wink and a tolerant chuckle. "Most of us have, I suppose. Eh? Ho-ho."

And with a grand wave of his hand, he stepped inside his car and sped away, leaving the man in the dark summer suit standing on the sidewalk staring after him, fairly agog.

Robert Frost

The Hardship of Accounting

Never ask of money spent
Where the spender thinks it went.
Nobody was ever meant
To remember or invent
What he did with every cent.

Colonel Stoopnagle (Frederick Chase Taylor)

The Farm Budget

A budget is a thing that when it is finally established, the job is to keep within it, but hardly anybody does, unless. Records show that the properly budgeted farm succeeds more frequently than the one where the method of anticipating expense and profit is done in the owner's head. That is, unless a storm comes along and ruins the wheat crop in five minutes. Then the budget goes all to pieces, unless it has been made for a period of years instead of just for one year. Then another storm comes along and fixes the several-year budget.

The principal drawback of a budget, as I see it, is that with one you can see your losses much better than without one.

Farmer A (funny name for a farmer) keeps a neat budget. He notices that he'll be able to anticipate 10,000 bushels of oats next year. Farmer B keeps no budget. He figures that if drought or storm keeps at a distance, he'll have 'several thousand' bushels of oats. Summer comes. Both crops of oats are nice, and everything looks hunky-dory for a fine harvest. Along about August 15th comes a terrific thunderstorm which wipes out both fields of oats. The budgeted fellow, A, goes to his budget-book and with tears in his eyes sees he has lost 10,000 bushels. B stands alongside the ruined crop, scratches his head, and declares: "Hm. Must have lost several thousand bushels." Now B's crop may have been 10,000 bushels, too, but he has the privilege of *thinking* it may have been only 5,000 bushels that he lost. So B goes ahead with his other work while the budgeted fellow sits looking at the red ink items on his budget-book until he eventually goes stark mad, almost.

I wouldn't want anyone to think that I'm against budgets on this account. If you want to keep a budget when you get your farm, please do so. But my suggestion is that you make the budget and then hide the book. You'll be a much happier, and therefore a much more productive farmer.

One year we kept a budget-book. Just to show you that budgets *can* work, here is a copy of ours:

CROP	ACRES PLANTED	PROBABLE YIELD	ACTUAL YIELD
Popcorn	5	80,000 bags	5 bags
Shredded wheat	2	400 boxes	1 box
Hominy grits	3	Oodles	Some
Grapenuts	7	6000 boxes	6 boxes
Chickweed	1	Scads	A teensy bit
Agar	¼	A mess	A mess
Skunk cabbage	13/16	Loads	500 loads

	COST	SELLING PRICE	NET LOSS
Popcorn	1345.67	.25	1345.42
Shredded wheat	456.32	.23	456.09
Hominy grits	577.02	1.68	575.34
Grapenuts	998.54	1.23	998.31
Chickweed	10.98	0.00	10.98
Agar	00.00	4.53	—
Skunk cabbage	00.07	123.42	—
Totals	3388.60	131.34	3386.14

Cost	3388.60
S. P.	131.34
Loss	3257.26
Plus Reserve For Error	128.88
Net Loss Above	3386.14

At first glance, this result looks a little disastrous. But when you consider that my wife found a purse containing $5,000, it doesn't come out so bad:

Purse	$5,000.00
Less net loss	3,386.14
Profit	1,613.86

So you see, with a little ordinary perspicuity, a bit of scrimping here and there, attention to details though it be odious, and a wife who is observant, the new farmer may turn a neat profit by carefully budgeting his expenses.

In all fairness, I should really show you how a farmer came out who kept no budget:

And at the end of the year it's easy to see that this man is just as happy as though he had spent half the time with his nose in a budget-book.

Thomas Malthus

Nature's Mighty Feast (excerpt)

A man who is born into a world already possessed, if he cannot get subsistence from his parents on whom he has a just demand, and if the society do not want his labour, has no claim of right to the smallest portion of food, and, in fact, has no business to be where he is. At nature's mighty feast there is no vacant cover for him. She tells him to be gone, and will quickly execute her own orders, if he does not work upon the compassion of some of her guests. If these guests get up and make room for him, other intruders immediately appear demanding the same favour. The report of a provision for all that come, fills the hall with numerous claimants. The order and harmony of the feast is disturbed, the plenty that before reigned is changed into scarcity; and the happiness of the guests is destroyed by the spectacle of misery and dependence in every part of the hall, and by the clamorous importunity of those, who are justly enraged at not finding the provision which they had been taught to expect. The guests learn too late their error, in counter-acting those strict orders to all intruders issued by the great mis-tress of the feast, who, wishing that all guests should have plenty, and knowing she could not provide for unlimited numbers, hu-manely refused to admit fresh comers when her table was already full.

119

William Wordsworth

On Malthus

Malthus! Thou shouldst be living in this hour:
The world hath need of thee: getting and begetting,
We soil fair Nature's bounty. Sweating
With 'dozer, spray and plough we dissipate our dower
In smart and thoughtless optimism, blocking the power
Of reason to lay out a saner setting
For reason's growth to change, adapt and flower,
In reason's way, to weave that long sought bower
Of sweet consistency. —Great Soul! I'd rather be
Like you, logic-driven to deny the feast
To those who would, if saved, see misery increased
Throughout this tender, trambling world.
Confound ye those who set unfurled
Soft flags of good intentions, deaf to obdurate honesty!

Scott Gordon

The Economics of the Afterlife

Economists have been extending their analytical methods into many new areas lately, but, so far as I know, no one has applied economics to the metaphysical aspects of theology. In this note I wish to show that this can be done, by examining one of the basic problems in metaphysical theology: the nature of the afterlife, or, to give it a somewhat more technical formulation, the ontology of Heaven.

I start with one postulate: that in Heaven there is no scarcity. As David Hume recognized, all conflict springs from scarcity, so it is not necessary to describe Heaven as characterized by justice, peacefulness, mutual love, etc., since these are derivatives from the no-scarcity postulate. One might wonder how economic analysis could be applied to a regime of no scarcity, but this is exactly the point: we can use the analysis, not to describe how to allocate resources efficiently, but to discover the characteristics Heaven must have if no such allocation is necessary.

Most theologians consider that scarcity would be absent if the inhabitants of Heaven were to enjoy everlasting life. What I wish to show is that this is neither a necessary nor sufficient condition for no scarcity.

I take "everlasting life" to mean that every inhabitant of Heaven is located on a time line which is, with certainty, expected to be infinite in duration. There is, then, an infinite amount of time available for each inhabitant. Does this mean that there is no scarcity of time? Not if Heaven time is like World time since, while it would be possible to do everything one wished to do sooner or later, one could not do everything *at the same time;* one could not, for example, play the harp and go swimming simultaneously.

Choices would have to be made as to which to do first; that is, time would have to be allocated despite its certain infinite duration. So, everlasting life is not a sufficient condition for no scarcity.

For Heaven to be characterized by no scarcity, it is necessary that Heaven time be different from World time. Tentatively, let us assume that Heaven time, in addition to being infinite in length, is also infinite in width. Instead of being represented by a Euclidian line which has length but no width, a Heaven time line would have both length and width and would be infinite in both dimensions. In such a regime, there would be no time constraint upon actions or experiences. This would be a condition of no scarcity, since at every instant there is an infinite amount of time.

This conception of time is sufficient to define a condition of no scarcity, but are both of its dimensions necessary? This is, clearly, not so. If Heaven time were infinite in width, then the inhabitants could have unlimited experiences simultaneously. The specification of infinite extent is therefore redundant or unnecessary.

I conclude from this that, if the basic postulate of Heaven is the absence of scarcity, then the afterlife will be exquisitely *intense* in experience but fleetingly *brief*. Perhaps the reason why most people display great reluctance to experience the bliss of Heaven is due to the fact that, being accustomed to thinking in terms of World time, where duration is of the essence, they find the brevity of Heaven time unappealing. Of course, in making this suggestion, I am assuming that most people have all along known intuitively what economics only just now has proven logically.

Philip H. Wicksteed

On the Diminishing Marginal Utility of Prayer (excerpt)

. . . [T]he same law [of diminishing marginal utility] holds in intellectual, moral, or spiritual as in material matters. . . . In a story of South America, after the war, we are told of a planter who, when warned by his wife in the middle of his prayers that the enemy was at the gate, concluded his devotions with a few brief and earnest petitions, and set about defending himself. Had he been a formalist those final petitions would never have been uttered at all; but under the circumstances the impulse to prayer, though sincere and urgent, became rapidly less imperative and exacting relatively to the urgency of taking steps for defence, as the successive moments passed. The most pious biographers of Alfred the Great praise him for "charging like a boar" at the Battle of Ashdown while his brother was still engaged in prayer; and an entirely devout and sincere person may find himself in the dilemma of having either to curtail (omit) family prayers or to hurry a guest over his breakfast and perhaps run him uncomfortably close for his train. If he shortens, but does not omit, the prayers, it shews that he attaches declining significance to his devotions as minute is added to minute. And in this we shall see nothing ludicrous, as soon as we give up the cant of the absolute in a world in which all things are relative.

Posthumous Humor and Other "After" Thoughts

Stephen B. Leacock, ridiculing the faith of classical economists in the ability of a 'general glut' to right itself, commented:

This is no doubt correct, if we admit that the 'righting' may take half a generation, may throw fifty million people out of work, and bring disorder, revolution, and blood shed widespread over the world. On those terms anything 'rights itself.' The Black Death righted labour; the Reign of Terror righted aristocracy; and the Great War righted nationality. It's a great world if you let it alone. . . . Imagine . . . anyone looking for light on the question of overproduction of to-day from the pages of the classical economists. They said it cured itself. It does. So does life.

John Maynard Keynes: In the long run we are all dead.

Larry E. Ruff: [P]ollution is an economic problem, . . . [but there are those who] pin their hopes on a moral regeneration or social revolution, apparently in the belief that saints and socialists have no garbage to dispose of.

George J. Stigler: . . . [T]he hereafter in which all problems are solved has been moved up to two months after the next election.

Stephen B. Leacock

A Resurrection of Adam Smith

Adam, Adam, Adam Smith,
   Listen what I charged you with!
      Didn't you say
         In the class one day
           That selfishness was bound to pay?
Of all your Doctrine, that was the Pith,
Wasn't it, wasn't it, wasn't it, Smith?

Don't you remember your book begins
With a Panegyric on making Pins?
         Didn't you say that the more we made
         The bigger would be External Trade?
We sold the pins and the Foreigners had 'em,
That was the Big Thought, wasn't it, Adam?

And didn't you say,—don't think it funny,
That the greatest thing in the world was money,
And didn't you say,—now please don't shirk,

That the basis of value was human work,
        And the Worker must be content with his lot
        Being worth precisely just what he got.
            Come don't evade it,
            Long-winded Scot,
            Just, whether you said it
              Or whether not?
And if you said it, you must confess
You have brought the World to a terrible Mess,
    For a hundred Years since your Grave was made
    We've been making Pins and Machines and Trade,
    All selfish as Hogs, whether rich as Sin
    Or as poor as Rats,—Ah! why begin
    To teach us about that fatal Pin!

How can you venture to look in the Face
    Of an honest fellow like Stuart Chase?
How can you dare to be blocking the way
    Of an Enterprise such as the NRA!

Smith, come up from under the sod
Tell me what did you do with God?
    You never named him, I understand,
    You called him (Book IV) an invisible hand;
    You gave him the system all geared and speeded
    With none of his Interference needed.
It wasn't worthy a man of your size,
Smith,—come up and apologize.

126

Part 4
Principles of Microeconomics I— A Nation of Shopkeepers

Introduction

At best, Adam Smith's humor is subtle—at worst, it is undetectable. Just the same, his irony and sarcasm qualify his writing for inclusion here. His reference to "a nation of shopkeepers" was a put-down of influence-peddling behind a British colonial policy that promoted profits for a favored few.

A scandalous example of government sponsorship of private profit, the South-Sea scheme, had occurred more than 60 years before the *Wealth of Nations*. The South Sea Company, chartered in 1711, was given exclusive rights by the government to trade in South America and the Pacific. Investors were promised a six percent return, but early birds received as much as 100 percent. Speculation in South-Sea stock reached the proportions of mania, largely because of the active roles of government officials, including the British king. In the bull market of early 1720, share values increased nearly 700 percent. By the end of the year, the bubble burst, the stock lost almost 90 percent of its value, people at all walks of life were wiped out, and charges of bribery brought down numerous government figures.

Alexander Pope's "An Inscription upon a Punch-Bowl," written in 1720, satirizes the "Jove-helps-those-who-help-themselves" attitude of South-Sea speculators that bull markets are immortal. The second verse appeared 12 years after the birth of the bear market. Stock markets offer a splendid example of supply and demand forces: bear markets are as likely as bull markets.

There is nothing more rare than a day in May, unless it is an honest annual report. George Chester's report to the 210 stockholders of Wisconsin Securities Company is candor with a "three-button dividend."

During the last decades of the twentieth century, Japanese leadership in automobile and steel production threatened to spill over into other areas of American preeminence such as computer technology. The Japanese announced a long-term project to develop thinking machines: artificial intelligence systems would think like people, understand language, make judgments, and draw conclusions.

If Rube Goldberg (1883–1970) were still around, the United States would have nothing to fear from Japanese competition, for Goldberg's inventions made thinking unnecessary. For over fifty years, Goldberg caricatured modern technology and the easy life with screwball projects that complicated simple things. Winner of the Pulitzer Prize for editorial cartoons in 1948, he is compared to Daumier and Cruikshank. According to the dictionary, "Rube Goldbergian" is a figure of speech for ridiculous contraptions. The cartoon takes the risk out of speculation with an "easy" test of stock market stamina.

In his piece on animal robots to "run machines," Clarence Day's entrepreneur tames what "was galloping around in the forest in hostile containers" to bring bottled milk to everyone's back door. The jest of the writing spares neither management nor worker. After graduating from Yale, Clarence Day (1874–1935) became a partner in his father's Wall Street brokerage firm, becoming a member of the New York Stock Exchange. His autobiographical *Life with Father* (1935) was made into a stage play.

While ideas and products can become outdated by time, the automobile industry is noted for "planned obsolescence." In "The Alarming Cost of Model Changes," George J. Stigler ridicules the "tail fins" of the publishing industry. His targets are textbook revisions and publications that would never make the "list of the 100 greatest books." As a good economist, Stigler refrains from value judgments and acknowledges "market conditions," noting what could have been saved in billions of dollars and reading time if nothing new had been published after 1900.

Rumor has it that Americans love their automobiles—but the

relationship began as a "marriage of convenience." Once viewed as mere transportation from here to there, the first cars were black, none had ashtrays, radios, heaters, tape decks, or air-conditioning. Eventually, Detroit's uncanny ability "to anticipate drivers' needs" with optional equipment made the car a substitute for legs, skates, and bicycles. Commuting gave rise to the traffic jam. In "The Permanent Traffic Solution," Harland Manchester (1898–1977) pictures a bizarre tomorrow when wheels cease to turn, the car is the home, and Detroit caters to "An Unmoveable Feast." Manchester contributed over 200 articles to *Scribner's, Harper's, Saturday Review, Saturday Evening Post, Reader's Digest,* and other magazines.

If public opinion surveys are correct, the familiar plea of voters, "get government off our backs," is nothing but rhetoric. Taxpayers want lower taxes but more public services, less regulation but more protection from foreign competition. Hector Breeze illustrates the best of all worlds: "compulsory laissez-faire . . . subsidized competition . . . and Japanese sales charts." The Breeze cartoons appeared in *Punch,* the British comic weekly that ceased to exist in 1992 after more than 150 years of social satire.

Historians of economic thought have dealt unkindly with Frédéric Bastiat (1801–50), the Frenchman whose career as an economist lasted little more than five years. Trained for business, Bastiat turned to economics through reading its literature. Karl Marx called his writing "sagacious blather . . . philistine sophistry,"[1] but Robert Heilbroner considered Bastiat's "*Economic Sophisms* . . . as close to humor as economics has ever come."[2] An avid free trader, Bastiat fought protectionism with journalistic ridicule. "Negative Railroad" is a response to a legislative suggestion of the benefits to local trade of a single toll on the Paris-Spain railroad. Why not, jeers Bastiat, place tolls at every city along the route so everyone can benefit?

The "Petition of the Candlemakers," a classic of economic literature, is Bastiat's only claim to fame in economics. Current arguments to protect American workers and producers from "cheap" foreign labor pale beside the candlemakers' case against the sun, a rival whose price is zero. Compare the essay to Jonathan Swift's early eighteenth-century "Petition of the Colliers . . ."

---

1. *The Grundisse,* ed. David McLellan (New York: Harper & Row, 1971), 54.
2. *The Worldly Philosophers* (New York: Simon and Schuster, 1980), 176.

(also in part 4) and Benjamin Franklin's 1784 "Economical Project" (part 7), both of which probably inspired Bastiat's essay. Bastiat admired Franklin and probably had a reading acquaintance with Swift.

Art Buchwald (1925–) was awarded the Grand Prix de la Humor by France in 1959. Buchwald was a syndicated columnist who lived in Paris while on the staff of the *New York Herald Tribune*. His humor is without malice. "Use Less, Pay More" is a comic exaggeration of the consumer's dilemma in an energy crisis. When the rate structure of large utilities is linked to the volume of output, conservation may not be "user friendly."

More than a century before Bastiat's essay, Jonathan Swift (1667–1745) writes of the "victuallers"—restaurant owners or tavern keepers—who seek a patent on "catoptrical" cooking with sunbeams, a culinary use of reflected light (maybe an eighteenth-century microwave). The "Petition of the Colliers, Cooks, Cookmaids, . . ." points out the dire effects on their livelihood as well as that of others when the "Catoptrical Victuallers" have a monopoly. The petitioners claim, furthermore, that solar-cooked food is dangerous to your health (it probably was not on the food pyramid).

Swift was dean of St. Patrick's in Dublin, and while he would have preferred to be in England, he championed the cause of the Irish. He graduated from Trinity College in Dublin, received a master's degree at Oxford, and was awarded a D.D. at Dublin. His *Travels into Several Remote Nations of the World,* by Lemuel Gulliver, was published anonymously in 1726.

John Arbuthnot (1667–1735) was a Scottish mathematician and physician to Queen Anne from 1705 to 1714. He was a member of the Scriblerus Club, wherein he collaborated with Swift and Alexander Pope in ridiculing bad literature. The "Petition of the Upholders" satirizes a British bill presented in 1724 to prohibit prescriptions of medications by anyone but physicians. Citing the harm to their business (i.e., burying the dead—upholders were morticians) the upholders describe what beneficial service they provide in a business where second opinions are not much good.

Adam Smith

Trade for the Public Good (excerpts)

. . . I have never known much good done by those who affected to trade for the public good. It is an affectation, indeed, not very common among merchants, and very few words need be employed in dissuading them from it.

It is not from the benevolence of the butcher, the brewer, or the baker, that we expect our dinner, but from their regard to their own interest. We address ourselves, not to their humanity but to their self-love, and never talk to them of our own necessities but of their advantages.

Alexander Pope

An Inscription upon a Punch-Bowl in the South-Sea Year of the Club, Chas'd with Jupiter placing Callista in the Skies & Europa with the Bull

Come, fill the South-Sea Goblet full;
The Gods shall of our Stock take care:
Europa pleas'd accepts the Bull,
And Jove with Joy puts off the Bear.

On Corruption, Av'rice, and Lucre's Sordid Charms (excerpt)

What made Directors cheat in South-sea year?
To live on Ven'son when it sold so dear.

. . . .

At length Corruption, like a gen'ral flood,
(So long by watchful Ministers withstood)
Shall deluge all; and Av'rice creeping on,
Spread like a low-born mist, and blot the Sun;
Statesman and Patriot ply alike the stocks,
Peeress and Butler share alike the Box,
And judges job, and Bishops bite the town,
And mighty Dukes pack cards for half a crown.
See Britain sunk in lucre's sordid charms.

Wisconsin Securities Company of Delaware
777 East Wisconsin Avenue—Suite 3090
Milwaukee, Wisconsin 53202

February 24, 1983
Aspen, Colorado

"When in doubt
   tell the truth."
    Mark Twain

To the 210 Stockholders of
Wisconsin Securities Company of Delaware

After a day of skiing, lounging in front of the fire in Bill Messinger's Aspen Square condominum, one becomes more philosophical about the difficulties of the past year. And a difficult year
it was! About the only good thing you can say about 1982 is that
the $22.00 cost of an all-day Aspen ski ticket (our informal infla-
tion guide) did not increase for the first time in memory. Also the
general stock market behaved rather well during the latter part of
the year.

It seems to be easier to make money than to hold on to it.

Two years ago our net assets totaled $29,332,818. A year ago
they were $25,300,803. By June 30, 1982 net assets had hit a low
of $20,718,842 only to recover modestly at year end to
$23,314,568. The problem was our substantial holding in Armco,
Inc. which during 1982 dropped in market value by 41.5 per cent.

In truth, it was a difficult year for both William Agee and
George Chester but George Chester still has a job thanks to his
many relatives.

133

1982 was not a good year for steel, oil field supplies, oil drilling, petroleum, fertilizer, titanium, foundries and those horrid Atari video games, in all of which areas Wisconsin Securities had substantial investments. Surprisingly, our foundry investment, Sandusky Foundry & Machine Company, did well during 1982 but the recession will finally catch up with it in 1983 when a loss is expected. Accordingly, no change was made during the year in the assigned value of Sandusky which now has become our largest holding at 23 per cent of our portfolio.

In contrast, banking, technology and especially medical technology performed well during 1982. Orion Pictures Corporation had a splendid price rise in 1982 of 149 per cent but unfortunately we purchased it too late in the year after it had matured. Scoa Industries and Metromedia both increased 85 per cent in value during the year but we sold these stocks too early in the year. Marshall & Ilsley Corporation increased 68.7 per cent in value during 1982. Boeing Company and Universal Foods both increased about 50 per cent in value during 1982. The big losers, in addition to Armco, were Beker Industries, down 28 per cent, Warner Communications, down 39 per cent, and Parker Drilling, down 52 per cent. We should have sold Parker Drilling when Stanley Stone told us to unload. He said we had the "stomach of a burglar" to hold on.

During 1982 net asset value per share declined from $397.98 to $366.74. This is a decline of 7.85 per cent compared with an increase in the Dow Jones Industrial Average of 19.6 per cent for the year. In comparison, the Baird list of forty Wisconsin stocks increased 23.5 per cent in value overall. The First Wisconsin Trust Company Special Equity Fund increased 30.9 per cent in unit value during 1982. It is surprising so few stockholders sold their Wisconsin Securities stock.

Our goal of doubling net asset value every ten years has not been met but we have doubled in approximately eleven years. We still have unrealized appreciation in excess of 21 million dollars.

Wisconsin Securities did increase its dividend in 1982 a modest 25 cents to $11.25. This was the *nineteenth* consecutive year of dividend increase but to accomplish this the directors had to pay out all of the net investment income of the Company ($9.83 per share) plus a portion of capital gains taken during the year ($1.42 per share out of capital gains of $6.60 per share). This is not part of the long-term game plan because long-term capital gains do not have to be distributed to stockholders under the personal holding company tax law.

Speaking of dividends, our aim is to pay a three-button dividend as soon as we can. The Aspen Emporium today charged me $4.00 to sew a button on my jacket.

At year end our one-half interest in Sandusky, our holding of 390,000 shares of Armco and our investments in banking represented exactly 63 per cent of our portfolio. The fortunes of Wisconsin Securities ride behind this troika. Sandusky was the surprise performer of the year earning $1,610,143, substantially the same amount as in 1981 but about half of what was earned in 1980. Of the $1,610,143 net earnings $679,600 was an accounting adjustment due to the LIFO inventory method resulting largely from liquidations of LIFO inventory. The year was a satisfactory year in a depressed economy with operating earnings of about one million dollars and total dividends of $177,000. Our share of the dividends was $88,500. The total stockholders' equity in Sandusky is now $18,478,121 but it would cost more than $50,000,000 to duplicate the facilities. This company has an enormous appetite for capital expenditures and the management and owners are committed to investing in the latest technology as needed. It is a tired dollar that is finally paid to Wisconsin Securities as a dividend and then paid out to Wisconsin Securities stockholders but in the meantime, year after year, the investment becomes more valuable. We record the value of Sandusky at $7,380,700 although the underlying total value of our investment is $9,239,060.

For those who do not read this report every year Sandusky specializes in the production of centrifugal castings for the paper machine industry. Much of the paper of the world is made on Sandusky suction rolls. Sandusky is able to melt and pour single heat castings weighing as much as 138,000 pounds of steel. Finished machine sizes range from 7 inches in diameter to 60 inches in diameter and up to 426 inches in length. A great deal of research and development goes into perfecting metallurgy for appropriate applications and maintaining exacting tolerances. The company was organized in 1904. It is now half owned by the Beloit Corporation and half owned by Wisconsin Securities Company. We could not have a better business partner.

One of the important steps completed during 1982 was a survey of the operations and profit goals of Sandusky made in conjunction with management by Richard Seaman, a former executive of Rexnord, Inc. The report will be very helpful in forward planning. More important, however, will be the state of the economy. To paraphrase Ernie Von Schledorn "Who do you know wants to buy a paper machine?"

During 1982 Armco, Inc. paid Wisconsin Securities $600,000 in dividends. Despite the decline in market value of Armco our investment in 390,000 shares at year end still represented an unrealized profit of over $4,000,000. This was the good news. The bad news was that for all of 1982 Armco had a net loss of $345,000,000, including an after-tax charge of $265,000,000 for closing steelmaking facilities and writing down the value of raw material assets, mainly iron ore. This was Armco's first annual operating loss in 44 years. In July of 1982 the quarterly dividend was reduced from 45 cents per share to 30 cents per share. In March of 1983 the quarterly dividend will be further reduced to 20 cents per share. To compensate partially for this loss of dividend income, we have reduced our bank borrowing by one million dollars, which will reduce substantially our interest expense.

Harry Holiday, Armco chairman and chief executive officer, stated "This has been the most difficult period for Armco since the Great Depression. It was an awful year and 1983 will be another difficult year." Despite all of this we continue to have great confidence in the Armco management and business strategy and have no plans to do any panic selling. At the appropriate time we plan to reduce our holding to 300,000 shares. In January we sold 10,000 shares at 18 reducing our holding to 380,000 shares.

During 1982 Wisconsin Securities paid no income taxes and received a $255,000 federal income tax refund. This was possible because we did not sell a substantial block of Armco stock. Our strategy was to avoid the 28 per cent capital gains tax by selling Armco shares over a period of years, to use the Armco dividend to meet our income requirements and to invest an increasing amount in low-yield, but high-growth, technology stocks. The strategy was only partially successful. Perhaps by 1984 the strategy will be more defensible.

In last year's report we predicted First Wisconsin Corporation would earn $30,000,000 in 1982. The Corporation actually earned $29,877,000 in 1982 before securities gains or losses. This amounted to $7.05 per First Wisconsin share of which $2.075 was paid out in dividends. Stockholders' equity increased by about $20,000,000. The First Wisconsin dividend year after year has

136

given Wisconsin Securities the financial stability to diversify into more exotic areas of untold growth but no immediate return. We fully support the concept of the First Wisconsin as a regional banking institution dedicated to the growth and prosperity of Wisconsin and its neighboring states and the development of the region's exports. We would like to see a more aggressive acquisition program, however, and believe the market would respond to such a development. Ed Tallmadge thinks First Wisconsin stock is a real bargain at about half of book value.

By tradition, our portfolio is divided with rather poor semantics into "manageable securities" and "long-term holdings". Sandusky, Armco and First Wisconsin are designated "long-term holdings" and the balance of the portfolio is considered "manageable". Ed Hipke, our investment advisor, has responsibility for the "manageable" portion although he sometimes quietly despairs of actions taken by the President.

Dear stockholders—don't stop reading until you have heard the Diasonics story. It would be like going to Aspen without seeing the 1983 Aspen Winternational, the biggest ski event in America. (I find I came to Aspen one week too early.) Wisconsin Securities owes a great debt to many Bills, to the late Bill Chester, Bill Brumder and Bill Vogel, to directors Bill Johnson and Bill Messinger, to Vice President Bill Chester, Jr., to Bill Murphy of Baird and Bill Berry, former CEO of NN Corporation before its merger into Armco Financial Services, but the Bill who could bill us for services rendered with most justification is Bill McDonald of F. Eberstadt & Co. The Eberstadt Connection has been more profitable than the French Connection.

Our investment in Beker Industries through Eberstadt is now part of history. We invested $50,000 and it became $6,000,000 in a relatively few years when we started selling out and reducing our holding to 100,000 shares. In July of 1981 Eberstadt again offered us an opportunity, this time to invest $480,000 in a private placement of Diasonics stock. We purchased 150,000 shares at $3.20 per share at the recommendation of Mr. Hipke. On December 31, 1982 this stock had an assigned value of $1,125,000 based on the last known sale. But the real story developed in 1983. The stock has been sold to the public at $22.00 per share and this week was the "darling of the hot new issues." We sold 25,000 shares in the registration to recoup our original investment and retain 125,000 shares with a market value in excess of $2,750,000. Your President wanted to sell 50,000 shares but was overruled by the directors who are now "gung ho" about this investment.

Also, we should note that Bill McDonald was also instrumental in bringing a number of technology stocks to our attention which are now included in our technology portfolio.

Despite all of the above the market value of our stock remained at $180 per share throughout 1982. A few shares have been sold at this price during 1983. The price is low compared with net asset value but probably high compared with yield.

The Dogcatcher of Aspen (excuse me, the Animal Control Officer of Pitkin County—Virginia Squier) is a loyal stockholder of Wisconsin Securities. I asked her to tell us how the younger generation of stockholders felt about the importance of dividends versus growth. Surprisingly, she gave equal importance to both. She said that dividends were important to a municipal employee in a vacation-priced town but that she did not want dividends at the sacrifice of long-term growth. This seems to approve of our twin goals, a dividend increase every year and doubling our net asset value every decade. Last year our directors approved a goal of a net asset value per share of $924.00 and a dividend of $20.00 per share by the year 1990. We'll worry about that tomorrow.

A few words about our directors. They have been wonderfully supportive of management during a trying year. Three new directors were elected during the year, Joseph F. Heil, Jr., George M. Chester, Jr. and V. Ross Read. We are trying to get the next generation involved with the election of George and Ross. Joseph F. Heil, Sr., Edward F. Pritzlaff and Norman M. Chester have become Directors Emeriti.

A few more words about our stockholders might be in order as well. We have five per cent more stockholders this year than last year. Frederick Ott once again doubled his holdings but when he saw the semi-annual report it was a little difficult to get payment. Stockholders include *Matthew* Feinstein, *Mark* McKoy, *Luke* Sims and *John* Yewer. Our spryest stockholder must surely be Norman Chester. The stockholder who writes the best letter is Robert Hine. The stockholder who has held Wisconsin Securities stock the longest is Edward Pritzlaff who acquired his first stock on March 18, 1921. Our youngest stockholder, Daphne Reynolds Chester, born today, February 24, 1983, is the daughter of director George M. Chester, Jr. (born February 25) and his charming wife, Laura (born February 26). This should cause a three-day holiday every year, perhaps enough time to come to Aspen. It is surely a good omen that Daphne Chester was born on a day when the Dow Jones Industrial Average attained a new all-time high which sent our net asset value once again over $400 per share.

George M. Chester
President

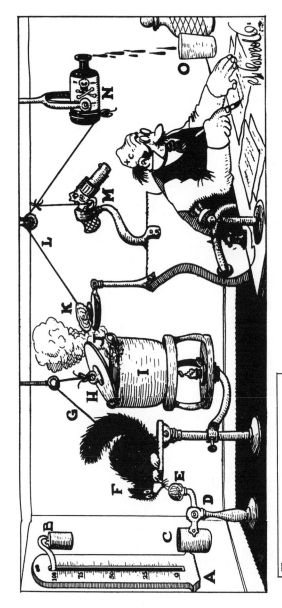

ELECTRIC INDICATOR (A) IS CONNECTED WITH TICKER IN STOCK BROKER'S OFFICE AND REGISTERS PRICE OF STOCK YOU OWN – WHEN ARM (B) DROPS TO ZERO, SHOWING YOU HAVE BEEN WIPED OUT, IT HITS WEIGHT(C) AND CAUSES LEVER(D) TO LIFT IMITATION NUT (E) WHICH IS REALLY MADE OF IVORY-SQUIRREL(F) JUMPS WITH PAIN WHEN IT'S TEETH BITE INTO IVORY NUT, CAUSING STRING(G)

TO LIFT LID (H) OF POT (I), LIBERATING FUMES OF HOT CHOWDER (J) - CLAM(K) DIVES INTO CHOWDER, PULLING CORD(L), WHICH SIMULTANEOUSLY SHOOTS PISTOL (M) AND EMPTIES BOTTLE OF POISON (N) INTO GLASS (O) – IF PISTOL SHOT DOES NOT END YOUR WORRIES, DRINK POISON.-IF YOU'RE STILL ALIVE AFTER THAT YOU'RE TOUGH ENOUGH TO GO BACK INTO THE STOCK MARKET.

Let Animals Run the Machines (excerpt)

The great age of invention was in prehistoric times, long ago. The era we live in is also an age of invention—our stupendous achievements have dwarfed all the past, in our eyes; but naturally the inventions of old were more basic than ours. The inventions of writing, and wheels; the invention of zero, of needles, and wheat, and of money were made by great men. And aside from these, there were some highly ingenious devices which were made in a field we are wholly neglecting today.

Consider, for instance, the man who invented the cow. It is hard for us even to imagine a home without milk: but once it was very much harder to imagine homes with it. In prehistoric times it would have been easier for a husband to bring his wife orchids, if she had desired such weeds, than a bottle of milk. There was plenty of milk in the world, yes, but what was it doing? It was galloping around in the forest, in hostile containers. No thief could rob one of these animals without getting hurt.

Then a genius was born: a genius who experimented with animals, as we do with chemicals. One winter—by accident probably—he got an idea: the astounding idea of having milk at his door every morning.

The job was a hard one. To begin with, which was the best animal? Cows were far from the obvious choice. In some parts of the world men had tried to use the golden-haired ground-sloth, a coarse monstrous creature which they kept in caves and milked them when they could. If they had succeeded we should have had sloths today in our fields, and our countryside poems and paintings would have been queerly different.

The curfew tolls the knell of parting day,
The lowing sloths wind slowly o'er the lea.

But the sloth was no good. Sloths have bad skin diseases in summer, they are wheezy at night, and every now and then there is a mean, fishy taste to their milk. These objections alone did not matter much perhaps in those days; but there was another, more serious: the sloth is monogamous. Commercially speaking, monogamy ruins a farm. When people found that every cow-sloth had to have her own bull, which the owner must tame, feed, and shelter, the sloth herds were scrapped.

At last a queer breed was tried out that looked even less promising. These were rough, horned, fiery beasts, running wild on the plains; as unlike our cows, almost, as iron ore is unlike a steamship. Yet that prehistoric genius saw in them first-class raw material for household machines that would manufacture milk every day.

People called him utopian, probably. Most inventors are laughed at. How did this one get help enough to capture those wild cows of old? It wasn't like digging for metals, which at least remain stationary. This raw material had to be chased, caught, and dragged home alive. And after he had slowly bred out their excessive mobility and speeded up the flow of their output, there was still much to do, before he could safely install them in the average household. Many users disliked being kicked while extracting the milk, and others complained, though in vain, of being gored by those horns. But with all its imperfections and dangers, this invention succeeded. It was a practicable and serviceable device for the production of milk, and with very few modifications we are using it yet.

Another great thinker in the meantime invented the hen. . . .

. . . Think of great future factories where interested wolverines work, their eyes shining with happy excitement as they gallop about, pulling levers. Every morning a flock of eager woodpeckers will be seen in the sky, with an aviator herding them up from Navesink to their carpenter-shop work in town. Ferryboats for the employees of New York manufacturing companies will steam over from Jersey, full of chattering squirrels to tend bobbins. And parents of children will summon a kangaroo nurse-girl, slip the babies into her pouch with a sandwich, and send them off for the day. They'd be out of the dusty town in two jumps, and away to some sunny hill, watching the elephants haying or gathering fruit. There might even be night schools or discussion clubs for the highest-grade workers—the Federated Grizzlies of America or the Order of Railway Raccoons. . . .

. . . [P]urely as a matter of business, why shouldn't it pay? It didn't pay at first to milk cows, but it has become very profitable. There would seem to be no limit to the profit a machine age could gain by using on its lower levels a new type of labor, that not only wouldn't strike for more wages but would get none at all.

George J. Stigler

The Alarming Cost of Model Changes: A Case Study

Vulgar luxury has always been condemned by men of high taste and income. Economists have lent some support to their displeasure, and I add my mite.

Franklin Fisher, Zvi Griliches, and Carl Kaysen have shown, in an article which will command wide and respectful attention, that if consumers had been content with the 1949 automobile, they would be saving over $700 per car by 1961.[1] They properly have left open the question whether improvements such as greater speeds and automatic transmissions were worth the cost, but after all, the 1949 cars ran, and kept out the rain.[2] Perhaps the $5 billion a year of extra costs had better alternative uses—higher tuition fees, more adequate farm subsidies, a violin in every home.

Their choice of the automobile industry was arbitrary, but reasonable; there has been much comment on over-elaborate automobiles; it is a large industry; and annual model changes are a prominent feature of its behavior. Of course, every sector—even public schools and health—displays a mixture of frivolous and genuine improvements, and eventually, let us hope, estimates of the costs of product changes will be available for all. I propose here to estimate the costs for an industry in which model changes have reached an almost unbelievable pitch.

The industry is publishing, and I was led to it by the com-

---

1. "The Costs of Automobile Model Changes Since 1949," *Journal of Political Economy*, October, 1962.
2. My 1950 Dodge was considerably more efficient in the latter role than in the former, however.

144

parison of editions of the same work. It is essentially correct that a man never changes, and seldom improves on, his views: certainly this is true of Ricardo (3 editions), Mill (7 editions), Marshall (8 editions), Böhm-Bawerk (3 editions), Walras (5 editions), Pigou (4 editions), Roscher (27 editions), etc. I suspect that the revision every five years of our textbooks reflects market considerations more than it expresses the march of scientific progress. The costs of this sort of minor amendment are not negligible—unlike the automobile, the older editions lose their usefulness.

But the phenomenon of change goes much deeper. Each year we publish about 11,000 books in the United States. Not *one* is in the list of 100 greatest books. Why must we have the *Rise and Fall of the Third Reich,* when the *Rise and Fall of the Dutch Republic* is a better book, and in the public domain? Is the *Tropic of Cancer* better (worse) than the works of the Marquis de Sade? What, precisely, are the respects in which Tennessee Williams surpasses Shakespeare? Samuelson (5 editions), Bach (3 editions), Harriss (4 editions) and others write our textbooks; is it abundantly clear that they are better books than the *Wealth of Nations?*

The economist cannot answer these questions. The answers rest on value judgments, which are not scientific, and the economist is a scientist. All the economist can do is report the facts. As Fisher, Griliches, and Kaysen say, we cannot tell a drunkard to stop drinking, but we can audit the bar bill. Or, to choose a metaphor without normative overtones, we cannot tell a nation to stop turning beautiful trees into waste paper, but we can weigh the ashes.

So let us assume that no new books were printed after 1900. This date is less arbitrary than 1949, I think, and in any event it yields bigger numbers. Some books of this earlier period would probably sell in only small quantities (I have in mind an item such as J. S. Mill's *An Examination of Sir William Hamilton's Philosophy, and of the Principal Philosophical Questions Discussed in His Writings* or Sinclair's 21 volume survey of Scotland in 1791–99), although without the diversion of the new models their markets would strengthen. Some books might even disappear (I have in mind such an item as Heinrich's *Phlogiston ist die Wahrheit*). But there would be an ample selection of reading matter: the books of 1900 and before could not run or keep out the rain, but they could furnish the minds of Newton, Gauss, Beethoven, and Goethe, of Jefferson and Lincoln and Dred Scott.

The stream of savings would be immense, and it would be fed

by a thousand hidden springs. Let me just cite four important components:

1. All books would be royalty free, with savings of perhaps 10 per cent on retail prices. The authors would usually have alternative products.
2. The plates of a typical book now print about 3,000 copies. This could be raised to at least 200,000 with a reduction of 98.5 per cent in composition costs. Easily another 30 per cent reduction in price. (This item alone exceeds the savings in the automobile study, as a percent of price.)
3. Advertising of books would fall, perhaps by 98 per cent. This would cut prices another 5 or 10 per cent.
4. In happy analogy to Fisher, Griliches, and Kaysen, books would get more mileage. Once a family outside Wisconsin grew up, its sturdily bound McGuffy Readers could be passed on to a second generation, and possibly a third. This would reduce costs by a factor of 2.5, making the aggregate saving perhaps 85 per cent of present costs.

I shall not pause to estimate indirect savings: houses could be smaller; people would not have to change the prescription of their glasses so often; teachers would not have to think up new examination questions; etc.

When we turn to newspapers, the savings would be even greater. There is nothing new under the sun, so it would be sufficient to print a dozen volumes of news once and for all: crimes, wars, women, colonies, frontier life, emancipation, and the Irish Question, for example. In addition to a saving of say 98 per cent on newspapers, there would be a substantial reduction in efforts by people to get into the news.

These savings are to be calculated in the billions of dollars, and the billions of hours of reader time. There would be some delay in the dissemination of new knowledge, few changes are without costs. I would beg the reader, however, to keep two facts in mind: most new knowledge is false; and the news got around in Athens.

The Permanent Traffic Solution

There were many contributing factors. Historians say that the Permanent Metropolitan Traffic Solution received its initial impetus from the electronic coffeemaker offered by Detroit as optional equipment in several 1972 automobiles. The devices appealed to New Jersey and Long Island commuters, who by that date were forced to rise at 5 A.M. to reach their Manhattan offices at 9, and often left home without breakfast.

Soon most cars had coffee machines, and it was a pleasant sight to see the accountants and media salesmen sipping the beverage during the long waits at the bridge and tunnel approaches, often forming jolly little groups, chatting and playing cards without a care in the world. Every half-hour or so a social-security number was called out over the public address system, and its owner waved a gay goodbye and drove on to the next stoppage point.

"Bottleneck clubs" were formed where lasting friendships ripened. Some groups played chess, others brought record players, and more serious motorists applied themselves to philosophy, science, or economics. The Neo-Anti-Keynesian School traces its origin to a club that met each morning for a spirited discussion hour on the Pulaski Skyway, as a brass plaque riveted to a steel girder now testifies.

Quick as always to anticipate drivers' needs, Detroit added toasters to 1973 models. Grills followed, and soon the haunting aroma of bacon gently mingled with the unburned hydrocarbon gases.

There were a few protests and letters to editors, but cultural anthropologists recalled that when our nation's founders were long absent from their hearths on stagecoach journeys, little blame attended their lapses.

Suburban mates, envious of the smart new highway life from which they were excluded, went to town with their husbands to shop for thread, one spool at a time. A thousand bridge clubs were formed on the Long Island Expressway alone, and teas and cocktail parties enlivened the long journey home. By this time the trek from Upper Montclair to Wall Street normally took several days, and one couple left Madison Avenue on the eve of Columbus Day and arrived home at Riverhead, Long Island, on New Year's Day.

Because of the new six-hour week and the portal-to-portal wage law, the extended travel time did not disrupt the business structure, or lessen the purchasing power of the delayed drivers. New industries arose. A fleet of spotless obstetrical trucks, operated by private industry under government subsidy, found business brisk, especially on the long concrete ribbon to Bucks County.

The Permanent Traffic Solution, foreseen only by a few ignored visionaries, came almost by accident. Consolidated Edison's overloaded cables broke down once more, and streets were dug up on strategic tunnel approaches. It was on a Friday before Labor Day. At 3:30 P.M., 150 police helicopters were patrolling the city's exits, shouting soothing advice to drivers. One, hovering low over the Queensborough Bridge, crashed into an ambulance and exploded. A commercial artist from Short Hills named Joe Bloch hit a hydrant on Varick Street and the area was flooded. By 5:45 P.M. all vehicles were motionless. The Mayor declared an emergency and fired Traffic Commissioner Barnes. The Salvation Army sent out soup kitchens on saddle horses.

From the Battery to the Bronx, from the North River to the East River, Manhattan streets were jammed with immovable traffic. The cars stayed there, for IBM computers quickly reported that the time needed to disentangle them would exceed the average obsolescence index of the vehicles. The Planners had finally achieved their goal.

Long trained in sedan living, the indomitable commuters were not seriously discommoded. Like the pioneer heroes of *Wagon Train,* and the early dog-cart victualers who bricked up their roving cafes, the home-workshop-conditioned citizens adjusted to their environment. And life was good. The morning sun glistened on dewy, cobwebbed clover-leaf crossings. Boys shot out traffic lights with air rifles. Roses rambled over Pontiacs. Seasons rolled by. People lived and died in their cars, and were happy. Swallows nested in the Lincoln Tunnel.

Compulsory Laissez-Faire

"What we need is a strong, authoritarian government with the courage to bring in compulsory laissez-faire."

Three cartoons by Hector Breeze, in *Punch*, September 24, 1975, p. 515. Permission granted by *Punch*.

Subsidized Competition

"If only we had a government subsidy we could be really competitive!"

Japanese Sales Charts

*"We have the very best sales charts, of course—
they're printed in Japan."*

A Negative Railroad

I have already remarked that when the observer has unfortunately taken his point of view from the position of the producer, he cannot fail in his conclusions to clash with the general interest, because the producer, as such, must desire the existence of efforts, wants, and obstacles.

I find a singular exemplification of this remark in a journal of Bordeaux.

Mr. Simiot puts this question:

Ought the railroad from Paris into Spain to present a break or terminus at Bordeaux?

This question he answers affirmatively. I will only consider one among the numerous reasons which he adduces in support of his opinion.

The railroad from Paris to Bayonne ought (he says) to present a break or terminus at Bordeaux, in order that goods and travelers stopping in this city should thus be forced to contribute to the profits of the boatmen, porters, commission merchants, hotel-keepers, etc.

It is very evident that we have here again the interest of the agents of labor put before that of the consumer.

But if Bordeaux would profit by a break in the road, and if such profit be conformable to the public interest, then Angouleme, Poitiers, Tours, Orleans, and still more all the intermediate points, as Ruffec, Chatellerault, etc., etc., would also petition for breaks; and this too would be for the general good and for the interest of national labor. For it is certain, that in proportion to the number of these breaks or termini, will be the increase in consignments, commissions, lading, unlading, etc. This system furnishes us the

153

idea of a railroad made up of successive breaks; *a negative railroad.*

Whether or not the Protectionists will allow it, most certain it is that the *restrictive principle* is identical with that which would maintain *this system of breaks:* it is the sacrifice of the consumer to the producer, of the end to the means.

Petition of the Manufacturers of Candles, Wax Lights, Lamps, Candlesticks, Street Lamps, Snuffers, Extinguishers, and of the Producers of Oil, Tallow, Rosin, Alcohol, and, Generally, of Everything Connected with Lighting (excerpt)

TO MESSIEURS THE MEMBERS OF THE CHAMBER OF DEPUTIES

GENTLEMEN,

You are on the right road. You reject abstract theories, and have little consideration for cheapness and plenty. Your chief care is the interest of the producer. You desire to emancipate him from external competition, and reserve the NATIONAL MARKET for NATIONAL INDUSTRY.

We are about to offer you an admirable opportunity of applying your—what shall we call it? your theory? No; nothing is more deceptive than theory; your doctrine? your system? your principle? but you dislike doctrines, you abhor systems, and as for principles, you deny that there are any in social economy: we shall say, then, your practice without theory and without principle.

We are suffering from the intolerable competition of a foreign rival, placed, it would seem, in a condition so far superior to ours for the production of light, that he absolutely INUNDATES our

NATIONAL MARKET with it at a price fabulously reduced. The moment he shows himself, our trade leaves us—all consumers apply to him; and a branch of native industry, having countless ramifications, is all at once rendered completely stagnant. This rival, who is no other than the sun, wages war to the knife against us, and we suspect that he has been raised up by PERFIDIOUS ALBION (good policy as times go); inasmuch as he displays toward that haughty island a circumspection with which he dispenses in our case.

What we pray for is that it may please you to pass a law ordering the shutting up of all windows, skylights, dormer windows, outside and inside shutters, curtains, blinds, bull's-eyes; in a word, of all openings, holes, chinks, clefts, and fissures, by or through which the light of the sun has been in use to enter houses, to the prejudice of the meritorious manufactures with which we flatter ourselves, we have accommodated our country—a country which, in gratitude, ought not to abandon us now to a strife so unequal.

We trust, gentlemen, that you will not regard this our request as a satire, or refuse it without at least previously hearing the reasons which we have to urge in its support.

And, first, if you shut up as much as possible all access to natural light, and create a demand for artificial light, which of our French manufactures will not be encouraged by it?

If more tallow is consumed, then there must be more oxen and sheep; and, consequently, we shall behold the multiplication of artificial meadows, meat, wool, hides, and, above all, manure, which is the basis and foundation of all agricultural wealth.

If more oil is consumed, then we shall have an extended cultivation of the poppy, of the olive, and of grape. These rich and exhausting plants will come at the right time to enable us to avail ourselves of the increased fertility which the rearing of additional cattle will impart to our lands.

Our heaths will be covered with resinous trees. Numerous swarms of bees will, on the mountains, gather perfumed treasures, now wasting their fragrance on the desert air, like the flowers from which they emanate. No branch of agriculture but will then exhibit a cheering development.

The same remark applies to navigation. Thousands of vessels will proceed to the whale fishery, and in a short time we shall possess a navy capable of maintaining the honor of France, and gratifying the patriotic aspirations of your petitioners, the under-signed candlemakers and others.

But what shall we say of the manufacture of ARTICLES DE PARIS? Henceforth you will behold gildings, bronzes, crystals, in candlesticks, in lamps, in lusters, in candelabra, shining forth, in spacious warerooms, compared with which those of the present day can be regarded but as mere shops.

No poor RESINIER from his heights on the seacoast, no coal miner from the depth of his sable gallery, but will rejoice in higher wages and increased prosperity.

Only have the goodness to reflect, gentlemen, and you will be convinced that there is, perhaps, no Frenchman, from the wealthy coalmaster to the humblest vender of lucifer matches, whose lot will not be ameliorated by the success of this our petition.

We foresee your objections, gentlemen, but we know that you can oppose to us none but such as you have picked up from the effete works of the partisans of free trade. We defy you to utter a single word against us which will not instantly rebound against yourselves and your entire policy. . . .

If you urge that the light of the sun is a gratuitous gift of nature, and that to reject such gifts is to reject wealth itself under pretense of encouraging the means of acquiring it, we would caution you against giving a death blow to your own policy. Remember that hitherto you have always repelled foreign products, BE-CAUSE they approximate more nearly than home products to the character of gratuitous gifts. To comply with the exactions of other monopolists, you have only HALF A MOTIVE; and to re-pulse us simply because we stand on a stronger vantage-ground than others would be to adopt the equation, $+ x + = -$; in other words, it would be to heap ABSURDITY upon ABSURDITY. . . .

. . . Make your choice, but be logical; for as long as you exclude, as you do, coal, iron, corn, foreign fabrics, IN PROPOR-TION as their price approximates to ZERO, what inconsistency would it be to admit the light of the sun, the price of which is already at ZERO during the entire day!

Art Buchwald

Use Less, Pay More

I went into Burberry's house one night, and much to my surprise, I found every light in his house on.

"Burberry, have you taken leave of your senses?" I said. "Don't you know there is an energy crisis?"

Burberry plugged in the toaster, the coffeemaker and the iron. "I know it," he replied. "And I'm trying to do something about it."

"By turning on all the lights and using all these electric gadgets?"

"That's right," he said, turning up the thermostat to 80. "You see, the electric companies say they can't make money if we conserve electricity. The only way we can bring prices down is if electric usage goes up."

"You're putting me on."

"I'm not putting you on," he said, plugging in his wife's hair dryer. "A few months ago the President and George C. Scott went on the air, separately of course, and said we had to conserve energy if we were going to be able to maintain our great way of life. So everyone cut down on using electricity. We turned off our lights, cut down our thermostats and reduced the use of all our electric appliances. They estimated the American people saved between ten percent and twenty percent during the winter. Everyone thought if he conserved, he would at least save money on his electric bills.

"Well, it turned out just the opposite. The electric companies all asked for rate increases because people weren't using enough of their product. It turns out they all want to be paid for electricity we haven't used."

"But that doesn't make sense," I said.

"What the hell does make sense about the energy crisis?" Burberry said. "My family froze their butts off this winter as a patriotic gesture, and now we find the electric companies want to put a surcharge on them."

"On your butts?"

"No, not on our butts, on our conservation methods.

"The electric companies are the only ones who want to charge you more for using less electricity. I cut down on smoking last year. The cigarette companies didn't send me a letter saying because I cut down on smoking they would have to charge me more a pack. We gave up high-priced steaks. My butcher didn't send me a bill for not eating steaks. Why should the electric companies send me a letter saying because I didn't use enough electricity I'm going to have to pay more for it?"

"I guess if they don't sell enough electricity to their customers, they lose money on it."

"Okay, so that means if I use more electricity, they'll make money and then be able to charge me less."

He yelled into the kitchen. "Honey, did you put the stove and oven on?"

"Burberry," I said, "I know what you say is true, but I think you've missed the point. Everyone is expected to make sacrifices during an energy crisis. I'm not talking about real sacrifices. What could be a greater sacrifice for an American than to use less electricity but at the same time compensate the electric companies by paying more for it? That's what George C. Scott and President Nixon were talking about when they asked you to turn your lights out."

By this time Burberry had turned on his vacuum cleaner, and I didn't hear his reply. But as an accomplished lip reader, I was just as glad I couldn't.

Jonathan Swift

To the Right Honourable
the Mayor and Aldermen
of the
City of London,
the
Humble Petition
of the
Colliers, Cooks, Cook-Maids, Blacksmiths,
Jackmakers, Braziers, and Others,

Sheweth, That whereas certain *virtuosi,* disaffected to the government, and to the trade and prosperity of this kingdom, taking upon them the name and title of the Catoptrical Victuallers, have presumed by gathering, breaking, folding, and bundling up the sun-beams, by the help of certain glasses, to make, produce, and kindle up several new focuses or fires within these his Majesty's dominions, and there to boil, bake, stew, fry, and dress all sorts of victuals and provisions, to brew, distil spirits, smelt ore, and in general to perform all the offices of culinary fires; and are endeavouring to procure to themselves the monopoly of this their said invention: We beg leave humbly to represent to your honours,

That such grant or patent will utterly ruin and reduce to beggary your petitioners, their wives, children, servants, and trades on them depending; there being nothing left to them, after the said invention, but warming of cellars and dressing of suppers in the winter-time. That the abolishing of so considerable a branch of the coasting-trade as that of the colliers, will destroy the navigation of this kingdom. That whereas the said catoptrical victuallers talk of making use of the moon by night, as of the sun by day, they will utterly ruin the numerous body of tallow-chandlers, and impair a very considerable branch of the revenue, which arises from the tax upon tallow and candles.

That the said catoptrical victuallers do profane the emanations of that glorious luminary the sun, which is appointed to rule the day, and not to roast mutton. And we humbly conceive it will be found contrary to the known laws of this kingdom, to confine, forestal, and monopolize the beams of the sun. And whereas the said catoptrical victuallers have undertaken, by burning glasses made of ice, to roast an ox upon the Thames next winter: we conceive all such practices to be an encroachment upon the rights and privileges of the company of watermen.

That the diversity of exposition of the several kitchens in this great city, whereby some receive the rays of the sun sooner, and others later, will occasion great irregularity as to the time of dining of the several inhabitants, and consequently great uncertainty and confusion in the dispatch of business; and to those who, by reason of their northern exposition, will be still forced to be at the expense of culinary fires, it will reduce the price of their manufacture to such inequality, as is inconsistent with common justice: and the same inconveniency will affect landlords in the value of their rents.

That the use of the said glasses will oblige cooks and cook-maids to study optics and astronomy, in order to know the due distance of the said focuses or fires, and to adjust the position of their glasses to the several altitudes of the sun, varying according to the hours of the day, and the seasons of the year; which studies, at these years, will be highly troublesome to the said cooks and cook-maids, not to say anything of the utter incapacity of some of them to go through with such difficult arts; or (which is still a greater inconvenience) it will throw the whole art of cookery into the hands of astronomers and glass-grinders, persons utterly unskilled in other parts of that profession, to the great detriment of the health of his Majesty's good subjects.

That it is known by experience, that meat roasted with sun-beams is extremely unwholesome; witness several that have died suddenly after eating the provisions of the said catoptrical victuallers; forasmuch as the sun-beams taken inwardly render the humours too hot and adust, occasion great sweatings, and dry up the rectual moisture.

That sun-beams taken inwardly shed a malignant influence upon the brain, by their natural tendency toward the moon; and produce madness and distraction at the time of the full moon. That the constant use of so great quantities of this inward light, will occasion the growth of quakerism, to the danger of the church: and of poetry, to the danger of the state.

That the influences of the constellations, through which the sun passes, will with his beams be conveyed into the blood; and when the sun is among the horned signs, may produce such a spirit of unchastity, as is dangerous to the honour of your worships' families.

That mankind, living much upon the seeds and other parts of plants, these being impregnated with the sun-beams, may vegetate and grow in the bowels, a thing of more dangerous consequence to human bodies than breeding of worms; and this will fall heaviest upon the poor, who live upon roots; and the weak and sickly, who live upon barley and rice-gruel, &c., for which we are ready to produce to your honours the opinions of eminent physicians, that the taste and property of the victuals is much altered to the worse by the said solar cookery, the fricassees being deprived of the *haut gout* they acquire by being dressed over charcoal.

Lastly, should it happen, by an eclipse of an extraordinary length, that this city should be deprived of the sun-beams for several months; how will his majesty's subjects subsist in the interim, when common cookery, with the arts depending upon it, is totally lost?

In consideration of these, and many other inconveniences, your petitioners humbly pray, that your honours would either totally prohibit the confining and manufacturing the sun-beams for any of the useful purposes of life, or, in the ensuing parliament, procure a tax to be laid upon them, which may answer both the duty and price of coals, and which we humbly conceive cannot be less than thirty shillings *per* yard square; reserving the sole right and privilege of the catoptrical cookery to the Royal Society, and to the commanders and crews of the bomb-vessels, under the direction of Mr. Whiston, for finding out the longitude; who, by reason of the remoteness of their stations, may be reduced to straits for want of firing.

And we likewise beg, that your honours, as to the forementioned points, would hear the reverend Mr. Flamstead, who is the legal officer appointed by the government to look after the heavenly luminaries, whom we have constituted our trusty and learned solicitor.

John Arbuthnot

Petition of the Upholders

Reasons Humbly Offered by the Company Exercising the Trade and Mystery of Upholders, against Part of the Bill, for the Better Viewing, Searching, and Examining Drugs, Medicines, Etc. 1724.

Being called upon by several retailers and dispensers of drugs and medicines about town, to use our endeavors against the bill now depending for viewing, etc. In regard of our common interest, and in gratitude to the said retailers and dispensers of medicines, which we have always found to be very effectual, we presume to lay the following reasons before the public against the said bill.

That the company of upholders are far from being averse to the giving of drugs and medicines in general, provided they be of such qualities as we require, and administered by such persons, in whom our company justly repose the greatest confidence; and provided they tend to the encouragement of trade, and the consumption of the woollen manufacture of this kingdom.

We beg leave to observe, that there has been no complaint from any of the nobility, gentry, and citizens, whom we have attended. Our practice, which consists chiefly in outward applications, having been always so effectual, that none of our patients have been obliged to undergo a second operation, excepting one gentlewoman, who, after her first burial, having burdened her husband with a new brood of posthumous children, her second funeral was by us performed without any further charges to the

---

In the year 1724, the physicians made application to parliament to prevent apothecaries dispensing medicines without the prescription of a physician.

164

said husband of the deceased. And we humbly hope, that one single instance of this kind, a misfortune owing merely to the avarice of a sexton, in cutting off a ring, will not be imputed to any want of skill or care in our company.

We humbly conceive, that the power by this bill lodged in the censors of the college of physicians to restrain any of his majesty's subjects from dispensing, and well-disposed persons from taking, what medicines they please, is a manifest encroachment on the liberty and property of the subject.

As the company, exercising the trade and mystery of upholders, have an undisputed right in and upon the bodies of all and every the subjects of the kingdom, we conceive the passing of this bill, though not absolutely depriving them of their said right, might keep them out of possession by unreasonable delays, to the great detriment of our company, and their numerous families.

We hope it will be considered, that there are multitudes of necessitous heirs, and penurious parents, persons in pinching circumstances with numerous families of children, wives that have lived long, many robust aged women with great jointures, elder brothers with bad understandings, single heirs of great estates, whereby the collateral line are for ever excluded, reversionary patents, and reversionary promises of preferments, leases upon single lives, and play-debts upon joint lives, and that the persons so aggrieved have no hope of being speedily relieved any other way, than by the dispensing of drugs and medicines in the manner they now are: burying alive being judged repugnant to the known laws of this kingdom.

That there are many of the deceased, who, by certain mechanical motions and powers, are carried about town, who would have been put into our hands long before this time, by any other well-ordered government: by want of a due police in this particular, our company have been great sufferers.

That frequent funerals contribute to preserve the genealogies of families, and the honours conferred by the crown, which are nowhere so well illustrated as on this solemn occasion; to maintain necessitous clergy; to enable the clerks to appear in decent habits to officiate on Sunday; to feed the great retinue of sober and melancholy men who appear at the said funerals, and who must starve without constant and regular employment. Moreover, we desire that it may be remembered, that, by the passing of this bill, the nobility and gentry will have their old coaches lie upon their hand, which are now employed by our company.

And we farther hope, that frequent funerals will not be discouraged, as it is by this bill proposed, it being the only method left of carrying some people to church.

We are afraid, that, by the hardships of this bill, our company will be reduced to leave their business here, and practice at York and Bristol, where the free use of bad medicines will be still allowed.

It is therefore hoped, that no specious pretence whatsoever will be thought sufficient to introduce an arbitrary and unlimited power for people to live (in defiance of art) as long as they can by the course of nature, to the prejudice of our company and the decay of trade.

That as our company are likely to suffer, in some measure, by the power given to physicians to dissect the bodies of malefactors, we humbly hope, that the manufacture of cases for skeletons will be reserved solely to coffin-makers.

We likewise humbly presume, that the interests of the several trades and professions which depend upon ours, may be regarded; such as that of hearses, coaches, coffins, epitaphs, and bell-ropes, stone-cutters, feathermen, and bell-ringers; and especially the manufacturers of crapes; and the makers of stuff; who use great quantities of old coffins, and who, considered in the consumption of their drugs, employ by far the greatest number of hands of any manufacture of the kingdom.

Part 5

Microeconomics II— Work and Play

Introduction

The basic concerns of economics are hidden in two statements: "You can't have your cake and eat it too" and "There's no such thing as a free lunch." At issue is the necessity to choose—and choice means cost.

This section deals with choices regarding time. In the economic sense, time is a commodity and a resource. It can be bought, saved, used, wasted, measured, served, and meted out. Time is unique in at least one respect, however. It cannot be accumulated. In 1863, J. O. Wallin described it thus:[1]

> Money you may waste.
> Money regain;
> Pile it in your chest,
> And thus retain.
> Now time, time, alas,
> Once it has elapsed,
> Never comes again;
> No seal whatever,
> Lock or bolt could ever
> Make it remain.

While the individual use of a 24-hour day varies according to taste and circumstance, everyone chooses between two activities:

---

1. "Tidens varde" in *Samlade Vitterhets-arbeten,* 5:e uppl., II delen, Adolf Bonnier, Stockholm, 1863, 190.

work and nonwork. But to define nonwork as leisure, as is customary in economics, puts the housewife in the unlikely position of mopping a floor for fun. To avoid confusion, work is defined here as market activity for which pay is received, all other activity—sleeping, eating, playing, meditating, mopping floors—being unpaid. And there is no free lunch. When Voltaire said, "Work keeps at bay three evils: boredom, vice, and need," he implied that the opportunity cost of a decision to work is the value of being bored, vicious, or needy—at no pay.

Decisions about the day's activities begin when people wake up, and because this normally occurs in the morning, the selections begin chronologically. Not everyone rises at dawn, of course, and some people can't make a decision until after a cup of coffee. But definitive data on waking reveal a median rising time of 7:22 A.M., a finding supported by traffic studies showing a lot of people going somewhere shortly thereafter.[2]

The three definitions of dawn, day, and decision making originally appeared in an Ambrose Bierce book entitled *The Cynic's Word Book,* published in 1906. Bierce attributes the fatalistic verse on "choice" to G. J., the fictitious Father Gassalasca Jape, S.J., one of Bierce's many pseudonyms.

In part 3, Philip H. Wicksteed applied the concept of diminishing marginal utility to prayer. Here he illustrates the idea with an "indolent young man" who budgets his time by evaluating "guilty and uneasy moments in bed" relative to other morning activities. Readers who have difficulty relating to the young man's intentions to walk are reminded that car ownership was not widespread in 1910 when the essay was written.

"Early to bed, early to rise" is usually attributed to Benjamin Franklin, but Aristotle (384–322 B.C.) said it first. Franklin loved nightlife and a party too much to practice what he preached. Whether Aristotle did is not known, but it is believed that he died of overwork around 322 B.C., at the age of 62, while Franklin lived to the ripe old age of 84. These conflicting results suggest the need for reexamination of the health benefits of early bedding and rising.

Benjamin Franklin's aphorisms were age-old proverbs that originally appeared in his *Poor Richard's Almanac.* When he included them in *The Way to Wealth,* a 1757 Preface to the *Almanac,* they achieved worldwide popularity in more than 150 edi-

---

2. See Reiz und Scheine, *Gutentag* (1903), 983.

tions and translations in every European language. Both the maxims and the first advertisement of the *Almanac* suggest the eclectic nature of the writings in this particular section. They are included for this reason.

One of the first things people do in the morning is brush their teeth. Or do they? It is hard to credit the results of tooth-brushing surveys, for how many respondents will admit that they don't brush after every meal? At any rate, Alan S. Blinder (1945–) rejects conventional models of toothbrushing in "The Economics of Brushing Teeth." His "human capital" approach proves to be a more reliable predictor of brushing habits than either the "bad taste in one's mouth" model or the "mother told me so" theory. While he includes denture wearers in his regression analysis, his exclusion of 189 toothless individuals attests to his careful attention to detail. Blinder's study contributes substantially to an area almost totally ignored in economics, "despite the fact that most economists brush their teeth." Blinder is the Gordon S. Rentschler Memorial Professor of Economics at Princeton, whose faculty he joined after receiving his Ph.D. degree at MIT. Appointed Vice-Chairman of the Federal Reserve Board by President Clinton in 1994, Blinder returned to Princeton in 1996.

In 1955, when he was Raffles Professor of History at the University of Singapore, C. Northcote Parkinson observed that "work expands so as to fill the time available for its completion." Firmly rooted in the tendency for officials to multiply subordinates and to make work for each other, Parkinson's Law is as valid today as it was when it was first published. Parkinson was born in 1909 at Barnard Castle, County Durham, England, graduated with honors from Cambridge's Emmanuel College in 1932, and earned a Ph.D. at the University of London in 1935.

Philip Musgrove (1940–) received his Ph.D. from MIT in 1974. He observes that the ratio of time taken to time expected tends to the value of "e." When no one's in a rush, jobs are completed on time. His bibliography gives scholarly weight to his study.

In "We Who Work at Night," Brooks Atkinson (1894–1984) presents a compelling argument for night work. His personifications of some of the night's attractions are enough to make day workers change to the late shift. "Grand Central Terminal," he writes, "dozes during the night . . . advertising displays are resting . . . the subway is quiet and lazy." Besides, "Day . . . looks haggard in the city by the time people have gotten through with it at five o'clock." Atkinson was a journalist and theater critic who joined the *New York Times* in 1922 as editor of the book review. He won a Pulitzer Prize for his reporting on the Soviet Union and, in 1972, was elected to the Theatre Hall of Fame and Museum.

Opportunity cost is central to economics, but its application to the institution of marriage is a bit unusual. This may explain the debates provoked by Gary North's "A Note on the Opportunity Cost of Marriage." North shows that if "a woman's place is in the home," an educated wife is a "very expensive mate." According to North, he should have married a high school dropout or an ignoramus with a penchant for pots and pans. After North's article was published, criticisms of his approach appeared in the same journal.

One, by Madelyn L. Kafoglis, offers criticism in "Marriage Customs and Opportunity Costs." Kafoglis writes that North confused two models, a conventional "market" model and an old-fashioned "woman's place is in the home" model. In the latter, Kafoglis writes, "There are no opportunity costs" by the nature of the contract. Furthermore, she says, even a "woman's place" model should account for the potential inexpensive tastes of educated wives.

In his own words, T. C. Bergstrom reaches "heights of pedantry" in his "boring reformulation" of M. A. El Hodiri's theory of sleeping. Bergstrom's finding in "Toward a Deeper Economics of Sleeping" that the average man *spends* exactly 9.231 hours per day in bed supports Hodiri's "first law of soporifics," but raises interesting questions and maybe a few eyebrows regarding Hodiri's "second law . . . [that] . . . most people *sleep* eight hours a day." Bergstrom drolly concludes that 1.231 hours must be allotted to "Activity X."

There is more irony than meets the eye in Millicent G. Fawcett's terse statement on "The Oldest Profession." From a current viewpoint, the flavor of the passage is Victorian, but its inclusion in an article entitled "Equal Pay, Equal Work" may have shocked 1918 readers. A strong advocate of women's rights, Millicent Fawcett (1847–1929) was married to Henry Fawcett, member of Parliament and professor of political economy at Cambridge. With her husband, Fawcett published a popular book in 1870, *Political Economy for Beginners*. Her efforts on behalf of women's suffrage and other female issues were supported by John Stuart Mill, a family friend.

At a time when many Americans plead "get government off

our backs," Arthur S. Levine brashly responds, "Let's bring government into the bedroom . . ." The author's graphical and tabular presentation of "official" census data on sexual resources gives his parody of income distribution an unexpected economic significance.[3]

<hr/>

3. In a related context, the Swedish economist Staffan B. Linder points out that "love has a negative income elasticity. It is an 'inferior' activity—although inferior in another sense than that employed by the moralist." Linder thus views "economic growth as a conceivable obstacle to sex." See *The Harried Leisure Class* (New York: Columbia University Press, 1970), 84.

Ambrose Bierce

Working Definitions—Dawn and Day

DAWN, n. The time when men of reason go to bed. Certain old men prefer to rise at about that time, taking a cold bath and a long walk with an empty stomach, and otherwise mortifying the flesh. They then point with pride to these practices as the cause of their sturdy health and ripe years; the truth being that they are hearty and old, not because of their habits, but in spite of them. The reason we find only robust persons doing this thing is that it has killed all the others who have tried it.

DAY, n. A period of twenty-four hours, mostly misspent. This period is divided into two parts, the day proper and the night, or day improper—the former devoted to sins of business, the latter consecrated to the other sort. These two kinds of social activity overlap.

On the Question of Choice

A leaf was riven from a tree,
"I mean to fall to earth," said he.

The west wind, rising, made him veer.
"Eastward," said he, "I now shall steer."

The east wind rose with greater force.
Said he, "'Twere wise to change my course."

With equal power they contend.
He said, "My judgment I suspend."

Down died the winds; the leaf, elate,
Cried: "I've decided to fall straight."

"First thoughts are best?" That's not the moral;
Just choose your own and we'll not quarrel.

Howe'er your choice may chance to fall,
You'll have no hand in it at all.

Philip H. Wicksteed

On the Diminishing Marginal Utility of Guilt (excerpt)

. . . [A] young man has made his arrangements to get up at a given hour, to take 30 minutes to dress, 30 minutes for breakfast and the paper, and 30 minutes to walk down to his office or lecture; but when he is called, a new claimant on the time he has so carefully distributed appears, in the shape of the luxury of staying where he is. He remembers hearing that it is bad for the constitution to get up suddenly, and he lies dreamily in bed cutting minutes off one after another of the three assignees of his time, till two-thirds of his resources are exhausted, and he springs out of bed to dress in 10 minutes, to breakfast in 5, and to run down in a quarter of an hour to keep his appointment. The significance of minutes in bed has encroached upon all the others, and by its pressure has revealed the fact that as you cut into them the significance of the minutes assigned to dressing, breakfast, and locomotion, rises unequally. There was a marginal balance at 30 minutes each, but the minutes taken off the time for getting to his appointment rise in significance more rapidly than those assigned to his toilet, and these again more rapidly than those assigned to his breakfast, and when at last these marginal significances, still equal to each other, rise to equality with the now declining value of guilty and uneasy moments in bed, the margins stand, as we have seen, at 5, 10, and 15 minutes. The thirtieth breakfast minutes and the thirtieth minute for walking had the same estimated significance, but as you recede the walking minutes rise in value so rapidly that you must go back to the fifth breakfast minute in order to find one as valuable as the fifteenth walking minute. . . .

. . . [W]e may think of our indolent young man, when he has fairly begun his day, carefully considering what expenditure of labour will pay best in the examination for which he is preparing, visited at certain moments by compunction as to the sordidness of this view, and genuinely allured (by the fascination of some subject) into the pursuit of knowledge for her own sake; or fraudulently persuading himself, in another mood, that he has a soul above mere utilitarian considerations, that knowledge of the world is better than University distinction, and that his acquaintance with the modern drama or with the points of dogs or horses is in more urgent need of marginal increments than his knowledge of the niceties of the syntax of a dead language. He too is, wisely or foolishly, administering his resources and endeavoring to bring marginal values into a proper balance with the terms on which alternatives are offered.

Maxims for Action

It is likewise well to rise before daybreak; for this contributes to health, wealth, and wisdom.

—Aristotle

Poor Richard says . . .

Early to bed, and early to rise, makes a man healthy, wealthy, and wise.

Laziness travels so slowly, that poverty soon overtakes him.

Sloth, like rust, consumes faster than labor wears, while the used key is always bright.

Diligence is the mother of good luck.

Employ thy time well if thou meanest to gain leisure.

Leisure is time for doing something useful.

Plough deep, while sluggards sleep, and you shall have corn to sell and to keep.

Let us then be up and doing.

He that riseth late, must trot all day, and shall scarce overtake his business at night.

How much more [time] than is necessary do we spend in sleep! . . . forgetting that the sleeping fox catches no poultry, and that there will be sleeping enough in the grave.

Let not the sun look down and say, inglorious here he lies.

Women and wine, game and deceit,
Make the wealth small, and the wants great.

Pride is as loud a beggar as want, and a great deal more saucy;
    'tis easier to suppress the first desire, than to satisfy all that
    follow it.

—Benjamin Franklin

The First Advertisement of Poor Richard's Almanac

Just published, for 1733, An Almanac, containing the Lunations, Eclipses, Planets' Motions and Aspects, Weather, Sun and Moon's Rising and Setting, High Water, etc; besides many pleasant and witty Verses, Jests, and Sayings; Author's Motive of Writing; Prediction of the Death of his Friend, Mr. Titan Leeds; Moon no Cuckold; Bachelor's Folly; Parson's Wine and Baker's Pudding; Short Visits; Kings and Bears; New Fashions; Game for Kisses; Katherine's Love; Different Sentiments; Signs of a Tempest; Death of a Fisherman; Conjugal Debate; Men and Melons; The Prodigal; Breakfast in Bed; Oyster Lawsuit, etc. By Richard Saunders, Philomat. Printed and Sold by B. Franklin.

Alan S. Blinder

The Economics of Brushing Teeth

The ever-growing literature on human capital has long recognized that the scope of the theory extends well beyond the traditional analysis of schooling and on-the-job training. Migration, maintenance of health, crime and punishment, even marriage and suicide, are all decisions which can usefully be considered from the human capital point of view. Yet economists have ignored the analysis of an important class of activities which can and should be brought within the purview of the theory. A prime example of this class is brushing teeth.[1]

The conventional analysis of toothbrushing has centered around two basic models. The "bad taste in one's mouth" model is based on the notion that each person has a "taste for brushing," and the fact that brushing frequencies differ is "explained" by differences in tastes. Since any pattern of human behavior can be rationalized by such implicit theorizing, this model is devoid of empirically testable predictions, and hence uninteresting.

The "mother told me so" theory is based on differences in cultural upbringing. Here it is argued, for example, that thrice-a-day brushers brush three times daily because their mothers forced them to do so as children. Of course, this is hardly a complete explanation. Like most psychological theories, it leaves open

Editor's note.—This paper derives from the Princeton oral tradition.

I wish to thank my dentist for filling in some important gaps in the analysis, and my colleague, Michael Rothschild, for insightful kibitzing. Support for this research is graciously solicited.

1. The analysis to follow can also be applied to such important problems as combing hair, washing hands, and cutting fingernails, as I hope to show in a series of future papers.

the question of why mothers should want their children to brush after every meal. But it does at least have one testable implication: that individuals from higher social classes will brush more frequently.

In these pages I describe a new model which is firmly grounded in economic theory and which generates a large number of empirically testable hypotheses. I then show that the predictions of the model are supported by the data.

The basic assumption is common to all human capital theory: that individuals seek to maximize their incomes. It follows immediately that each individual does whatever amount of toothbrushing will maximize his income. The "mother told me so" model can be considered as a special case where the offspring only does as he or she is told, but the mother's decisions are governed by income maximization for the child. Thus, offspring will behave *as if* they maximized income.

An example will illustrate the usefulness of the model. Consider the toothbrushing decisions of chefs and waiters working in the same establishments. Since chefs generally come from higher socioeconomic strata, the "mother told me so" model predicts that they will brush more frequently than waiters. In fact, it has been shown that the reverse is true (Barnard and Smith 1941). Of course, the human capital model predicts precisely this behavior. On the benefits side, chefs are rarely seen by customers and work on straight salary. Waiters, by contrast, are in constant touch with the public and rely on tips for most of their income. Bad breath and/or yellow teeth could have deleterious effects on their earnings. On the cost side, since wages for chefs are higher, the opportunity cost of brushing is correspondingly higher. Thus, the theory predicts unambiguously that chefs will brush less. It is instructive to compare this rather tight theoretical deduction with Barnard and Smith's glib attribution of the observed differences to the different hygiene standards in the birthplaces of the individuals. (The chefs were born mostly in France, while the waiters were largely Brooklynites.)

I. Review of the Literature

A substantial literature on dental hygienics exists. It is ironic that economists are almost completely unaware of these studies, despite the fact that most economists brush their teeth.

The best empirical study was conducted by a team of researchers at the University of Chicago Medical Center in 1967. They compared tooth-brushing habits of a scientifically selected sample of 27 sets of twins who had appeared in Wrigley's chewing gum commercials with a random sample of 54 longshoremen. The twins brushed their teeth an average of 3.17 times per day, while the longshoremen brushed only 0.76 times daily. The difference was significant at the 1 percent level. As noneconomists, the doctors advanced two possible explanations for this finding: either twins had a higher "taste for brushing" than nontwins, or the Wrigley Company deliberately set out to hire people with clean teeth. Further study, they concluded, would be needed to discriminate between these two hypotheses (Baker, Dooley, and Spock 1968). The human capital viewpoint makes the true explanation clear enough. Earnings of models depend strongly on the whiteness of their teeth. On the other hand, no direct connection has ever been established between the income of longshoremen and the quality of their breath.

Another recent contribution was a survey of professors in a leading Eastern university. It was found that assistant professors brushed 2.14 times daily on average, while associate professors brushed only 1.89 times and full professors only 1.47 times daily. The author, a sociologist, mistakenly attributed this finding to the fact that the higher-ranking professors were older and that hygiene standards in America had advanced steadily over time (Persons 1971). To a human capital theorist, of course, this pattern is exactly what would be expected from the higher wages received in the higher professorial ranks, and from the fact that younger professors, looking for promotions, cannot afford to have bad breath.

II. A Theoretical Model of Toothbrushing

Let w be the wage rate of an individual; let J be an index of his job; and let B be the time spent brushing his teeth. With no loss of generality, I can reorder the jobs so that jobs with higher J are the jobs where clean teeth are more important. The assumed wage function is therefore

$$w = w(J, B), \qquad w_B \geq 0, \qquad w_{BJ} = w_{JB} \geq 0. \qquad (1)$$

Since jobs have been reordered, there is no a priori presumption about the sign of w_J. It is also assumed that $w(\cdot)$ is continuous, twice differentiable, and semistrictly quasi-concave in the non-negative orthant.

Each individual is assumed to maximize his income:

$$Y = w(J, B)(T - B) + P, \tag{2}$$

where T is the fixed amount of time per period available for working or brushing[2] and P is the (exogenously determined) amount of unearned income.[3] That is, each individual selects a value of B to maximize (2). The necessary condition for a maximum is[4]

$$w_B(J, B)(T - B) - w(J, B) = 0. \tag{3}$$

Several important implications follow from (3). First, since both w and w_B are presumptively positive, (3) implies that $T - B$ must be positive. In words, the theory predicts that no person will spend every waking hour brushing his teeth—an empirically testable proposition not derivable from either the "bad taste" or "mother told me" models.

Second, (3) can be rewritten

$$\frac{B}{T - B} = \frac{Bw_B}{w} \tag{4}$$

In words, the ratio of brushing to nonbrushing time is equated to the partial elasticity of the wage with respect to brushing time. So individuals in jobs where wages are highly sensitive to brushing will devote more time to brushing than will others—as indicated in the verbal discussion. Also, for any two jobs with equal w_B's but unequal w's, (3) implies that the higher-wage person will brush less due to his greater opportunity cost.

Finally, consider the important case where (1) is linear in B (though possibly nonlinear in J):

$$w = \alpha(J) + \beta(J)B, \qquad \alpha \geq 0, \qquad \beta \geq 0. \tag{1'}$$

---

2. It is assumed, for simplicity, that these are the only possible uses of time. The model can easily be extended to accommodate an arbitrary number of uses of time, as is not shown in an appendix.

3. A more general model would allow for the possibility that cleaner teeth can lead to a larger inheritance, that is, $P(B)$ with $P'(B) > 0$. For evidence of this, see "Toothpaste Heir Disinherited for Having Bad Breath," *Wall Street Journal*, April 1, 1972, p. 1.

4. Since w is assumed semistrictly quasi-concave, this is also sufficient for a weak maximum.

Substituting into (3) and solving yields

$$B = \frac{T}{2} - \frac{\alpha}{2\beta} \tag{5}$$

In jobs where brushing is immaterial to success, $\beta \to 0$, so (5) calls for a corner maximum with $B = 0$. Thus, we have a second strong prediction from the model: such persons will never brush. At the other extreme, as the ratio α/β approaches zero, (5) implies $B \to T/2$. In words, individuals whose wages depend almost exclusively on the whiteness of their teeth (M.C.'s of television quiz shows are a good example) will spend approximately half their lives brushing. Again, no sociological theory can generate predictions as strong as this.

III. A Regression Model

The implications of the model can be put to an empirical test thanks to a recent cross-section study of American adults in the civilian labor force conducted by the Federal Brushing Institute. In its Survey of Brushing, the institute collected data on toothbrushing frequency and many socioeconomic characteristics of 17,684 adults in 1972. From these data, the following regression model was formulated:

$$NBRUSH = a_0 + a_1 AGE + a_2 WAGE + a_3 NTEETH \\ + a_4 S + a_5 EXP + a_6 FDUM + a_7 Y + u. \tag{6}$$

The dependent variable is the number of times teeth were brushed during the year. AGE is included as a proxy for the number of years remaining before the individual's teeth fall out. Viewing brushing as a human investment clearly implies that $a_1 < 0$. $WAGE$, of course, measures the opportunity cost of time; so $a_2 < 0$. $NTEETH$ is the number of teeth in the person's mouth. Since brushing time is nearly independent of the number of teeth brushed, having more teeth should certainly encourage more brushing. S and EXP are, respectively, years of schooling and work experience. They are included because this is a human capital model; although there are no a priori expectations about the signs of a_4 and a_5, both should have high t-ratios. $FDUM$ is a dummy for persons who live in an area with fluoridated water supply, included since there is some substitution in the production function for good teeth between brushing and fluoridating the water. Finally, Y is nonlabor income, which enables us to estimate the income effect on toothbrushing frequency.

Since I have argued above that *WAGE* should depend on *NBRUSH*, equation (6) was estimated by the instrumental-variables technique. Denture wearers were included in the sample, but 189 people with no teeth at all were omitted from the analysis. The empirical results are reported below, with standard errors in parentheses:

$$NBRUSH = 2.04 - 0.006 \; AGE - 0.096 \; WAGE + 0.054 \; NTEETH$$
$$(0.63) \quad (0.001) \qquad (0.001) \qquad (0.009)$$
$$+ \; 0.0043 \; S - 0.0022 \; EXP - 0.146 \; FDUM$$
$$(0.0002) \quad (0.0001) \qquad (0.027)$$
$$+ \; 0.0006 \; Y, \quad R^2 = .79, \quad SE = 0.056.$$
$$(0.0002)$$

By any standards the results are very good. The R^2 is very high for cross-section work, indicating that the data have been successfully mined. All the variables suggested by the theoretical model are highly significant and, wherever the theory implied a priori sign restrictions, they are satisfied.

In summary, the survey data strikingly confirm the predictions of the theoretical model of toothbrushing presented here. Of course, this is only one of many possible tests of the theory. But it does point out the usefulness of human capital concepts in understanding dental hygiene. Hopefully, these results will stimulate renewed interest in such questions on the part of economists.

References

Baker, M. D.; Dooley, C.; and Spock, B. "Brushing by Longshoremen and Twins: A Case Study." *Q. J. Orthodontics* 3 (1968): 377–462.

Barnard, C., and Smith, L. "Brushing Proclivities of Restaurant Employees in New York City." *Rev. Periodontics and Dentistics* 7 (1941): 1–2.

Persons, T. "Dental Hygiene and Age: A Sociological View." *J. Dental Soc.* 11 (1971): 1–243.

C. Northcote Parkinson

Parkinson's Law (excerpt)

Work expands so as to fill the time available for its completion. General recognition of this fact is shown in the proverbial phrase "It is the busiest man who has time to spare." Thus, an elderly lady of leisure can spend an entire day in writing and dispatching a postcard to her niece at Bognor Regis. An hour will be spent in finding the postcard, another in hunting for spectacles, half an hour in a search for the address, an hour and a quarter in composition, and twenty minutes in deciding whether or not to take an umbrella when going to the mailbox in the next street. The total effort which would occupy a busy man for three minutes all told may in this fashion leave another person prostrate after a day of doubt, anxiety, and toil.

Granted that work (and especially paperwork) is thus elastic in its demands on time, it is manifest that there need be little or no relationship between the work to be done and the size of the staff to which it may be assigned. A lack of real activity does not, of necessity, result in leisure. A lack of occupation is not necessarily revealed by a manifest idleness. The thing to be done swells in importance and complexity in a direct ratio with the time to be spent. This fact is widely recognized, but less attention has been paid to its wider implications, more especially in the field of public administration. Politicians and taxpayers have assumed (with occasional phases of doubt) that a rising total in the number of civil servants must reflect a growing volume of work to be done. Cynics, in questioning this belief, have imagined that the multiplication of officials must have left some of them idle or all of them able to work for shorter hours. But this is a matter in which faith and doubt seem equally misplaced. The fact is that the number of the officials and the quantity of the work to be done are not related to each other at all. The rise in the total of those employed is governed by Parkinson's Law, and would be much the same whether the volume of the work were to increase, diminish, or even disappear. The importance of Parkinson's Law lies in the fact that it is a law of growth based upon an analysis of the factors by which that growth is controlled.

The validity of this recently discovered law must rest mainly on statistical proofs, which will follow. Of more interest to the general reader is the explanation of the factors underlying the general tendency to which this law gives definition. Omitting technicalities (which are numerous) we may distinguish, at the outset, two motive forces. They can be represented for the present purpose by two almost axiomatic statements, thus: (1) "An official wants to multiply subordinates, not rivals" and (2) "Officials make work for each other."

To comprehend Factor I, we must picture a civil servant, called A, who finds himself overworked. Whether this overwork is real or imaginary is immaterial, but we should observe, in passing, that A's sensation (or illusion) might easily result from his own decreasing energy: a normal symptom of middle age. For this real or imagined overwork there are, broadly speaking, three possible remedies. He may resign; he may ask to halve the work with a colleague called B; he may demand the assistance of two subordinates, to be called C and D. There is probably no instance in civil service history of A choosing any but the third alternative. By resignation he would lose his pension rights. By having B appointed, on his own level in the hierarchy, he would merely bring in a rival for promotion to W's vacancy when W (at long last) retires. So A would rather have C and D, junior men, below him. They will add to his consequence; and, by dividing the work into two categories, as between C and D, he will have the merit of being the only man who comprehends them both.

It is essential to realize, at this point, that C and D are, as it were, inseparable. To appoint C alone would have been impossible. Why? Because C, if by himself, would divide the work with A and so assume almost the equal status which has been refused in the first instance to B; a status the more emphasized if C is A's only possible successor. Subordinates must thus number two or more, each being kept in order by fear of the other's promotion. When C complains in turn of being overworked (as he certainly will) A will, with the concurrence of C, advise the appointment of two assistants to help C. But he can then avert internal friction only by advising the appointment of two more assistants to help D, whose position is much the same. With this recruitment of E, F, G, and H, the promotion of A is now practically certain.

Seven officials are doing what one did before. This is where Factor II comes into operation. For these seven make so much work for each other that all are fully occupied and A is actually working harder than ever. An incoming document may well come before each of them in turn. Official E decides that it falls within the province of F, who places a draft reply before C, who amends it drastically before consulting D, who asks G to deal with it. But G goes on leave at this point, handing the file over to H, who drafts a minute, which is signed by D and returned to C, who revises his draft accordingly and lays the new version before A.

What does A do? He would have every excuse for signing the thing unread, for he has many other matters on his mind. Knowing now that he is to succeed W next year, he has to decide whether C or D should succeed to his own office. He had to agree to G going on leave, although not yet strictly entitled to it. He worried whether H should not have gone instead, for reasons of health. He has looked pale recently—partly but not solely because of his domestic troubles. Then there is the business of F's special increment of salary for the period of the conference, and E's application for transfer to the Ministry of Pensions. A has heard that D is in love with a married typist and that G and F are no longer on speaking terms—no one seems to know why. So A might be tempted to sign C's draft and have done with it.

But A is a conscientious man. Beset as he is with problems created by his colleagues for themselves and for him—created by the mere fact of these officials' existence—he is not the man to shirk his duty. He reads through the draft with care, deletes the fussy paragraphs added by C and H and restores the thing back to the form preferred in the first instance by the able (quarrelsome) F. He corrects the English—none of these young men can write grammatically—and finally produces the same reply he would have written if officials C and H had never been born. Far more people have taken far longer to produce the same result. No one has been idle. All have done their best. And it is late in the evening before A finally quits his office and begins the return journey to Ealing. The last of the office lights are being turned off in the gathering dusk which marks the end of another day's administrative toil. Among the last to leave, A reflects, with bowed shoulders and a wry smile, that late hours, like grey hairs, are among the penalties of success. . . .

. . . [D]etailed statistical analysis of departmental staffs would be inappropriate in such a work as this. It is hoped, however, to reach a tentative conclusion regarding the time likely to elapse between a given official's first appointment and the later appointment of his two or more assistants.

Dealing with the problem of pure staff accumulation, all the researches so far completed point to an average increase of about 5.75 per cent per year. This fact established, it now becomes possible to state Parkinson's Law in mathematical form, thus:

In any public administrative department not actually at war, the staff increase may be expected to follow this formula:

$$x = (2k^m + l)/n$$

where k is the number of staff seeking promotion through the appointment of subordinates; l represents the difference between the ages of appointment and retirement; m is the number of man-hours devoted to answering minutes within the department; and n is the number of effective units being administered. Then x will be the number of new staff required each year.

Mathematicians will, of course, realize that to find the percentage increase they must multiply x by 100 and divide by the total of the previous year, thus:

$$100 \ [(2k^m + l)]/yn \ \%$$

where y represents the total original staff. And this figure will invariably prove to be between 5.17 per cent and 6.56 per cent, irrespective of any variation in the amount of work (if any) to be done.

The discovery of this formula and of the general principles upon which it is based has, of course, no emotive value. No attempt has been made to inquire whether departments ought to grow in size. Those who hold that this growth is essential to gain full employment are fully entitled to their opinion. Those who doubt the stability of an economy based upon reading each other's minutes are equally entitled to theirs. Parkinson's Law is a purely scientific discovery, inapplicable except in theory to the politics of the day. It is not the business of the botanist to eradicate the weeds. Enough for him if he can tell us just how fast they grow.

Philip Musgrove

Why Everything Takes 2.71828. . .
Times as Long as Expected

It is widely observed, and almost as widely lamented, that everything takes longer than one expects. However, most attempts to explain why deadlines are missed and budgets overrun go no farther than Murphy's (n.d.) often-quoted aphorism. Blaming the phenomenon on unrealistic expectations, as Handtvefer (1982) does, cannot explain why expectations are not revised after repeated disappointment. The problem presents both a theoretical challenge to economic science and an issue of great practical importance; a procedure for predicting delays could save a lot of money and frustration. In the absence of constraints on the time available for a job, it turns out that the ratio of time taken to time expected tends to $e = 2.71828 \ldots$ for a job consisting of an infinite number of steps. Shorter jobs exceed the expected time by ratios less than e but never less than 2. Constraints on time, when the time available is less than what is expected to be needed for completion, only make matters worse.

I. Delays in Steps and in Jobs

A "job" is just something one wants to get done—and can tell whether it has been finished or not. A "step" is a physically essential part of a job, performed in sequence with other steps; completing the last step means finishing the job. To avoid considering intervals between steps, a step is not regarded as finished until the next step is begun.

The first question then is, how does delay in a step affect the job of which the step is a part? Procrastinateur (1971) appears to have been the first to show that a delay in one step introduces an equal proportional, rather than absolute, delay in the entire project. Studying 283 large civil engineering projects,[1] in each of which one step triggered delay in the job, he found that a one-month step delay could slow down the project by as much as two years, even when nothing else went exogenously wrong. I have obtained very similar results using a large sample from the PAO Register (1969 et seq.), which includes military as well as civilian projects discriminated by presidential administration, cabinet agency or contractor responsible, and the state in which the project occurred. None of these variables is significant.[2]

These results can be summarized in

PROPOSITION 1: *If S and P are step and project time, respectively, and DS and DP are step and project delays, then*

$$1 + DP/P = \prod_{i=1}^{N} (1 + DS_i/S_i)$$

where i = 1,2, . . ., N are the project steps.

II. Number of Steps and Step Delays

The finding that job delays are proportional to step delays is initially counterintuitive, but is plausible once one considers that the delayed step interrupts the schedule of work, causes overtime or stretch-outs to avoid overtime, and even produces delays in previously executed steps which have to be tested or repeated to make sure they do not suffer the same error which caused the delay. Procrastinateur's research also suggests that job delay does not depend on where in the project the delayed step or "foul-up" occurs, contradicting Harnischfeger's (1976) hypothesis that delays hurt most if they happen near the beginning or end of a project.[3] A still more puzzling result is that the complexity or differentiation of the steps does not seem to matter: this contradicts the intuitive notion that a step is a quite arbitrary element

---

1. All of them, to be sure, designed and executed by Frenchmen.
2. When highway projects alone are studied, the dummy for Massachusetts is almost significant ($t = 1.83$).
3. Harnischfeger's hypothesis, while incorrect for delays, may still be valid for "step problems" of other types—for example, if the job is an airplane flight, with takeoff the first step and landing the last one.

of a project, and that complex steps can be made into simple ones by subdivision. This should permit better control and less delay, but if simple and complicated steps are equally dangerous as sources of delay, nothing can be gained by adding to the number of steps. A project such as raising a pyramid, in which each step consists of placing a single stone but some are harder to seat than others, might offer a test of this issue. Unfortunately, Bloch's (1948) estimates of delays due to fractures and accidents at Giza are hotly disputed by other scholars, and anyway are too vague for quantitative analysis.[4]

Procrastinateur did not include the *number* of steps in his analysis, but when it is included, the apparent paradox disappears. Smythe (1976), studying the limits on the division of labor in manufacturing, discovered that step delay tends to be inversely proportional to the number of steps in a process, confirming that subdivision of labor yields a gain at the level of individual steps. Her results give

PROPOSITION 2: $E(DS/S) = 1/N$, *with* var(DS/S) *of order* $1/N^2$.

Combining Propositions 1 and 2 then establishes

Theorem 1: As a job is continuously subdivided into steps, the time actually taken to complete it tends to e times the time anticipated for its completion.

Proof: It is straightforward: substitution of Proposition 2 into Proposition 1 gives:

Time Required/Time Expected = $R_N = (1 + 1/N)^N$
and lim $R_N = e$, as $N \to \infty$.

Passing to the limit removes the arbitrariness in the definition of a step. The ratio nevertheless converges: a job of arbitrarily many steps does not take forever to complete, in accord with experience.[5] It is an immediate corollary that even a job of only one step takes on average twice as long to finish as expected, since $N = 1$ means $R_N = 2$.

---

4. Bloch sometimes relies on the number of days the Pharaoh spent sulking, which, even if correctly reported by the scribes, is a poor proxy for delay in construction.

5. So-called "interminable" jobs are the proper domain of Murphy's Law.

Suppose A is the total time available for a job (exogenously determined by the "boss"), and that the average anticipated time required for a step is T, so that NT is the total time the job is expected to take. Define $m = NT/A$ as the share of the available time that the job is expected to use. If N and A tend to infinity at the same rate, holding m constant, then the probability of actually completing x steps in an interval T is described by the Poisson distribution,

$$p(x) = e^{-m}m^x/x!$$

where x is a random variable because the steps vary in length or difficulty. The rapid decline in $p(x)$ as x increases reflects the unlikelihood of "catching up" a delayed step by completing an additional step in a later interval.[6] The terms $m^x/x!$ sum to e^m over all nonnegative values of x.

If $m = 1$, so that the time appears to be just adequate, the project will in fact take $2.71828\ldots$ times as long to complete as anticipated. What happens if the time available *ex ante* appears to be too short? If $m = 2$, for example, the ratio of time taken to time expected becomes e^2 or $7.3891\ldots$: trying to squeeze a project into half the required time makes it take not twice as long to finish as was anticipated, but nearly eight times as long. This explains Shaughnessy's (1937) finding that attempts to speed up projects by unrealistic deadlines actually end by slowing them down.[7] Letting C be the time taken to complete a project, the foregoing establishes

Theorem 2: $R = C/NT \to \exp(NT/A)$, as N, $A \to \infty$, for T constant.

It is a corollary of this theorem that a job can actually be completed in exactly the time expected—a result which Theorem 1 does not permit—but only on condition that it be expected to use a negligible fraction of the available time. The proof is direct:

---

6. A complete theory of personal stress reduction is built on this by Orff (1969).

7. Shaughnessy's results for Soviet labor productivity are violently disputed by Vodkapiu (1937), who—curiously—published first. Subsequent evidence, however, tends to vindicate Shaughnessy.

$R = 1$ requires $\exp(NT/A) = 1$, from which $NT/A = 0$. This result also accords with experience: the only jobs finished on time are those for which nobody is in a hurry.

References

Bloch, Pyramus, "'Y' Raise Sixteen Stones," *Review of Archae-oeconomics,* Special Issue on Ancient Public Works, May 1948, *22,* 68–94.

Handtvefer, Luke, "Micro-Rational Expectations, or Learning by Doing (Wrong)," *Ausgezeichnetter Stiftung,* June 1982, *3,* 1–11.

Harnischfeger, Harold, "Project Delays, Cost Overruns and the Right Way to Run a Railroad," *Journal of Marginal Management,* Spring 1976, *41,* 37–50.

Murphy, N. M., *If Anything Can Go Wrong,* Secaucus: Nullo Modo Press, n.d.

Orff, Hans, "One Thing at a Time," *Journal of Statistics and Self-Fulfillment,* February 1969, 1, 3–28.

Procrastinateur, Jean-Jacques, "Les Retards dans Les Grands Projets de Construction Civile," *Annales de l'Académie des Imperfections,* Juillet 1971, *83,* 115–32.

Shaughnessy, Brendan O., "Stakhanovism, Speed-ups and Reduced Productivity," *Soviet Management Studies,* April 1937, *10,* 68–101.

Smythe, Adele, "The Precision of Labor is Limited by the Extent of the Market," *American Economic Journal,* Smith Bicentennial Number, September 1976, *138,* 25–62.

Vodkapiu, Ivan Akakievitch, "Shto Znayet Shaughnessy?," *Akademia Naukonomika CCCP,* March 1937, *19,* 1–3.

U.S. Partial Accounting Office, *Register of Federally Financed Projects,* Vol. XLIII, *Contract and Actual Dates and Costs of Completion,* Washington: USGPO, 1969 et seq.

We Who Work at Night

Don't waste sympathy on the people who work at night. Since they go on duty when most people go to bed, they are sometimes pitied for the sacrifice they make. Don't pity them. At any rate, don't pity me. I am one of them; for thirty years I have worked in a New York City morning-newspaper shop that does not really come to life until after sundown.

When I reach the brilliantly lighted office at 10:30 or 11 from my evening assignment everyone is wide awake. The organization is at peak strength—scores of reporters, copy-readers, and editors working under pressure in outward harmony. Enough edited copy goes upstairs in the pneumatic tubes at the peak hour to fill a small book, though no one appears to be rushing. Upstairs the printers are setting type on clattering machines, absorbed and industrious but not excited.

In daytime this bustle of activity would go unnoticed amid the general busyness of the city. Then our plant is no more inter-esting than the offices, hotels, garages, restaurants, and theatres in the neighborhood. But it is a conspicuous and vivid place at night. It puts to shame the indolence of our part of the city. Most of the other people have locked up and gone home. Don't pity us. We pity you. We are preparing a report of the world's activities. It will vitally concern you when you start reading it tomorrow morning.

But I wonder whether anybody gets as much pleasure out of reading the newspaper as we do out of putting it together at midnight at the bright center of a network that covers the globe. In the back of their heads most newspapermen never forget that it is a dramatic job done with a new script every night. And when the edition has gone to press the world outside the office seems like an anti-climax. It is ordinary, prosaic, soft.

For anyone working in a city at night the hours surrounding dawn can be almost lyrical. All the work in the world would be suffused with glory if it could be done during the tender hours when the day is forming. Gradually, along the avenues, the automobiles extinguish their driving lights as the king of lights begins to climb the eastern sky. The streets and buildings look clean, relaxed, and promising. There is no anger in the city at dawn. It is quiet and motherly; the silent buildings shelter the sleeping multitudes from the harshness of the world.

What happens? For there is no use denying that the pell-mell, bedlam city of nine and ten in the morning or five and six in the afternoon has lost the rosy promise of the dawn. The streets and buildings look ugly and fretful. At rush hour the subway is a savage place, a rebuke to civilization. Everyone seems to have a grievance. People go through the familiar routine of pushing into the cars as if they were in a sullen trance. Even the best of them wear a subway mask that hides their true personalities.

As citizens we are at our worst in the pitiless glare of daytime. Day may be good in itself. But it looks haggard in the city by the time people have gotten through with it at five o'clock.

"Day tells less of distance, more of detail; less of peace, more of contest; less of immortality, more of the perishable," wrote Frank Bolles, the New England essayist, at the turn of the century.

As night-workers we must guard against a temptation to patronize those who work by day. In point of fact, we are no better than anyone else—that is, I suppose we are not. But the act of going solemnly to work while other people are sitting at home in their slippers, gaping at television, playing at cards, or possibly carousing, induces a feeling of puritanical piety, as though we were the only responsible people in the world.

We must have almost inhuman strength of mind, for example, not to feel sanctimonious when we decline an invitation to dinner or a frivolous party with the invincible argument: "I'm sorry, I have to work that night." A statement like that makes us sound consecrated.

We can also point out that many of the essential community services are performed at night. The wholesale fruit market on New York's lower West Side, for example, guarantees fresh fruit in our homes during the day by being open for business at night. The fruit is loaded, unloaded, opened, graded, and bid on by men who sleep by day and unlimber their muscles after the sun goes down. And the same is true of bakeries, fish markets, and other food suppliers.

When is the slatternly debris of the day cleaned up in the office buildings? By night, of course. You owe your clean desk and empty wastebasket to ministering angels of the night whom you never see.

When are the tracks of the subway repaired and replaced? At night, when the schedule is lightest.

The city would soon run down if it were not for hundreds of mechanics and service employees who work on the equipment at night when the city is not clogged with millions of hurrying people.

The magnificence of our harbors is not conspicuous by day. In the first place, the water is filthy from sewage disposal and industrial waste. In the second place, the waterfront is frowsy— an erratic system of piers, lofts, and warehouses, built without plan.

Night restores the magnificence that man has chipped away. The harbor looks refreshed and lustrous. On the night of a full moon, which streaks the black water with patches of liquid silver, New York Harbor is a glorious place. Squalor gives way to the enchantment and mystery of lights: lights in the windows of waterfront lofts, where men work all night on freight and cargo; garlands of lights on the ferries that look like royal barges; and, in my own New York harbor, the soft effulgence of the Statue of Liberty floodlights, the exultant blaze in her upstretched hand. The Statue of Liberty looks more like the shrine it is by night than by day. In fact, the whole harbor looks like Coleridge's Xanadu, the walls and towers girdled round with radiance and splendor. And every light means that someone is awake, alert, organized.

There is never an hour of the night when tugs are not grinding the water with their propellers. There can be a very pleasant informality about night life. It doesn't seem quite so fierce or impersonal as by day. Seat yourself in the pilot house of a tug working down the bay, and listen to the radio messages coming from the night dispatcher of the Moran Towing Co. on the brightly lighted twenty-fifth floor of 17 Battery Place: "17 to the *Moira*. You'll pass a Dalzell tug pretty soon. She's going up to Newark. Give her a toot and tell Joe to call Tom at home." Or: "17 to the *Anne*. When you get to Pier 1 send me up a cup of coffee, will you? I'd appreciate it. Thanks."

The long night watches are uncommonly sociable. There's time for gossip and banter.

People in general are likely to be more amiable at night. Note the complete reversal in the tone of radio programs: After being crisp and calculated all day, they subside into general conversation after midnight—substituting sociability for showmanship.

The cab drivers I ride with say that they prefer to work at night. Passengers are in a gayer mood and tip more generously. One driver told me he earns $700 more a year by working nights.

After midnight the subway is quiet and lazy. Descending into the Rector Street station about 1 A.M. recently, I was astonished to hear the station clock ticking. It had never occurred to me that subway clocks tick in the same soothing rhythm that the clocks have at home.

There is also something relaxing about the way the Grand Central Terminal dozes during the night. The advertising displays that give the terminal a nervous alertness by day are now unlighted and resting. The vibrating drone or rumble that is the blending of a thousand little conversations is now stilled. All the shops are closed. All but two of the brilliantly lighted ticket windows are marked "Closed. Closed. Closed."—with peremptory lack of interest in commercial affairs.

Flanked by neat piles of freshly-printed newspapers, the attendants at the Terminal's newsstands stare in a trance at the people who come to buy. After the last important train has left, a gang of fifty porters takes charge of the terminal. Some, with wide brooms, sweep the concourse floor in long furrows, with a practiced twisting motion that gives the rows of dirt a jaunty edge. Then others mop and squeegee the marble floor. Like a civilized person preparing for bed, the Grand Central washes off the grime of the day.

It is possible that the creative mind works most fruitfully during the hours of darkness, undistracted by the details and the nervous tempo of the day. "The soul of man is alive only in the nighttime," Shelley said. For the imagination travels farthest when distance, no longer limited by the visible landscape of the day, extends into the universes of stars that light celestial lamps millions of miles off through the dark corridors of space.

The heavens not only declare the glory of God but play hob with ordinary calculations. Space is limitless at night. Time is a new dimension. The light that reaches us tonight from Betelgeuse in the constellation of Orion started toward the earth in the time of John Milton, three centuries ago.

Ideas that seem too ambitious by day look more plausible by night against the grand geography of the heavens. The negations of the day, based on the bitter experience of the race, may not be final. "Perhaps there is hope," the heavens say.

Hideki Yukawa, who won the Nobel Prize for Physics in 1949 in recognition of his work on the function of the meson in the atom, found that night was the time when his mind was most creative. "When you work in the daytime," he said, "it is easy to do your *regular* work. It is hard, though, to get anything but conventional notions. Lying awake at night I have thought of some very interesting things. Almost always, in the morning, these things have turned out to be untrue. But once in a great while, one of them has been true and unusual. This was the way, at night, that I thought of the meson theory."

"Morning's at seven," Browning cried with blithe enthusiasm. After years of sleeping late, I confess that his cheerfulness makes me slightly ill. It reminds me of too many times when I have been routed out of bed to conform to the inhuman schedules of the world.

Last year my wife and I returned from England in the dazzling, blue-ribboned steamship *United States*. While we were dashing across the Atlantic we were swathed in luxury and encouraged to believe that we were too genteel to cope with the harsh realities of the world. But at what time did the *United States* dock in New York? Seven o'clock!

Overwrought stewards, who had no confidence in the discretion of passengers, started blasting us out of bed at five, and gave us breakfast at topspeed in the bedlamite dining room. They treated us like livestock that had lost its market value. We were lined up for the port doctor and immigration officers, examined, processed, stamped, and reminded that the obsequious grandeur of the voyage had been only a brief illusion. As a night-worker I can better reconcile myself to reality early in the afternoon. I am convinced that it is better for a man to get up when he has *finished* sleeping, free of the tyranny of the alarm clock or anything else.

"The night was made for the day, not the day for the night," Emerson declared. I wonder.

I wonder whether the leisure should not come before the work, so that the work might be better balanced? A man should not tackle every day mechanically. Let him take a little time to consider the possibility of doing something fresh before the day is over. It is pleasant not to have to plunge furiously, immediately on rising, into an automatic work schedule that leaves one no margin for improvisation. The best time for work is after sundown, when patience is unharried by pressure from the world outside.

Who inaugurated the custom of working by day? It was a serious mistake.

Gary North

A Note on the Opportunity Cost of Marriage

One of the most important conceptual breakthroughs made by the nineteenth-century marginalists was the "alternative cost" doctrine. Prior to the 1870's, men were not used to thinking in such terms. How could a piece of land which required no operating expenses other than taxes be an economic burden? They seldom thought of the possibility that the land could be sold and the receipts put to some alternative use, such as earning interest in a bank. It did not occur to them that the interest foregone in any such investment should be calculated as an operational expense and therefore deducted from total profits.

All this is quite elementary; any competent college sophomore majoring in economics is aware of it. Yet from the actions of some of my professional colleagues—even those in the economics department—it would seem that the full implications of the doctrine have not made themselves felt in this century, let alone in the nineteenth. The condescending smiles we use in reference to the misconceptions of nineteenth-century accounting and business practices might better be reserved for ourselves.

Consider, for example, the marriage patterns of most college-trained males. There is a noticeable tendency for college men and graduate students to marry women who are also attending or have attended college. People tend to marry those from similar educational and social backgrounds (or, as Professor Keith Berwick has put it, "You marry the person who's most available when you're most vulnerable"). Yet the man who chooses an educated or professionally trained woman to be his wife is selecting a very expensive mate. I am not referring to the obvious increased costs: for example, her more expensive tastes, which have been fostered by her broadened educational perspective, or her previous dating of well-heeled college men whose allowance checks have helped to raise her standards of "the good life" (thus making her subject to a "marital Deusenberry effect" if she marries someone of average means). The latter case shows that it is a smart procedure to marry only girls who have limited their dating to graduate students on small fellowships. Nevertheless, these are peripheral issues. What is more important is something rather different: the opportunity costs of an educated wife.

A friend of mine is a classic, and somewhat tragic, example. He is an assistant professor of history, earning about $8,500 a year. He is a good family man, as is evidenced by his three fine children and a large mortgage. He is married to a remarkable woman who holds a Ph.D. in physics. If she were to offer her talents to any of the numerous industrial firms in the area she could probably earn a starting salary of $12,500, and possibly a good deal more. Thus, my friend finds himself in a distressing condition: his costs of running his household probably approach $20,000 a year. From this we can deduct the benefits he receives from his wife's homemaking abilities (which, she admits, are not very inspiring), say, $5,000, thus reducing his costs to some $15,000. If, as we are told, "a woman's place is in the home," then his wife is costing him a small fortune annually—almost twice as much as his paycheck would seemingly allow. When one considers the even greater salary she forfeits as each year passes, the staggering cost of his marriage comes into focus: some top-flight physicists earn $50,000 a year!

This, of course, is an exceptional case. Not all historians are married to physicists. But the basic point is clear: only my friend's ignorance of fundamental economic principles could have led him to select such a financially disastrous mate. A woman with that kind of education should not be married to anyone making less than $45,000 a year; no one else could afford such a costly housekeeper.

His only possible hope rests in his children. If they should all earn Ph.D.'s in the sciences, or become extremely successful businessmen, then his returns in his old age may compensate for the foregone costs of his shockingly uneconomic marriage. Sadly, the man is burdened with three daughters. The tragedy of this man's economic life is almost overwhelming.

No prospective historian should ever consider courting a woman with anything beyond a junior college education. An M.A. in history ought to locate some high school dropout; anything else is really a luxury he cannot afford. The best kind of wife, from the point of view of contemporary economics, is obviously an uneducated woman who has become a masterful housekeeper and/or cook. In marrying someone like this, a man not only forfeits a small opportunity cost in her lost salary but simultaneously gains the services of a relatively costly household servant. Of course, there is a certain degree of unpatriotic action involved in this. By removing her from the market, he lowers the nation's GNP, and insofar as GNP figures are propaganda devices of the nation involved, he may be hurting the U.S. Information Agency's effort abroad. But his personal economic gains may offset any political commitment he may have.

I have limited myself to historians here, since their position economically seems most obvious. Clearly, further research needs to be done along these lines, relating the opportunity-cost concept to marriage expenses for a large number of educational and occupational groups. The professional economist should realize how a neglected application of economic reasoning to a vital practical problem may be furthering economic disaster in thousands, possibly millions, of families throughout America and even the world. Something must be done to correct the situation. I can only hope that my small contribution will stimulate further research along these lines.

Madelyn L. Kafoglis

Marriage Customs and Opportunity Costs

Gary North's tongue-in-cheek analysis of the "opportunity cost" of marriage (*Journal of Political Economy*, March/April 1968) raises interesting questions about domestic economics. North examines the situation of an $8,500 assistant professor of history married to a woman whose market value as a physicist is $12,500. Since a woman's place is in the home, this man foregoes $12,500 in cash, gains a middling housekeeper with expensive tastes, and finally finds himself with "opportunity costs" exceeding income in a marriage that is "shockingly uneconomic" and "financially disastrous." North concludes (facetiously?) that "the best kind of wife, from the standpoint of contemporary economics, is obviously an uneducated woman who has become a masterful housekeeper and/or cook." My concern is not with those who already have married educated women—their costs are sunk—but with the young, college-trained male, who, taking North seriously, might break off a blossoming courtship with a still hopeful Ph.D. candidate. I am also concerned with North's interpretation of opportunity cost which (a) confuses two different models and the assumptions appropriate to each and (b) implicitly introduces assumptions concerning property rights in the wife's income.

In the premarital planning period, the prospective groom must select between two women, one of whom is highly educated, the other, to use North's characterization, a junior college dropout. I assume he is to select so as to maximize the present value of his expected real income. If these calculations are made on the basis of a "woman's place is the home" marital contract, the forgone market earnings of the educated woman are not admissible as an opportunity cost to the male, the female, or anyone else after the vows are traded. They are, by contractual agreement, an irrelevant alternative. Given the "woman's place" contract, the choice of a wife will hinge on the candidate's housekeeping abilities, the expensiveness of her tastes, and other attributes which are admissible in the "woman's place" model.

North's impressions lead him to predict that even in these circumstances the scales will tip in favor of the dropout. However, he must admit that there are other impressions which might tip the scales in favor of the Ph.D. In the first place, the educated woman's tastes, contrary to North, may not be more expensive. Since she is educated, she may appreciate the "best things in life" like free library books rather than "vain" things like furs. One might wish to assume that the educated woman will search these things out— especially if she majored in economics at the University of Chicago where the search for free goods and spillovers is intense. As for her housekeeping and other capabilities as a wife, the decision can go one way or the other. The services will be qualitatively different and will be evaluated differently by different men. I conclude that, on the basis of the "woman's place" model, economic theory cannot predict the rational choice.

It is true that, on the date of the marriage contract, the investment in the bride's education must be written off. At this point, a lump-sum loss is imposed on the bride, her father, taxpayers, and others who contributed to her education. But since the groom to this point has been uninvolved, this is not his concern. If, on the other hand, the husband pays for his wife's education, irrationality begins to creep in. It is irrational for a man to educate his own (or anyone else's) wife beyond the minimum needed for her place. Since many husbands and fathers do behave in just this Pygmalion-like manner, there must be more to a woman's education than North can handle. In any case, it is not uneconomic to marry an educated woman, although it may be irrational to pay for her education. If it is not uneconomic to marry an educated woman, why should the situation become uneconomic after marriage?

The dilemma in North's analysis arises because he refuses to stick with his assumptions. Having married the Ph.D. physicist within the "woman's place" model, the assistant professor of history, who earlier had been blinded by love, casts a longing glance at the market, sees a $12,500 price tag on his wife, and becomes

205

aware of more options than he would have had if he had married the dropout. Unfortunately, these options are foreclosed by his marital contract and, of course, he is presumptuous in ever supposing that these are *his* options. His costs increase as his presumptuous claims to property increase. What can he do? He can try to recontract his marriage on the basis of a market model. If he can convince his wife to enter the labor market, he might be better off than if he had married the dropout. Joint maximization is likely to result in the wife's working part time, while the husband assumes a greater share of the housekeeping duties. The distributional bargain is more difficult to predict. If he can persuade his wife to give him the new paycheck—to which he has no strong claim by virtue of the original "woman's place" contract—he will clearly be better off. On the other hand, under present legal arrangements, the wife may claim both paychecks. However, any recontract should lead to mutual gain, and the husband should wind up somewhat better off than if he had married the dropout.

My counsel differs from North's. If at the date of the marriage it is decided firmly not to recontract away from the "woman's place" model, one should marry for love. The market value of education has little to do with it. However, if there is a probability of recontracting, one should choose education (assuming love is equal or blind). If recontracting is possible and love is not equal, one must evaluate that classic tradeoff—love or money. Finally, I do not overlook the possibility of love and money.

North confuses the economics of a market model with those of a "woman's place" model. He calculates by the former, but agrees to live by the latter. There are no opportunity costs in terms of foregone market values in the "woman's place" model. And, even if we weaken our assumptions to admit market value, the male has only a skimpy claim to such values.

I would have had no cause to disagree with North if the dowry system were in force. Under this system, the father who paid for his daughter's education would have been rewarded; the husband would have received exactly what he bargained for and could quite properly define his woman's place in or out of the market, depending on his tastes, her productivity, and the state of the market. Many years ago rational men established such a rational system. But women, without benefit of economic analysis, reacted against being sold—on the mistaken assumption that a zero price eliminates claims on the merchandise. It seems that we have found another "externality." Externalities are usually defined as "social" costs and benefits that escape the market model. In this case, we have a market value which has escaped the "woman's place" model. This suggests that externalities ought to be defined as discrepancies between alternative legal and social arrangements.

We have learned what we already know: marital customs and institutions prevent rational maximization in a significant number of cases. But we have also discovered an unhinged externality—the market value of a wife's services. Finally, we have gained the insight that the interpretation of opportunity cost will vary, depending on property and other contractual arrangements.[1]

---

1. For a fuller treatment of the subject of opportunity cost in a new analytical context, see James M. Buchanan, *Cost and Choice* (Chicago: Markham Publishing Co., 1969).

T. C. Bergstrom

Toward a Deeper Economics of Sleeping

Exhaustive study of Professor M. A. El Hodiri's tedious, yet curiously superficial analysis of the economics of sleeping has led to a powerful and remarkably boring reformulation of Hodiri theory.[1]

As Hodiri astutely observes, it is difficult to deny that a sensible man would seek to maximize $U(x, y) = x^2y$ where x is daily consumption and y is the fraction of the day spent in bed. Hodiri supposes that daily consumption equals daily income, which in turn equals the daily wage rate, w, times the fraction of the day one spends out of bed.[2] Hence $x = w(1 - y)$. But then $U = w^2(1 - y)^2y$. By substituting all real numbers between zero and one into this expression, the reader will quickly verify that U is maximized when $y = \frac{1}{3}$. Thus Hodiri asserts that, regardless of the wage rate he receives, a sensible man will sleep $\frac{1}{3} \times 24 = 8$ hours per day.

Had Hodiri been more deeply embedded in the profundities of economic literature, he could hardly have closed his eyes to the abundance of platitudinous evidence that some reap who do not sow. This fertile observation makes two things obvious. One is that the Hodiri equation, $x = w(1 - y)$, must be replaced by $x =$

---

1. It would be difficult to underestimate the importance of El Hodiri's contribution in enabling the author to achieve these heights of pedantry. Historians of thought could no doubt find many wearisome parallels in the advance of science. Though I do not presume to have mounted the shoulders of a giant, I hope that I have trod gently on the toes of El Hodiri.

2. Professor J. T. Little of Washington University, St. Louis, in an unpublished note, maintains that not all time out of bed is spent in productive labor. However, there is reason to suppose that Little's observations have been confined to a pathological sample of the labor force.

$w[(1 - y) + (R/w)]$ where R is daily earnings from nonlabor sources. The proper substitution for $U = x^2y$ is then $U = w^2[1 - y + (R/w)]^2y$. Consequently, U is maximized when $y = \frac{1}{3}[1 + R/w)]$. This inescapable truth would appear to rend Hodiri theory all to pieces. How can it be that sensible men have always slept 8 hours unless R/w has always been both constant and zero?

Resolution of this fearsome paradox will display once again to the jaded reader the beauty and the mystery of Economic Fairyland. Observe that the source of nonwage income is called "capital." Where r is the daily interest rate, K is the stock of capital, and N is the size of the labor force, the average daily nonwage income is $R = rK/N$. Then $R/w = (1 - y)rK/(1 - y)wN$. Since total daily labor income is $(1 - y)wN$, $rK/(1 - y)wN$ is the ratio of capital's share to labor's share of national income, which is well known to have been remarkably constant over time and is in fact equal to $\frac{1}{4}$. Hence in all historical epochs, the average value of R/w has been $(1 - y)\frac{1}{4}$. Recalling that $y = \frac{1}{3}[1 + (R/w)]$, making the appropriate substitution, and solving for y, we have $y = \frac{5}{13}$. Now $\frac{5}{13} \times 24 = 9.231$ hours. Thus have we elegantly vindicated Hodiri's tiresome "first law of soporifics," namely, "In all epochs the average man has spent the same amount of time in bed."

There remains a yawning chasm between Hodiri's banal "second law of soporifics" which is "most people sleep 8 hours a day" and our unassailable demonstration that the average man has always spent 9.231 hours per day in bed. As in the science of astronomy, the existence of the planet Pluto was first conjectured as a consequence of a remarkable deviation of planetary orbits from those predicted by pure theory, so must we conjecture that the average man spends 1.231 hours per day in bed doing something other than sleeping. I eagerly await the announcement that some penetrating theorist or tireless data-massager has actually discovered Activity X.

Reference

El Hodiri, M. A. "The Economics of Sleeping." Unpublished manuscript, University of Kansas, 1973.

209

Millicent G. Fawcett

The Oldest Profession: Unequal Pay, Equal Work (excerpt)

There is one trade in which women receive higher wages than men for the same work. I AM NOT GOING TO REVEAL WHAT IT IS; but I will say that I believe the employment of women in it is a fashion and denotes a superior social status on the part of the employer, for which they are willing to make a considerable payment.

Arthur S. Levine

Sex and the Democrats: Liberalism's New Frontier (excerpt)

Without a Major Government Sexual Initiative, Warns an Expert, Our Nation Is Surely Headed toward Totalitarianism.

Whither liberalism? That is the profound dilemma that confronts us. The old New Deal coalition that once supported large-scale government programs is in disarray. Fortunately, there is a promising new arena for fresh liberal policy initiatives that could revitalize the faded dream of progressive change in this country—while offering the Democratic Party an unmatched opportunity to reassert its power. Potentially, this issue could generate the visceral appeal of the Progressive Era campaign against industrial abuses, the hope for the nation's downtrodden that Franklin Delano Roosevelt once offered, and the dream of equality inspired by the Great Society and Martin Luther King, Jr. It is an issue that touches all our lives, rich and poor, black and white, and it would allow the Democratic Party to claim a vast new constituency, to speak once again as the party of the "little guy," the average American.

The anguish, disaffection, and loneliness surrounding our sexual lives are a growing national scandal. We have become a nation divided into "haves" and "have-nots." How much longer can this sexual inequity continue without fundamentally threatening the national polity? The "invisible hand" that supposedly governs the sexual marketplace is simply no longer working, and our totally unregulated free enterprise system for meeting and mating has become as antiquated as the unchecked industrialism of the late nineteenth and early twentieth centuries.

No civilized country in the world today assumes that those who can't fend for themselves should starve to death on the street;

211

yet we callously disregard the needs of those unfortunate citizens who are starving for the food of life—love, or its nearest approximation: sexual pleasure. Jimmy Carter once described justice as "love in action." We should now realize that love is "sex in action," and that our society is very far indeed from realizing the promise of universal sexual fulfillment that has always been an integral part of the American Dream.

A few grim statistics tell the story. A recent Harris poll noted that on any given Saturday night over 75 percent of the American population will either not have a date, be stuck with someone they can't stand, or have to go home alone after spending too much money. The pornography business, fueled by sexual frustration and loneliness, generated $25 billion in revenues last year, larger than the gross national products of Afghanistan, Zambia, and South Yemen combined.

But what is truly appalling about today's crisis is the persistence of widespread sexual inequities among adults. There are only a limited number of compatible, eligible, and attractive partners available at any one time, yet the odds against finding such "perfect loves" have risen from one in ten in 1950 to one in 5,000 today, according to a study done by the Brookings Institution.[1] This scarcity of sexual resources is compounded by the disparities in their distribution. Not unlike the laissez-faire economy of the late 1800s, today's sexual marketplace is plagued by "robber baron" types who monopolize too much of the sexual action, leaving little or nothing for those lower down the scale.

Indeed, as the following chart from the 1980 Census illustrates, the distribution of sexual resources, as measured by the number of sexual interfaces during the previous seven-day interval, has actually become *less* equal since 1950:

Distribution of Sexual Resources, Per Capita, 1950–1980

Shares of action	1950	1980
Lowest quintile	0.0%	0.0%
Second quintile	7.0%	6.0%
Third quintile	18.6%	17.5%
Fourth quintile	26.4%	27.0%
Fifth quintile	48.0%	49.5%

Source: U.S. Bureau of the Census, *Current Population Reports: Sexual Income, 1980,* Series P-60, no. 118 (March 1982), p. 226.

1. Brookings Institution, *Sexual Priorities in the 1980s,* 1981, p. 72.

If you break out the highest quintile, which includes everyone from happily married couples to famous movie directors, the disparities are even more shocking. If this quintile's 49.5 percent of the 1980 action is converted, for calculation's sake, to a base figure of 100 percent, we see the following disturbing results:

Distribution of Sexual Resources, Per Capita, Highest Quintile, 1980

Shares of action	
Warren Beatty	20%
Mick Jagger	15%
Hugh Hefner	10%
Germaine Greer	8%
Billy Dee Williams	6%
Rudolf Nureyev	5%
All others	36%

Source: *Sexual Income, 1980, loc. cit.*, p. 227, *Cosmopolitan*, "Who's Sleeping with Whom," June 1982.

Even those upsetting figures may mask the true disparities at work. We have yet to confront seriously the existence of a permanent sexual underclass in this country, seething with deep-seated frustration and anger that takes a toll in everything from random violence to alcoholism. The sexual underclass includes not only those whose physical or mental handicaps prevent them from forming relationships, but those who are too boring, unattractive, or shy. The number of Americans who are currently unable to find sex may be as high as 20 million—the highest figure since World War II—not counting Andy Warhol, Father Theodore Hesburgh, and others who have dropped out of the sex force altogether.

This underclass is a time bomb ticking away in our society. Unless we move quickly to end their frustrations, we may see their drives distorted into ugly political movements. . . .

As a nation we have yet made no serious attempt to deal with the problems of this underclass. A congenitally shy individual with a face like a pizza is expected to "sink or swim" when it comes to finding mates. What have we offered him in the way of training to allow him to compete in the ruthlessly competitive sexual marketplace? . . .

In a just society, individuals with true romantic merit would be expected to do very well for themselves. In fact, today's unregulated marketplace allows fly-by-night operators with little more

213

than some fast patter and a few gold chains on their hairy chests to dominate the scene. . . .

In short, no one is adequately served by a free market run amok. Yet our laissez-faire policy responses remain stuck in the nineteenth century. It is time to launch a bold program that deals realistically with the sexual inequities in our society—a program that can serve as the cornerstone of a new progressive coalition. . . .

The benefits of government-sponsored sex become more apparent when we look at the issue of productivity. Few economists have bothered to address the role sexual malaise plays in the declining output of the American worker, but it's obvious that if too many workers spend their weekends in a draining, futile search for companionship, the frustration will impact on the workplace in declining productivity, fatigue, and substance abuse. Thus, increasing the sexual experience available to each employee could pay off in a big way, as the following chart shows:

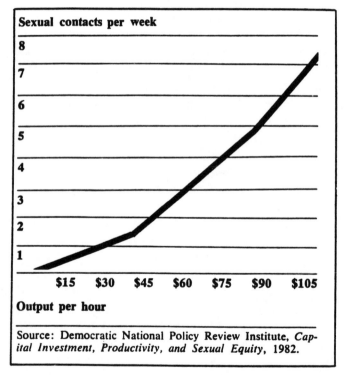

Source: Democratic National Policy Review Institute, *Capital Investment, Productivity, and Sexual Equity*, 1982.

For this reason, many forward-looking companies are beginning to provide dating services and increased opportunities for on-the-job socializing in order to spur worker productivity. These

efforts should be encouraged by our tax system and by subsidies for promising pilot programs, such as IBM's "Friendly Worker" program. Promoting corporate initiatives, though, isn't enough, which is why the government should be the "pimp of last resort."
. . .

Some critics say that the government role should end once a relationship has begun, but those of us who have studied this issue closely disagree. If a couple breaks up, it's only fair that the government—which may have helped bring them together—should provide them some support during the post–break-up period. Unloved Compensation Assistance would be available only to those who had been involuntarily dismissed from a relationship, and qualified heartbroken would have to provide documentation showing a good-faith effort to find new lovers on their own.

Because of the importance of sex to a sound economy and a strong national defense, a top priority of the next Democratic administration should be the establishment of an Inter-Agency Task Force on Sexual Affairs. Among the agencies that should be included are the Department of Interior's Office of Offshore Drilling, the Consumer Product Safety Commission, the truth-in-advertising section of the Federal Trade Commission, the General Services Administration, the Solicitor General's Office, and the Tennessee Valley Authority.

The political appeal of all of these proposals is obvious. At any given time, tens of millions of Americans are thinking about sex. Now, for the first time, the Democrats have an opportunity to capitalize on this obsessive interest with a concrete political program. Sexual concerns cut across race, class, and sex lines, and a constituency composed of the sexually downtrodden would flock to support any party offering them new hope.

Undoubtedly, there will be those who will look at this bold new program and say, "Let's keep the government out of the bedroom." But to those querulous critics, I respond, "Let's bring government *in*to the bedroom and kick loneliness *out*." It is hard to believe that in a country as great and rich as ours, there are still Americans who go to bed alone each night. But until the tragic plight of the *other* "Other America" is resolved, we will never reach our true greatness as a nation, and I, for one, can know no peace.

Part 6
Principles of Macroeconomics I— Fiscal Foolishness, Monetary Madness

Introduction

Hilaire Belloc (1870–1953) was a French-born poet, historian, and essayist. George Bernard Shaw dubbed Belloc's friendship with G. K. Chesterton the "Chesterbloc." Born in France, Belloc became a British citizen in 1902. The short excerpt, entitled "Economic Imaginaries," is an ironic effort to unravel the mystery of income generation. Written in 1924, it looks suspiciously like groundwork for a Keynesian multiplier. One thing seems certain. Belloc's charming puzzle is not an inflationary tale, for who would pay the price of a song for a loaf of bread?

Stephen B. Leacock's humorous excerpt on "The Balance of Trade in Impressions" was written in 1922. As an economist he was probably aware that positive net exports of that year were 80 percent lower than the favorable 1919 balance of $4 billion. Whether Leacock attributes this drop to the selling of American "genius . . . at twenty cents a word" cannot be determined.

The topical nature of political cartoons frequently renders them obsolete, but Honoré-Victorin Daumier's lithograph is an exception. His metaphorical drawing of the myth of Sisyphus illustrates both the burden of the budget and the futility of trying to balance it. The theme is as applicable to government fiscal deficits today as it was in 1869, as budget makers always seem doomed to the Hadean punishment of the Corinthian king.

Honoré-Victorin Daumier (1808–79), a French political caricaturist, was sentenced to prison in 1832 for a scatological caricature of Louis-Philippe, the king of France. The drawing was a spoof of "Gargantua," hero of the famous Rabelaisian satire. Daumier served more than six months in jail for the offense.

Ambrose Bierce applies his sardonic humor to the spending habits of kings and the heartrending acts of tax collectors. The king graciously responds to his tax collectors' pleas of insolvency with a sharp scheme to exempt them from the "head tax." He removes the tax "base."

According to the *Punch* excerpt, the difficulty of receiving exact change in the form of sheep and lambs for a "1000-pound bullock" note leads to the discovery of "bullion."

At one time, banks accepted checks written on menus, napkins, and scraps of paper, provided there were adequate funds on deposit. This practice is, at best, in ill repute. A. P. Herbert's "Board of Inland Revenue *v.* Haddock; Rex *v.* Haddock: The Negotiable Cow" is a medium-rare insight into legal tender. If pecuniary derives from the Latin "pecus," for cow, can cows be counted in M-1? In trying to pay his income taxes with a promissory cow, Herbert's Mr. Haddock is sued by the tax collector and arrested for causing a disturbance. Noting that the cow is appropriately stamped as a bill of exchange, the judge dismisses the case. Even if it walks like a cow, moos like a cow, and looks like a cow, it may be negotiable. It may even be a cash cow.

Sir Alan Patrick Herbert (1890–1971) was an English barrister who never practiced law. A member of Parliament for Oxford University, Herbert joined *Punch* in 1924. He campaigned against jargon and officialese.

In nineteenth-century Britain and the United States, when bank notes began to circulate as a medium of exchange, controversy arose between "currency" and "banking" schools. Advocates of the first favored "hard" money like gold and silver, while banking proponents favored a judicious use of "paper" money, or credit, based on the needs of trade. Alexander Pope's verses on gold and paper-credit point out uses and abuses of both.

Ogden Nash plays on the idea that "if you can borrow money, you don't need it—if you need it, you can't borrow it." Nash (1902–71) pioneered in a special kind of humorous verse that often violated conventional rules of rhyme and meter. In

218

"Bankers Are Just Like Anybody Else, Except Richer," Nash employs onomatopoeia to describe the sound of money as "clinks and clanks" and "rustling of . . . bills." He was on the staff of the *New Yorker*.

In "Money," Gertrude Stein (1874–1946) drolly reflects on whether money is the same to those who "vote to spend it" as to fathers who always say "no" when asked for it. She concludes that "when you earn it" you know the difference between one million dollars and three dollars. When you vote it, "it all sounds the same."

Gertrude Stein studied at Radcliffe from 1893 to 1897, then attended Johns Hopkins medical school until 1902. She emigrated to Paris in 1903, where her home became a mecca for a coterie of artists that included Hemingway, Picasso, Matisse, and others.

For thousands of years money has stubbornly resisted precise definitions and descriptions. Aristotle viewed it as a "veil," but other philosophers equate it to some five-letter word more often than not. The name-calling section, "Reflections on Money," shows an ineluctable fascination with lucre, dating from biblical times. Opinions range from manna to "trash."

"Alfred Martial, Unemployed" is a pseudonym for an economist who shall remain anonymous. The name is presumably a play on both Alfred Marshall, the neoclassical economist, and Marcus Valerius Martialis (ca. 40–104 A.D.), Roman epigrammatist. Martialis, whose name is Latin for the god Mars, was noted for his puns, parodies, and ambiguities. The style of "Biological Analogies for Money" is more Martialis than Marshall. After considering a number of "near-misses" in body analogues, Martial concludes that money must be "Bile" because the greenness of national currencies is statistically significant.

Hilaire Belloc

Economic Imaginaries (excerpt)

Now assessment of these services creates an enormous body of economic imaginaries, and to show you how they may do so I will give you an extreme and ludicrous case.

Supposing two men, one of whom, Smith, has a loaf of bread, and the other of whom, Brown, has nothing. Smith says to Brown: "If you will sing me a song I will give you this loaf of bread." Brown sings his song and Smith hands over the bread. A little later Brown wants to hear Smith sing and he says to him: "If you will sing me a song I will give you this loaf of bread." A little later Smith again wants to have a song from Brown. Brown sings his song (let us hope a new one!) and the loaf of bread again changes hands and so on all day.

Supposing each of these transactions to be recorded in a book of accounts. There will appear in Smith's book: "Paid to Brown for singing songs two hundred loaves of bread," and in Brown's book: "Paid to Smith for singing songs two hundred loaves of bread." The official who has to assess the national income will laboriously copy these figures into his book and will put down: "Daily income of Smith, 200 loaves of bread. Daily income of Brown, two hundred loaves of bread. Total, 400 loaves of bread." Yet there is only one *real* loaf of bread there all the time! The other 399 are imaginary.

Now with a ludicrous and extreme example of this sort you may say: "That is all very well as a joke, but it has no bearing on real life." It has. That is exactly the sort of thing which is going on the whole time in a highly developed economic society.

220

Stephen B. Leacock

The Balance of Trade in Impressions (excerpt)

For some years past a rising tide of lecturers and literary men from England has washed upon the shores of our North American continent. The purpose of each one of them is to make a new discovery of America. They come over to us travelling in great simplicity, and they return in the ducal suite of the AQUITANIA. They carry away with them their impressions of America, and when they reach England they sell them. This export of impressions has now been going on so long that the balance of trade in impressions is all disturbed. There is no doubt that the Americans and the Canadians have been altogether too generous in this matter of giving away impressions. We emit them with the careless ease of a glow-worm, and like the glow-worm ask for nothing in return.

But this irregular and one-sided traffic has now assumed such great proportions that we are compelled to ask whether it is right to allow these people to carry away from us impressions of the very highest commercial value without giving us any pecuniary compensation whatever. English lecturers have been known to land in New York, pass the Customs, drive up-town in a closed taxi, and then forward to England FROM THE CLOSED TAXI ITSELF ten dollars' worth of impressions of American national character. I have myself seen an English literary man—the biggest, I believe: he had at least the appearance of it—sit in the corridor of a fashionable New York hotel and look gloomily into his hat, and then FROM HIS VERY HAT produce an estimate of the genius of America at twenty cents a word. The nice question as to whose twenty cents that was never seems to have occurred to him.

221

I am not writing in the faintest spirit of jealousy. I quite admit the extraordinary ability that is involved in this peculiar susceptibility to impressions. I have estimated that some of these English visitors have been able to receive impressions at the rate of four to the second; in fact, they seem to get them every time they see twenty cents. . . .

In the course of time a very considerable public feeling was aroused in the United States and Canada over this state of affairs. The lack of reciprocity in it seemed unfair. It was felt (or at least I felt) that the time had come when some one ought to go over and take some impressions off England. The choice of such a person (my choice) fell upon myself. By an arrangement with the Geographical Society of America, acting in conjunction with the Royal Geographic Society of England (to both of whom I communicated my proposal), I went at my own expense. . . .

Like Sisyphus.

G. J. (Ambrose Bierce)

Death and Taxes: Head-Money

In ancient times there lived a king
Whose tax-collectors could not wring
From all his subjects gold enough
To make the royal way less rough,
For pleasure's highway, like the dames
Whose premises adjoin it, claims
Perpetual repairing. So
The tax-collectors in a row
Appeared before the throne to pray
Their master to devise some way
To swell the revenue. "So great,"
Said they, "are the demands of state
A tithe of all that we collect
Will scarcely meet them. Pray reflect:
How, if one-tenth we must resign,
Can we exist on t'other nine?"
The monarch asked them in reply:
"Has it occurred to you to try
The advantages of economy?"
"It has," the spokesman said: "we sold
All of our gay garrotes of gold;
With plated-ware we now compress
The necks of those whom we assess.
Plain iron forceps we employ
To mitigate the miser's joy
Who hoards, with greed that never tires,
That which your Majesty requires."
Deep lines of thought were seen to plow

Their way across the royal brow.
"Your state is desperate, no question;
Pray favor me with a suggestion."
"O King of Men," the spokesman said,
"If you'll impose upon each head
A tax, the augmented revenue
We'll cheerfully divide with you."
As flashes of the sun illume
The parted storm-cloud's sullen gloom,
The king smiled grimly, "I decree
That it be so—and, not to be
In generosity outdone,
Declare you, each and every one,
Exempted from the operation
Of this new law of capitation.
But lest the people censure me
Because they're bound and you are free,
'Twere well some clever scheme were laid
By you this poll-tax to evade.
I'll leave you now while you confer
With my most trusted minister."
The monarch from the throne-room walked
And straightway in among them stalked
A silent man, with brow concealed,
Bare-armed—his gleaming axe revealed!

The Introduction of Bullion (excerpt)

The early Italians, says *Punch,* used cattle as currency, instead of coin; and a person would sometimes send for change for a thousand-pound bullock, when he would receive twenty fifty-pound sheep; or, perhaps, if he wanted *very* small change, there would be a few lambs among them. The inconvenience of keeping a flock of sheep at one's bankers, or paying in a short-horned heifer to one's private account, led to the introduction of *bullion.*

A. P. Herbert

Board of Inland Revenue v. Haddock; Rex v. Haddock: The Negotiable Cow

'Was the cow crossed?'

'No, your worship, it was an open cow.'

These and similar passages provoked laughter at Bow Street to-day when the Negotiable Cow case was concluded.

Sir Joshua Hoot, K.C. (appearing for the Public Prosecutor): Sir Basil, these summonses, by leave of the Court, are being heard together, an unusual but convenient arrangement.

The defendant, Mr. Albert Haddock, has for many months, in spite of earnest endeavours on both sides, been unable to establish harmonious relations between himself and the Collector of Taxes. The Collector maintains that Mr. Haddock should make over a large part of his earnings to the Government. Mr. Haddock replies that the proportion demanded is excessive, in view of the inadequate services or consideration which he himself has received from that Government. After an exchange of endearing letters, telephone calls, and even cheques, the sum demanded was reduced to fifty-seven pounds; and about this sum the exchange of opinions continued.

On the 31st of May the Collector was diverted from his respectable labours by the apparition of a noisy crowd outside his windows. The crowd, Sir Basil, had been attracted by Mr. Haddock, who was leading a large white cow of malevolent aspect. On the back and sides of the cow were clearly stencilled in red ink the following words:

To the London and Literary Bank, Ltd.

Pay the Collector of Taxes, who is no gentleman, or Order, the sum of fifty-seven pounds (and may he rot!).

£57/0/0.   (Albert Haddock)

Mr. Haddock conducted the cow into the Collector's office, tendered it to the Collector in payment of income-tax and demanded a receipt.

Sir Basil String: Did the cow bear the statutory stamp?

Sir Joshua: Yes, a twopenny stamp was affixed to the dexter horn. The Collector declined to accept the cow, objecting that it would be difficult or even impossible to pay the cow into the bank. Mr. Haddock, throughout the interview, maintained the friendliest demeanour[1]; and he now remarked that the Collector could endorse the cow to any third party to whom he owed money, adding that there must be many persons in that position. The Collector then endeavoured to endorse the cheque—

Sir Basil String: Where?

Sir Joshua: On the back of the cheque, Sir Basil, that is to say, on the abdomen of the cow. The cow, however, appeared to resent endorsement and adopted a menacing posture. The Collector, abandoning the attempt, declined finally to take the cheque. Mr. Haddock led the cow away and was arrested in Trafalgar Square for causing an obstruction. He has also been summoned by the Board of Inland Revenue for non-payment of income-tax.

Mr. Haddock, in the witness-box, said that he had tendered a cheque in payment of income-tax, and if the Commissioners did not like his cheque they could do the other thing. A cheque was only an order to a bank to pay money to the person in possession of the cheque or a person named on the cheque. There was nothing in statute or customary law to say that that order must be written on a piece of paper of specified dimensions. A cheque, it was well known, could be written on a piece of notepaper. He himself had drawn cheques on the backs of menus, on napkins, on handkerchiefs, on the labels of wine-bottles; all these cheques had been duly honoured by his bank and passed through the Bankers'

---

1. *'Mars est celare martem.'* (Seiden, *Mare Clausun:,* lib. I, c. 21)

Clearing House. He could see no distinction in law between a cheque written on a napkin and a cheque written on a cow. The essence of each document was a written order to pay money, made in the customary form and in accordance with statutory requirements as to stamps, etc. A cheque was admittedly not legal tender in the sense that it could not lawfully be refused; but it was accepted by custom as a legitimate form of payment. There were funds in his bank sufficient to meet the cow; the Commissioners might not like the cow, but, the cow having been tendered, they were estopped from charging him with failure to pay. (Mr. Haddock here cited *Spowers* v. *The Strand Magazine*, *Lucas* v. *Finck*, and *Wadsworth* v. *The Metropolitan Water Board*.)

As to the action of the police, Mr. Haddock said it was a nice thing if in the heart of the commercial capital of the world a man could not convey a negotiable instrument down the street without being arrested. He had instituted proceedings against Constable Boot for false imprisonment.

Cross-examined as to motive, witness said that he had no cheque-forms available and, being anxious to meet his obligations promptly, had made use of the only material to hand. Later he admitted that there might have been present in his mind a desire to make the Collector of Taxes ridiculous. But why not? There was no law against deriding the income-tax.[2]

Sir Basil String (after hearing of further evidence): This case has at least brought to the notice of the Court a citizen who is unusual both in his clarity of mind and integrity of behaviour. No thinking man can regard those parts of the Finance Acts which govern the income-tax with anything but contempt. There may be something to be said—not much—for taking from those who have inherited wealth a certain proportion of that wealth for the service of the State and the benefit of the poor and needy; and those who by their own ability, brains, industry, and exertion have earned money may reasonably be invited to surrender a small portion of it towards the maintenance of those public services by which they benefit, to wit, the Police, the Navy, the Army, the public sewers, and so forth. But to compel such individuals to bestow a large part of their earnings upon other individuals, whether by way of pensions, unemployment grants, or education allowances, is manifestly barbarous and indefensible. Yet this is the law. The original and only official basis of taxation was that

---

2. Cf. Magna Carta: *'Jus ridendi nulli negabimus.'*

individual citizens, in return for their money, received collectively some services from the State, the defence of their property and persons, the care of their health or the education of their children. All that has now gone. Citizen A, who has earned money, is commanded simply to give it to Citizens B, C, and D, who have not, and by force of habit this has come to be regarded as a normal and proper proceeding, whatever the comparative industry or merits of Citizens A, B, C, and D. To be alive has become a virtue, and the mere capacity to inflate the lungs entitles Citizen B to a substantial share of the laborious earnings of Citizen A. The defendant, Mr. Haddock, repels and resents this doctrine, but, since it has received the sanction of Parliament, he dutifully complies with it. Hampered by practical difficulties, he took the first steps he could to discharge his legal obligations to the State. Paper was not available, so he employed instead a favourite cow. Now, there can be nothing obscene, offensive, or derogatory in the presentation of a cow by one man to another. Indeed, in certain parts of our Empire the cow is venerated as a sacred animal. Payment in kind is the oldest form of payment, and payment in kind more often than not meant payment in cattle. Indeed, during the Saxon period, Mr. Haddock tells us, cattle were described as *viva pecunia*, or 'living money', from their being received as payment on most occasions, at certain regulated prices.[3] So that, whether the cheque was valid or not, it was impossible to doubt the validity of the cow; and whatever the Collector's distrust of the former it was at least his duty to accept the latter and credit Mr. Haddock's account with its value. But, as Mr. Haddock protested in his able argument, an order to pay is an order to pay, whether it is made on the back of an envelope or on the back of a cow. The evidence of the bank is that Mr. Haddock's account was in funds. From every point of view, therefore, the Collector of Taxes did wrong, by custom if not by law, in refusing to take the proffered animal, and the summons issued at his instance will be discharged.

As for the second charge, I hold again that Constable Boot did wrong. It cannot be unlawful to conduct a cow through the London streets. The horse, at the present time a much less useful animal, constantly appears in those streets without protest, and the motor-car, more unnatural and unattractive still, is more numerous than either animal. Much less can the cow be regarded as

---

3. Mandeville uses *Catele* for 'price'. (Wharton's Law Lexicon)

an improper or unlawful companion when it is invested (as I have shown) with all the dignity of a bill of exchange.

If people choose to congregate in one place upon the apparition of Mr. Haddock with a promissory cow, then Constable Boot should arrest the people, not Mr. Haddock. Possibly, if Mr. Haddock had paraded Cockspur Street with a paper cheque for one million pounds made payable to bearer, the crowd would have been as great, but that is not to say that Mr. Haddock would have broken the law. In my judgment Mr. Haddock has behaved throughout in the manner of a perfect knight, citizen, and taxpayer. The charge brought by the Crown is dismissed; and I hope with all my heart that in his action against Constable Boot Mr. Haddock will be successful. What is the next case, please?

Alexander Pope

On the Demand for Gold (excerpt)

What Nature wants, commodious Gold bestows,
'Tis thus we eat the bread another sows:
But how unequal it bestows, observe,
'Tis thus we riot, while who sow it, starve.
What Nature wants (a phrase I much distrust)
Extends to Luxury, extends to Lust:
And if we count among the Needs of life
Another's Toil, why not another's Wife?
Useful, I grant, it serves what life requires,
But dreadful, too, the dark Assassin hires:
Trade it may help, Society extend;
But lures the Pyrate, and corrupts the Friend:
It raises Armies in a Nation's aid,
But bribes a Senate, and the Land's betray'd.
. . . .
What Riches give us let us then enquire:
Meat, Fire, and Cloaths. What more? Meat, Cloaths, and
    Fire.

Blest Paper-Credit! (excerpt)

Blest paper-credit! last and best supply!
That lends Corruption lighter wings to fly!
Gold imp'd by thee, can compass hardest things,
Can pocket States, can fetch or carry Kings;
A single leaf shall waft an Army o'er,
Or ship off Senates to a distant Shore;
A leaf, like Sibyl's, scatter to and fro
Our fates and fortunes, as the winds shall blow:
Pregnant with thousands flits the Scrap unseen,
And silent sells a King, or buys a Queen.

Ogden Nash

Bankers Are Just Like Anybody Else, except Richer

This is a song to celebrate banks,
Because they are full of money and you go into them and all
    you hear is clinks and clanks,
Or maybe a sound like the wind in the trees on the hills,
Which is the rustling of the thousand dollar bills.
Most bankers dwell in marble halls,
Which they get to dwell in because they encourage deposits and
    discourage withdralls,
And particularly because they all observe one rule which woe
    betides the banker who fails to heed it,
Which is you must never lend any money to anybody unless they
    don't need it.
I know you, you cautious conservative banks!
If people are worried about their rent it is your duty to deny
    them the loan of one nickel, yes, even one copper
    engraving of the martyred son of the late Nancy Hanks;
Yes, if they request fifty dollars to pay for a baby you
    must look at them like Tarzan looking at an uppity ape
    in the jungle,
And tell them what do they think a bank is, anyhow, they had
    better go get the money from their wife's aunt or ungle.
But suppose people come in and they have a million and they
    want another million to pile on top of it,
Why, you brim with the milk of human kindness and you urge
    them to accept every drop of it,
And you lend them the million so then they have two million

and this gives them the idea that they would be better
    off with four,
So they already have two million as security so you have no
    hesitation in lending them two more,
And all the vice-presidents nod their heads in rhythm,
And the only question asked is do the borrowers want the money
    sent or do they want to take it withm.
But please do not think that I am not fond of banks,
Because I think they deserve our appreciation and thanks,
Because they perform a valuable public service in eliminating
    the jackasses who go around saying that health and
    happiness are everything and money isn't essential,
Because as soon as they have to borrow some unimportant money
    to maintain their health and happiness they starve to
    death so they can't go around any more sneering at good
    old money, which is nothing short of providential.

Gertrude Stein

Money

Everybody now just has to make up their mind. Is money money or isn't money money. Everybody who earns it and spends it every day in order to live knows that money is money, anybody who votes it to be gathered in as taxes knows money is not money. That is what makes everybody go crazy.

Once upon a time there was a king and he was called Louis the fifteenth. He spent money as they are spending it now. He just spent it and spent it and one day somebody dared say something to the king about it. Oh, he said, after me the deluge, it would last out his time, and so what was the difference. When this king had begun his reign he was known as Louis the Well-beloved, when he died, nobody even stayed around to close his eyes.

But all the trouble really comes from this question is money money. Everybody who lives on it every day knows that money is money but the people who vote money, presidents and congress, do not think about money that way when they vote it. I remember when my nephew was a little boy he was out walking somewhere and he saw a lot of horses; he came home and he said, oh papa, I have just seen a million horses. A million, said his father, well anyway, said my nephew, I saw three. That came to be what we all used to say when anybody used numbers that they could not count well anyway a million or three. That is the whole point. When you earn money and spend money everyday anybody can know the difference between a million and three. But when you vote money away there really is not any difference between a million and three. And so everybody has to make up their mind is money money for everybody or is it not.

That is what everybody has to think about a lot or everybody

236

is going to be awfully unhappy, because the time does come when the money voted comes suddenly to be money just like the money everybody earns every day and spends every day to live and when that time comes it makes everybody very unhappy. I do wish everybody would make up their mind about money being money.

It is awfully hard for anybody to think money is money when there is more of it than they can count. That is why there ought to be some kind of system that money should not be voted right away. When you spend money that you earn every day you naturally think several times before you spend more than you have, and you mostly do not. Now if there was some arrangement made that when one lot voted to spend money, that they would have to wait a long time, and another lot have to vote, before they vote again to have that money, in short, if there was any way to make a government handle money the way a father of a family has to handle money if there only was. The natural feeling of a father of a family is that when anybody asks him for money he says no. Any father of a family, any member of a family, knows all about that.

So until everybody who votes public money remembers how he feels as a father of a family, when he says no, when anybody in the family wants money, until that time comes, there is going to be a lot of trouble and some years later everybody is going to be very unhappy.

In Russia they tried to decide that money was not money, but now slowly and surely they are coming back to know that money is money.

Whether you like it or whether you do not money is money and that is all there is about it. Everybody knows it. When they earn it and spend what they earn they know it they really know that money is money and when they vote it they do not know it as money.

That is the trouble with everybody, it is awfully hard to really know what you know.

When you earn it and spend it you do know the difference between three dollars and a million dollars, but when you say it and vote it, it all sounds the same.

Of course it does, it would to anybody, and that is the reason they vote it and keep on voting it. So, now please, everybody, everybody everybody, please, is money money, and if it is, it ought to be the same whether it is what a father of a family earns and spends or a government, if it isn't sooner or later there is disaster.

Reflections on Money

For the love of money is the root of all evil.

—1 Timothy 6.10 (King James version)

Money burned a hole in his pocket.

—A saying with sixteenth-century origins.

Money is like a sixth sense without which you cannot make a complete use of the other five.

—W. Somerset Maugham
(*Of Human Bondage,* chap. 51, 1915)

Time is money.

—Benjamin Franklin
("Advice to a Young Tradesman," 1748)

A feast is made for laughter, and wine maketh merry; but money answereth all things.

—Ecclesiastes 10.19 (King James version)

Biological Analogies for Money:
A Crucial Breakthrough

During the seventeenth century, economists of the Mercantilist School gained insight into the functioning of the aggregate economy by exploring evident similarities between the *Body Politic* and the *Body Natural*. However, in the wake of Adam Smith's refutation of the Mercantilist position, this method has fallen into almost total disuse. One might say that the Body was thrown out with the Bathwater. Increasingly, mathematized physical analogies have replaced biological ones, until today Rostow's vision of the developing economy as passing through the life cycle of a bird stands as the only instance of a biological analogy that has achieved contemporary success.

This dissertation seeks phoenix-like to resuscitate the time-honored method of biological analogy by settling once and for all what constitutes the proper biological analogue for money. As Milton Friedman and Robert Keale ("Love doth much, but money doth all," 1615) both hold, money plays a critical role in the determination of the level of economic activity. It follows that, until someone solves the conundrum of money's biological analogue, biological models of the aggregate economy will lack proper focus.

The problem is approached in two ways. First, we examine the various analogues proposed by seventeenth-century theorists. It could be that in the profession's rush to physical (mathematical)

A dissertation completed at the Neoplastic Institute of Technology in 1968.

models a valid prior solution has been overlooked.[1] Then, we focus on the essential functions and attributes of money to determine precisely what Bodily Organ, Principle, or Substance performs parallel functions in the Body Natural.

Our review of the literature reveals no fully satisfactory solutions, but does uncover five near-misses:

1. *Money is fat.*
   Money is but the Fat of the Body-Politick, whereof too much doth as often hinder its Agility, as too little makes it sick. 'Tis true that as Fat lubricates the motion of the Muscles, feeds in want of Victuals, fills up uneven Cavities, and beautifies the Body, so doth Money in the State quicken its Action, feeds from abroad in the Time of Dearth at Home; even accounts by reason of its divisibility, and beautifies the whole, altho more especially the particular persons that have it in plenty. (William Petty, 1665)

2. *Money is spirit.*
   Money is the *vitall spirit* of *trade* and if the spirit faile, needs must the Body faint. (Edward Misselden, 1622)

3. *Money is blood.*
   [Money is] . . . as useful in the Body Politick as Blood in the Veins of the Body Natural, dispersing itself and giving Life and Motion to every Part thereof. (Samuel Lamb, 1659)

4. *Money is muck.*
   Money is like Muck, not good except it be spread. (Thomas Manley, 1625)

5. *Money is Muscle (specifically, the "sinews of war").*
   . . . War is become rather an expense of money than men, and success attend those that can most and longest spend money: whence it is that princes' armies in Europe are become more proportionable to their purses than to the number of their people. (James Whiston, 1693)

These analogies stress the role of money in economic circulation, but they ignore certain of its other important attributes. In particular, none of these analogies are consistent with the fact

---

1. Although this is not a particularly promising hypothesis, a dissertation must review the literature in any case.

(proved for the first time in this thesis) that national currencies show a statistically significant tendency to be *green*.

On the other hand, recognizing this fact (and ignoring the almost equally significant incidence of red monies[2]) virtually solves our problem. *Money must be Bile.*[3] This is a substance of the proper color and one which plays a critical role in the production of Fat, Muscle and Muck, as well as in the circulation of the Blood. Moreover, when Bile ceases to flow, the Spirit must "faile."

While identifying money with Bile is only the first step on a long analogical-analytical road, its implications are decidedly anti-Keynesian. Whereas Keynes (in the last sentence of his *Essays in Persuasion*) views economists as dentists, we hold that economists do the work of internists: an insight that may well touch off a Martiallian Revolution.

---

2. We reject the hypothesis that money is red because of that color's recessive (in the Mendelian sense) connotations: (1) not all money is "hot"; (2) not all money is injected via expenditure deficits; and (3) monetary theory assumes free-world institutions.

3. This finding has important policy implications. First, close reading of the literature on international monetary reform indicates that the overriding obstacle to agreement on an international reserve currency has been the selection of an appropriately persuasive acronym. Our work suggests that units of this currency should be termed Basic International Liquidity Effusions (*Base Internationale Liquide d'Effusions*).

Second, the central bank rather than being an inflationary engine is now seen to be the liver of the economy, so that instead of speaking of an *overheated* economy macroeconomists should use the more precise term *choleric*.

Part 7

Macroeconomics II—
Policy Folly

Introduction

To introduce this last section, Bill Schorr's cartoon illustrates
trends in economic policy from Keynesian to "bum," a promising
candidate for a theory of "irrational expectations."

For anyone who has a problem sorting out this "liberal-
conservative" stuff, help is on the way—or, more appropriately,
on the couch. In "A Crypto-Liberal Takes the Cure," Herbert
Stein reveals what *he* learned while in a horizontal position.

Christopher U. Light's parable of the people of Xanadu
equals a first lesson in basic macroeconomic policy. The Priests of
the Invisible Hand fall into disrepute when the Great Drought
descends on the land. All they can offer to boost unemployment is
promises, promises (sounds familiar, doesn't it?). Consequently,
the Xanaduans turn for advice to a Philosopher from Atlantis with
a remarkable resemblance to John Maynard Keynes. The Xanadu
government engages in deficit finance, hires unemployed workers
as Civil Servants, and creates a "cute little creature named Stagflation." Finally, a Student of the Master suggests growth. A revolutionary idea. Christopher Light (1937–) received his Ph.D. in
1971 from Washington University. He is a freelance writer.

Any reader still confused about the true meaning of inflation
and unemployment is referred to Kenneth E. Boulding's illustrated
verse for the former and to Pogo for the latter. Boulding's whimsy
and Pogo's profoundness remove all lingering doubt. Pogo, the
creation of Walt Kelly (1913–73) was launched in 1948. With

Pogo, Kelly introduced the whimsical pearls of wisdom so familiar to fans: "We have met the enemy, and he is us."

From any standpoint taxation is a grievous issue. On the one hand, taxpayers are aggrieved to be forced to surrender payments on assets and earnings. Governments grieve the taxpayers further by what and how they tax. In "How to Raise Taxes without Grieving the Subject," Jonathan Swift relates two ways to simplify the tax system, each based on assessing traits of character. Either tax vice, or vice versa, virtue. In the first plan, neighborly stool pigeons determine the extent of "vice and folly." The second and far simpler proposal has greater potential for maximizing revenue. With taxes based on self-assessments of the virtuous traits people value most in themselves, what individuals would describe themselves as other than witty, brave, generous, wise, well-dressed, honest, and handsome?

It is possible that Mark Twain's promise not to use profanity in discussing "house rent and taxes" would exempt him from taxation under Swift's neighborly stool pigeon approach. Whether he would exempt himself by the "self-evaluation" plan is questionable.

As a result of the adjustment in tax laws some years back, American couples with two incomes pay a smaller "marriage penalty" than formerly. In A. P. Herbert's "court case," written some 60 years ago, an economics professor and his wife are charged by the British crown with evasion of taxes when they divorce, continue to live together, and pay lower taxes. The sympathetic judge directs for acquittal with some Swiftian remarks on marriage as a "taxable luxury."

Stephen B. Leacock explains that there is such a thing as a "painless tax": it is a tax on somebody else.

After partying all night, Benjamin Franklin's "Subscriber" makes an "early to bed, early to rise" proposal. Upon discovering that "it is daylight when the sun rises," he suggests "An Economical Project" to replace artificial light with free sunshine. Enforcement procedures consist of taxes on shuttered windows, a sunset curfew, and other government regulations. Contrast this 1784 essay with Frédéric Bastiat's "Petition of the Candlemakers" (in part 4), written about 60 years later.

John Trever's use of M. C. Escher's trompe l'oeil art likens President Reagan's economic package to an uphill waterfall.

William A. Paton (1889–1991) was Professor Emeritus of Accounting and Economics at the University of Michigan's Business School. His name has been memorialized at the School. Paton's allegorical dream of a tank of hot stew turns into a nightmarish Malthusian feast. A mad scramble of "every man for himself" ensues when some diners begin to "draw out" more than they "pour in." Readers may "draw out" their own conclusions regarding the analogy.

No sane person would suggest war as a solution to unemployment, yet its economic advantages are well known. Evoe's verse, written on the eve of World War II, suggests that a cooperative effort to rearm and dump the hardware in the ocean would be mutually advantageous to all nations. Besides, the kiddies would love it. Evoe was the pseudonym for Edmund George Valpy Knox (1881–1971), English humorist, writer, and parodist.

To pay for a deficit, governments can either borrow in the bond market or raise taxes. No one likes taxes, and bonds must be serviced. Linhart Stearns proposes that the government go "public" with an equity issue. By tying earnings to the level of government spending, the "Red-White-and-Blue Chip" stock is certain to replace IBM as the growth stock of tomorrow.

Like a rose, a structural deficit by any other name is still a deficit. Or, as Gertrude Stein might phrase it, "Is a deficit a deficit, or is it a deficit?" When taking the ten-minute quiz on "Rubik's fiscal policy," readers are cautioned not to look at the answers first.

To put the deficit in perspective, consider this: deficits add to debt; stack the 1992 U.S. debt in $1000 bills and it will be 196 miles high; in dollar bills it will take 200,000 years (plus or minus a few hundred) to count. Worse yet, make the debt international, state it in Mouseville currency, and foreign mice might start demanding cheese for their "rallod" holdings. See "Confronting the Cheese Crisis" from the Morgan Guaranty Trust Company.

The story goes that the Laffer curve originated as a drawing on a restaurant napkin in 1974, when its author illustrated the effects of high taxes to a presidential advisor. The lack of applause from leading economists may be due to the fact that most economists were taught at their mothers' knees not to write on napkins.

Martin Gardner's article spoofs the Laffer curve with an innovative substitute, the neo-Laffer (NL) curve. The key to the NL curve, which resembles an unraveled sweater, is the "technosnarl," an idea suggested by the statistician Diaconis.

During the depression of the 1930s, unemployment rates rose almost to 25 percent in the United States. It is generally agreed that rearmament and World War II "solved" the problem. Clarence Day's "Edible Workers," written in the 1930s, is a mockery with a moral, suggesting a solution to unemployment that is "viable" or "unviable," depending upon which view of the dinner table one has.

The health care problem is primarily one of runaway costs, costs that consistently exceed the rate of inflation. In the deregulated market of Joan Beck's "Modest Proposals on Health Costs," medical services are on a par with food, Fords, and airline tickets. Bargain-minded consumers benefit from twofers, discounts, and disease-of-the-month specials.

Despite his apparent dislike for Ireland, where he lived most of his life, Jonathan Swift sympathized with the poverty and misery of the Irish people. His concern following a winter famine in the early eighteenth century prompted what has been described as the greatest satire: "A Modest Proposal." Written in 1729, the theme is infanticide.

Kenneth E. Boulding implicitly acknowledges his debt to Jonathan Swift in "The Green Stamp Plan." His voucher proposal for population control pits the pros (philoprogenitives) of procreation against the cons (phoboprogenitives) to set the price of "legal" children.

Christmas is the season to be jolly, whether Santa Claus is a Keynesian, a Monetarist, a supply-sider, an independent, or a bum. Two verses play on Clement Moore's " 'Twas the Night before Christmas." Milton Friedman is Martin S. Feldstein's Santa in a verse presented originally before a group at Harvard, where Feldstein is George F. Baker Professor of Economics. He was Chairman of the Council of Economic Advisers (CEA) under Ronald Reagan, resigning in 1984. Feldstein is president and CEO of the National Bureau of Economic Research.

Jolly St. Ron (Reagan) wears the red suit to "let them eat jelly beans" in Alan S. Blinder's "Christmas, Revisited," published in January 1983. The lampoon of Reagan's policies uses sharp and hard-hitting analogies to make its points during a season of high unemployment (over 10 percent) and a deficit approaching the hundred billions. It seemed large at the time. By 1992, it had more than tripled.

Larry Johnson's cartoon illustrates Blinder's line, "They knew in a moment it must be St. Ron." Dispensing a jelly bean handout, St. Ron apparently has Recovery in the bag.

When all is said and done, including this anthology, can economists be trusted? Pat Oliphant's cartoon seems clearly opposed to feeding the CEA monkeys any more bananas, but someone slipped them some fruit. Or slipped *on* some fruit.

".... FIRST I WAS A KEYNESIAN .... NEXT I WAS A MONETARIST...THEN A SUPPLY-SIDER ... NOW I'M A BUM.... "

Herbert Stein

A Crypto-Liberal Takes the Cure

"So, Mr. Stein. You are back on the couch. I thought we straightened you out already."

"That was five or six years ago, when I was afraid I might be a Keynesian."

"Then what happened?"

"With your help, I learned that we are all Keynesians now and there are no longer any Keynesians. That made me see that I couldn't be a Keynesian and that it didn't matter if I was."

"So why are you back here?"

"Well, I have this terrible fear that I may be a Liberal. I wake up at night in a cold sweat, after dreaming that I am a Liberal. And when I go into the dining room at the American Enterprise Institute I hear people whispering, 'Liberal,' 'Liberal.'"

"Is that so awful?"

"Oh, it really is. It's the *L* word. It stands for Left, Lewd, Lecherous, Libertine, Lazy, Lascivious, Loafer, Lenin, and Marx."

"Marx doesn't start with an *L*."

"I know, but it's close. Another important thing is this. Being a Liberal is not like being a Democrat. Being a Democrat or a Republican is like having the red pieces or the black pieces in a checkers game. It doesn't have any moral implications. But being a Liberal is Ba-a-ad. You can be a good Democrat if you're not Liberal and you can be a bad Republican if you are Liberal."

"Then what do you call people who are not Liberal?"

"A Crypto-Liberal Takes the Cure," in Herbert Stein, *On the Other Hand . . .* (Washington, D.C.: The AEI Press, Published for the American Enterprise Institute, 1995), pp. 61–63.

"That's interesting. Only the intelligentsia call themselves conservatives. A politician who says that his opponent is a Liberal doesn't say that he himself is a conservative. He usually says only that he himself is not Liberal. Sometimes he might say that he is American."

"What makes you think that you might be a Liberal?"

"I suppose it's mainly something about taxes. I seem to be soft on taxes."

"You mean that you love taxes, that you're a taxophiliac?"

"No, I don't love taxes, but when I say to myself, 'Taxes 20 percent of GNP, result bliss; taxes 21 percent of GNP, result misery,' I get mixed up. I forget how it goes and sometimes I get it backward."

"Have you been doing anything to try to correct this condition?"

"Yes, I've been trying to read my lips. I stand in front of a mirror trying to read my lips saying, 'No New Taxes!'"

"What happens when you do that?"

"All I see is a silly old man standing in front of a mirror saying 'No Nude Actress!' to himself."

"That hardly seems to be enough. After all, even President Reagan raised taxes."

"He's a special case. For ordinary folk, taxes are a litmus test. Anyway, that isn't all."

"Aha! So what else is there?"

"I'm worried about this 'card-carrying member' thing."

"You don't mean that you are a member of the ACLU!"

"Oh, no. But when this card-carrying business started I went through my wallet and found that I'm a card-carrying member of the AARP, the AAA, the Cosmos Club, and the D.C. Video Rental Club."

"That all seems safe enough to me."

"Oh, you can't be sure. I haven't studied all the things these organizations stand for and checked them out against the certified list of 'Liberal' positions. The AARP wants to spend more government money for old people. The AAA wants to spend more money for roads. The Cosmos Club has just voted to admit women after 100 years of segregation. And the video rental club has adult films in the back room. That's all pretty worrisome. You never know what they might find out."

"I have a feeling you're holding back. Is there something else you ought to tell me before we begin?"

"Doctor, can I count on you to keep this completely confidential?"

"Who can count on anything? But you can tell me."

"Well, there are two things. When I was a boy in school and learned the Pledge of Allegiance we didn't say 'under God' and that still doesn't sound natural to me. Also, I have to confess that I know only one stanza of the Star Spangled Banner. So, what do you advise, doctor?"

"It looks like a pretty clear case. So, you're a Liberal. You should come out of the closet and admit it. Then you could move to Sweden. There are many Liberals there and they are accepted in society."

"But I'm not a Liberal. I can't admit to being something I'm not. That's my whole problem. I feel guilty when I'm not."

"What makes you think that you're not a Liberal? Everything you've said today sounds like a Liberal."

"There are lots of things. I helped to raise money for Ronald Reagan's campaign in 1980. I'm for Bush this year. I'm for SDI and a big defense budget. I'm for aid to the Contras. I want not only to balance the budget but to run a surplus. I'm for a tight, anti-inflationary monetary policy. I'm against middle-class subsidies, like the farm program. I'm against 'industrial policy' and protectionism. I could give you a much longer list.

"And yet, when people divide the world into black and white, Liberals and Conservatives, I'm not sure where I belong and I'm afraid of where other people would put me."

"So, So! That makes the problem a little harder. Let me think for a minute."

"I'm waiting."

"All right. This is my advice. We wait until the day after the election. If Dukakis wins, I think you will quickly discover all by yourself that you are not a Liberal. If Bush wins, I'll see you three times a week starting Monday, November 14, at 11 o'clock."

"Thank you, doctor." *(October 1988)*

Christopher U. Light

The Birth of Stagflation: A Fable

Once upon a time in the land of Xanadu, which lies to the east of Atlantis and to the north of Timbuktu, there existed but three classes of workers: Farmers, Pinmakers, and government employees who were called Civil Servants.

Pinmakers and Civil Servants bought their food from the Farmers. Civil Servants and Farmers bought pins from the Pinmakers so their wives could pin together cloth for clothing they made for their families. This cloth came as manna from heaven and was called "exogenous." The government bought pins to hold together pieces of paper, for this was long before the technological breakthrough of the paper clip. And the government provided services for the Farmers and Pinmakers and collected taxes to pay for these services.

In number the Farmers were largest. The Pinmakers were next, and the Civil Servants in those days were few.

In normal years all those who wished to work at their chosen trades could do so. All that was produced was purchased and consumed. And there was equilibrium throughout the land.

In some years, however, a drought came, and farm income fell. Farmers' wives had to make do with last year's dresses and did not buy pins. Many Pinmakers found themselves unemployed and unable to buy food, so they cultivated their backyards to feed their families. The price of pins fell and, after an initial rise, so did the price of food.

At times in other years the neighboring country of Timbuktu placed a large order for pins. Pinmakers went on overtime, and their wives were induced to work part time in the pin factories, but the Farmers' wives could not, for they were unskilled. Employ-

252

ment rose; incomes rose and so did the price of pins and, later, of food.

Over many cycles of drought and prosperity the People noticed that whenever employment fell so did prices. When employment rose, prices rose too. They began to ask why. The Priests of the Cult of the Invisible Hand answered the People and said that it was in the nature of things, that it was part of the order of the universe, and that for prices to rise when employment was falling or for prices to fall when employment was rising would be unnatural.

One time the drought was especially severe, and the next year the wives of the Farmers and Civil Servants were afraid and saved their income instead of buying pins. And they continued to do this even unto the third year, long after the drought was over. Most of the Pinmakers were now unemployed, and the Farmers planted their crops but marketed little. The People were starving, and the government was paralyzed. But the Priests of the Cult of the Invisible Hand said, "Fear not. Wait. The market will clear." And the People looked to the heavens waiting for the market to clear. But employment and prices continued to fall.

In one of those years a Philosopher from Atlantis came into Xanadu. He saw the shuttered pin factories and the People starving in the streets, and he asked the government, "Why do you permit this?"

The government replied, "There is nothing we can do. We must wait for the market to clear."

"Nonsense," growled the Philosopher. "You must create effective demand. You, the government, must buy pins now and stockpile them against the year when Timbuktu again places its large order. The deficit you run will be made up by raising taxes in the year that Timbuktu again orders pins."

The Priests of the Cult of the Invisible Hand were aghast, and their forecasts were dire. "If that is done," they warned, "we shall never again have equilibrium."

"Blither your equilibrium," shouted the Philosopher. "You shall have prosperity."

Then the Priests of the Cult of the Invisible Hand appealed to the People. "When Timbuktu orders those pins," they cautioned, "you will not enjoy the super prosperity you normally enjoy in those years. You will be slaving on overtime for nothing because the government will tax away your extra earnings to make up the deficit."

253

"We shall accept that," said the People, "for then we shall have stability."

The government did as the Philosopher urged, and it worked. Normalcy returned. Equilibrium was restored except for the warehouse full of pins waiting for the next Timbuktu order.

But the order from Timbuktu did not come for many years.

In the meantime there was another severe drought, and again there was no recovery the next year even though the rains came. Despite the abundance of apples on the trees and grain in the fields, employment, output, and prices continued to fall until once again People were starving in the streets.

The government said, "We must once again follow the Philosopher's teaching. But since our warehouses are filled to the bursting point with pins, we cannot buy more pins. Instead we will hire some of the unemployed Pinmakers and train them to be Civil Servants. We will pay them, and that will create effective demand."

And again it worked, and recovery came.

When Timbuktu finally placed a very large order that cleared out the warehouses, the Priests of the Cult of the Invisible Hand went to the government and said, "You must release the Pinmakers you have hired and allow them to return to the pin factories, or there will be a shortage of pins."

"We cannot," replied the government. "They have greatly reduced the work burden on our regular Civil Servants, and therefore they are obviously productive. Besides, we need them. Government can be a stabilizing force only if it is big. Let the Pinmakers' wives fill the empty places in the pin factories." Then, to ensure that the Pinmakers did not return to private industry, the government increased their wages to parity with the pin factories but did not require productive labor of them.

When the lean years came again, they were not as bad as before because the government was big. Nevertheless, many Pinmakers were out of work. Reasoning that it was as effective and less burdensome to hire as Civil Servants unemployed Pinmakers than to purchase and stockpile their pins, the government did just that. Many of these unemployed Pinmakers were the wives of former Pinmakers who themselves had been hired as Civil Servants previously.

Something new happened this time, something that could not have happened before the government discovered the principle of effective demand. The wives and children and grandchildren of the Farmers now entered the labor force, not to seek work in the pin factories, for they were not born to the trade and could not be trained, but in hopes of being employed as Civil Servants to help create effective demand.

The government did hire many of the Farmers' relatives, but could not employ them fast enough to keep up with their entry into the labor force. So it happened that unemployment rose. At the same time the pin factories were unable to find enough skilled Pinmakers, so output fell, and some of the factories were shuttered. But the government kept right on trying to create effective demand by hiring the unemployed and paying them through deficits. The Civil Servants had money and attempted to buy pins. But the output of pins was falling, and all they did was to bid up the price of pins. So prices and wages rose *pari passu*, but output fell.

The Priests of the Cult of the Invisible Hand were horrified. "You have done the unspeakable," they cried out. "You have made unemployment and prices rise simultaneously. You have made an inflationary depression. You have created an unnatural monster that will rise up one day and devour the nation."

But the Priests of the Cult of the Invisible Hand were by now few in number and were growing old. So the government replied that this was not a monster at all but a cute little creature named Stagflation and, in any case, was a necessary outcome if the government was to provide stability. And the People believed.

In time Stagflation grew, and the People began to fear it. "The Philosopher misled us," the People cried out, and the Cult of the Invisible Hand came back but as an underground movement, for in those days it was no longer safe to be a member. The government was again paralyzed, but it could not turn to the Philosopher for advice, for he had died.

One day a second Philosopher from Atlantis, a Student of the Master, came into Xanadu and saw the monster that had been created. "You have strayed from the Master's advice," he said. "You have blundered. When you purchased pins beyond your immediate needs, perhaps you did right. You did indeed end the depression.

"The next time, though," he went on, "you did not purchase pins. You merely hired the Pinmakers and pretended they were productive. There was, and is, no demand from the People for the work these new Civil Servants do. You could have done the same thing by printing money and giving it to the unemployed."

"But that would be wrong," the government replied.

"Exactly," agreed the Student of the Master.

"It would be immoral," said the Priests of the Cult of the Invisible Hand.

"It would be neither moral nor immoral," replied the Student, who believed philosophy to be positive rather than normative. "It would be wrong because it, too, would create this monster."

"What should we do now?" asked the government. "We cannot order the Farmers' wives to leave the labor force. And we certainly cannot dismiss Civil Servants. What can we do?"

Although shaking his head in dismay at these constraints, the Student replied, "There is a possible answer. You might try growth, which can be achieved in a couple of ways. You could develop new technology, or you could increase your population to raise more Pinmakers. I would advise trying both."

So the government reclassified those Civil Servants who had been Pinmakers and were therefore experts in fastener technology and placed them in a laboratory with orders to develop a substitute for the pin that would be a technological breakthrough.

After that the government went to the wives of the Farmers and of the Pinmakers and of the Civil Servants and urged them to have more children. But they refused, for then they could not have gone to work for the government to help create effective demand. So the government took the pill away from them, and there was growth—but that's another fable for another time.

Moral: If you would follow the advice of a Philosopher, make sure that both blades of his shears are sharp.

Kenneth E. Boulding

The Inflationary Spiral

The horrid Spiral is unending:
He feeds on Deficits and Spending,
And ever round and round will drift
Till stopped by Taxes or by Thrift.

POGO

Jonathan Swift

How to Raise Taxes without Grieving the Subject (excerpt)

In the school of political projectors I was but ill entertained; the professors appearing, in my judgment, wholly out of their senses, which is a scene that never fails to make me melancholy. These unhappy people were proposing schemes for persuading monarchs to choose favourites upon the score of their wisdom, capacity, and virtue; of teaching ministers to consult the public good; of rewarding merit, great abilities, and eminent services; of instructing princes to know their true interest, by placing it on the same foundation with that of their people; of choosing for employments persons qualified to exercise them; with many other wild impossible chimaeras, that never entered before into the heart of man to conceive; and confirmed in me the old observation, "That there is nothing so extravagant and irrational, which some philosophers have not maintained for truth." . . .

. . . I heard a very warm debate between two professors, about the most commodious and effectual ways and means of raising money, without grieving the subject. The first affirmed, "The justest method would be, to lay a certain tax upon vices and folly; and the sum fixed upon every man to be rated, after the fairest manner, by a jury of his neighbors." The second was of an opinion directly contrary; "To tax those qualities of body and mind, for which men chiefly value themselves; the rate to be more or less, according to the degrees of excelling; the decision whereof should be left entirely to their own breast." The highest tax was upon men who are the greatest favourites of the other sex, and the assessments, according to the number and nature of the favours

259

they have received; for which they are allowed to be their own vouchers. Wit, valour, and politeness were likewise proposed to be largely taxed, and collected in the same manner, by every person's giving his own word for the quantum of what he possessed. But as to honour, justice, wisdom, and learning, they should not be taxed at all, because they are qualifications of so singular a kind, that no man will either allow them in his neighbour, or value them in himself.

The women were proposed to be taxed according to their beauty and skill in dressing, wherein they had the same privilege with the men, to be determined by their own judgment. But constancy, chastity, good sense, and good nature, were not rated, because they would not bear the charge of collecting.

Mark Twain

House Rent, Taxes, and Profanity (excerpt)

Being a stranger, it would be immodest and unbecoming in me to suddenly and violently assume the associate editorship of the *Buffalo Express* without a single explanatory word of comfort or encouragement to the unoffending patrons of the paper, who are about to be exposed to constant attacks of my wisdom and learning. . . .

I shall not make use of slang or vulgarity upon any occasion or under any circumstances, and shall never use profanity except in discussing house rent and taxes. Indeed, upon second thought, I will not even use it then, for it is unchristian, inelegant, and degrading—though to speak truly I do not see how house rent and taxes are going to be discussed worth a cent without it.

A. P. Herbert

Rex v. Pratt and Merry:
The Tax on Virtue

At the Old Bailey to-day Mr. Justice Plush declined to allow this case, a prosecution by the Crown, to go to the jury. He said:

In this unusual and painful case the defendants are charged with a conspiracy to cause a public mischief by diminishing the revenue. The female defendant, May Merry, is a distinguished actress earning a considerable income of her own. The male defendant, Mr. Pratt, is, or rather was, her husband, and he is a professor of economics, equally distinguished but not so prosperous. The couple lived happily together for fourteen years, and there was issue of the marriage three children.

Among their friends and neighbours they were regarded as a model couple; and in the spring of last year much surprise and consternation were caused by the news that the wife was filing a petition for a dissolution of marriage. The news was true, as it sometimes is, and a dissolution was duly decreed, the custody of the children being granted to the wife. But two days after the decree absolute was pronounced the two defendants again took up residence together in their London house; and there they have cohabited ever since, with their family, happily, according to the evidence, but technically in sin.

The writer of an anonymous letter brought these facts to the notice of the King's Proctor, who was asked to make an inquiry upon the ground that the divorce must have been obtained collusively or in other ways have been an abuse of the processes of law. The King's Proctor held that he was *functus officio*, that is, he had no status or excuse for interference in a matter which had been finally determined by the Court. The papers in the case showed without question that the divorce had been duly obtained according to the forms and practices of that queer branch of the law; but, not being wholly satisfied by his inquiries, he referred the matter to the Public Prosecutor.

The defendants, when challenged, made no secret of their position. Mr. Pratt had caused himself to be divorced strictly according to the forms of law, in order to free himself from the excessive burden of income-tax and surtax imposed upon him by the married state. While the couple were married their incomes were added together and assessed for taxation purposes as one income, and the impecunious husband was responsible for the tax upon the whole, though he was quite unable at law to get at a penny of his wife's money if she should see fit to withhold it. Further, though his own income never came near to the exalted regions of surtax or super-tax, he was compelled by the bulking of the two incomes to pay super-tax upon most of his own modest earnings; and if at any time his wife had declined to pay he might have been sent to prison for refusing to pay surtax on an income which has never qualified for it.

Resenting this position and without consulting his wife, he provided her with evidence which would formally justify her in seeking a divorce; and formally she took advantage of it. There is no evidence of connivance or collusion; and if there had been anything of the sort we must assume that the learned President of the Divorce Court would have discovered it. The wife may have known what was in the husband's mind after he took the fatal step, but it is not suggested that she knew before. The necessary facts were proved, and the motive of the parties is not material so far as the law of divorce is concerned; nor is there any law against a divorced couple living happily ever after.

The Crown, then, was in the familiar position of one who wants to find fault but cannot say why, smelling an offence but unable to identify it; and the Crown now says that the facts disclose an unlawful conspiracy not to defraud but to diminish the revenue. There is no doubt that the revenue has been diminished. Now that the parties are single they are separately assessed; each of them enjoys a 'personal allowance' of £100 instead of an allowance of £150 between them; Mr. Pratt pays only the ordinary income-tax upon his slender income; he is not responsible for the taxes on his wife's; and the total contribution to the revenue of the two of them is substantially less.

It is, no doubt, an undesirable thing to act deliberately in such a way as to diminish the revenue; but it need not necessarily be unlawful. A successful surgeon, for example, who decides that he will retire at forty and live quietly in a tub will diminish the revenue by the amount of the tax upon his former earnings. If we all decided to sell all that we have and give it to the poor we should cause an alarming fall in the revenue and probably an economic crisis. A solemn thought. But we should not be liable to an indictment for conspiracy.

In other words, it is an offence to evade income-tax but not to avoid it. If every loving couple in the land decided that they would refrain from marriage because of the extra taxation which it involves they could not be punished by any existing law. Yet it would be a great mischief. For it has always been regarded as the public policy of the land that those who love each other should marry and have children. Accordingly the law of the land makes it easy to enter the married state but extremely difficult to leave it; and the children of married persons have still certain advantages (though these are diminishing) over the children of those who are not. There are various provisions which reflect the same policy—a contract or legacy, for example, restraining a person from marriage is void.

One would expect to find, then, that the law of income-tax, being the only law that in the modern State has any real importance, would be framed in conformity with the same venerable policy; that it would say to Mr. and Mrs. Pratt, 'Since you have taken upon yourselves the responsibility of matrimony, the upkeep of a house and the rearing of a family, which are institutions dear to the State, you shall pay less by way of taxation than you would have paid if you had remained two independent celibates or lived together without the lawful tie.'

What we do find is the exact opposite. The State said to Mr. Pratt, 'You are married, therefore you shall pay more.' And Mr. Pratt replied, 'Then I will not be married.' In other words, we have here a direct conflict between a modern Act of Parliament and the public policy of the land as expressed in other Acts of Parliament and the principles of the Common Law. This is no new or exceptional thing; for many Acts of Parliament in these days appear to have been made by men walking in their sleep—by a Legislature whose right hand is not aware what its left hand doeth. If we are asked to enforce such statutes we have no alternative but to obey. But the present case is different. We are asked to extend the vague and elastic law of conspiracy to cover a set of facts not hitherto contemplated—to create, in effect, a new offence. We are not ready to do so. We cannot find that at law the defendants have done anything wrong. It is as if the State had said, 'You have a motor-car. We shall tax you for it,' and the Pratts had replied, 'Then we will get rid of the motor-car.'

Counsel for the Crown seemed to suggest that the defendants had no cause for complaint, because together they were well off and could afford to pay the extra taxes. But the principle is the same whether the married persons are rich or poor. It is in effect a tax upon marriage and a tax upon virtue, and no man can be punished for evading such a tax unless Parliament expressly says so. It may be that the policy of Parliament has changed and that marriage is to be regarded in future as a taxable luxury. Without doubt much revenue could be extracted from such a popular commodity. Marriages, like intoxicating liquors, might be graded according to their strength; and the most passionate, happy, or fruitful couples could be made to pay more than the lukewarm or miserable. There are possibilities here. But until Parliament has declared its will we are bound by the Common Law.

I find that there is here no evidence of a Common Law conspiracy, and I shall direct the jury to acquit the defendants. Further, I think that they have done good service in drawing attention to a grave evil, and I recommend that £6,000 be paid to them out of public funds.

Stephen B. Leacock

A Painless Tax (excerpt)

Man is born unto trouble. He no sooner solves one problem than unkind fate sets him another. A few years ago it seemed as if there were only two serious problems in the world—the Drink Problem and the Sex Problem. Both these have been solved and set aside— one by the Eighteenth Amendment and the other by the Nineteenth. Women may now vote as much and as often as they care to; as for drink, one never hears it mentioned—or not above a whisper.

With these two problems settled, we might have expected peace. But it was not to be. All of a sudden there has come into the world a new trouble in the form of the Tax Problem.

A few years ago none of us ever thought about taxes. Such feeble taxes as we had we smoked in our cigars or drank with our lager beer and never knew that they were there. There was a little grumbling over the dog tax, but that was all.

Now everything is changed. The whole of what used to be called the civilized world is overwhelmed in money trouble.

It is always easy to know what the world is thinking about by observing the comic paper and the stage "gag" of the comedian. A few years ago the Suffragette with the Ax was the favorite subject of merriment. Now it is the Puzzled Citizen with his Income Tax Return.

The whole of the United States at the present moment buzzes like a beehive with tax discussion. Some think that the taxes ought to fall upon the rich. Others think that they should remain upon the poor. People who have no income claim that the income tax is the ideal method of taxation. People who do not smoke favor very strongly the levy of more taxes on tobacco. People who ride in street cars want to tax motors. Married people believe in taxing bachelors. The manufacturer wants to tax the farmer and the farmer says that he has nothing left. The only general agreement found is in the idea of taxing somebody else.

Benjamin Franklin

An Economical Project

To the Authors of the Journal of Paris:

Messieurs:—You often entertain us with accounts of new discoveries. Permit me to communicate to the public, through your paper, one that has lately been made by myself, and which I conceive may be of great utility.

I was the other evening in a grand company, where the new lamp of Messrs. Quinquet and Lange was introduced, and much admired for its splendor; but a general inquiry was made, whether the oil it consumed was not in proportion to the light it afforded, in which case there would be no saving in the use of it. No one present could satisfy us in that point, which all agreed ought to be known, it being a very desirable thing to lessen, if possible, the expense of lighting our apartments, when every other article of family expense was so much augmented.

I was pleased to see this general concern for economy, for I love economy exceedingly.

I went home, and to bed, three or four hours after midnight, with my head full of the subject. An accidental sudden noise waked me about six in the morning, when I was surprised to find my room filled with light; and I imagined at first that a number of those lamps had been brought into it; but, rubbing my eyes, I perceived the light came in at the windows. I got up and looked out to see what might be the occasion of it, when I saw the sun just rising above the horizon, whence he poured his rays plentifully into my chamber, my domestic having negligently omitted, the preceding evening, to close the shutters.

I looked at my watch which goes very well, and found that it was but six o'clock; and still thinking it something extraordinary that the sun should rise so early, I looked into the almanac, where I found it to be the hour given for his rising on that day. I looked forward, too, and found he was to rise still earlier every day till towards the end of June; and that at no time in the year he retarded his rising so long as till eight o'clock. Your readers, who with me have never seen any signs of sunshine before noon, and seldom regard the astronomical part of the almanac, will be as much astonished as I was, when they hear of his rising so early; and especially when I assure them *that he gives light as soon as he rises.* I am convinced of this. I am certain of my fact. One cannot be more certain of any fact. I saw it with my own eyes. And, having repeated this observation the three following mornings, I found always precisely the same result.

Yet it so happens that, when I speak of this discovery to others, I can easily perceive by their countenances, though they forbear expressing it in words, that they do not quite believe me. One, indeed, who is a learned natural philosopher, has assured me that I must certainly be mistaken as to the circumstance of the light coming into my room; for it being well known, as he says, that there could be no light abroad at that hour, it follows that none could enter from without; and that of consequence, my windows being accidentally left open, instead of letting in the light, had only served to let out the darkness; and he used many ingenious arguments to show me how I might, by that means, have been deceived. I owned that he puzzled me a little, but he did not satisfy me; and the subsequent observations I made, as above mentioned, confirmed me in my first opinion.

This event has given rise in my mind to several serious and important reflections. I considered that if I had not been awakened so early in the morning I should have slept six hours longer by the light of the sun, and in exchange have lived six hours the following night by candle-light, and the latter being a much more expensive light than the former, my love of economy induced me to muster up what little arithmetic I was master of, and to make some calculations which I shall give you, after observing that utility is, in my opinion, the test of value in matters of invention, and that a discovery which can be applied to no use, or is not good for something, is good for nothing.

I took for the basis of my calculation the supposition that there are one hundred thousand families in Paris, and that these families consume in the night half a pound of bougies, or candles, per hour. I think this is a moderate allowance, taking one family with another; for though I believe some consume less, I know that many consume a great deal more. Then estimating seven hours per day as the medium quantity between the time of the sun's rising and ours, he rising during the six following months from six to eight hours before noon, and there being seven hours, of course, per night in which we burn candles, the account will stand thus:

In the six months between the 20th of March and the 20th of September there are

Nights	183
Hours of each night in which we burn candles	7
Multiplication gives for the total number of hours	1,281
These 1,281 hours multiplied by 100,000, the number of inhabitants, give	128,100,000
One hundred twenty-eight millions and one hundred thousand hours spent at Paris by candle-light, which, at half a pound of wax and tallow per hour, gives the weight of	64,050,000
Sixty-four millions and fifty thousands of pounds, which, estimating the whole at the medium price of thirty sols the pound, makes the sum of ninety-six millions and seventy-five thousand livres tournois	96,075,000

An immense sum, that the city of Paris might save every year by the economy of using sunshine instead of candles!

If it should be said that people are apt to be obstinately attached to old customs, and that it will be difficult to induce them to rise before noon, consequently my discovery can be of little use, I answer, *Nil desperandum*. I believe all who have common-sense, as soon as they have learnt from this paper that it is daylight when the sun rises, will contrive to rise with him, and, to compel the rest, I would propose the following regulations:

First. Let a tax be laid of a louis per window on every window that is provided with shutters to keep out the light of the sun.

Second. Let the same salutary operation of police be made use of, to prevent our burning candles, that inclined us last winter to be more economical in burning wood; that is, let guards be placed in the shops of the wax and tallow chandlers, and no family be permitted to be supplied with more than one pound of candles per week.

Third. Let guards also be posted to stop all the coaches, etc., that would pass the streets after sunset, except those of physicians, surgeons, and midwives.

Fourth. Every morning, as soon as the sun rises, let all the bells in every church be set ringing; and if that is not sufficient, let cannon be fired in every street, to wake the sluggards effectually, and make them open their eyes to see their true interest.

All the difficulty will be in the first two or three days, after which the reformation will be as natural and easy as the present irregularity; for, *ce n'est que le premier pas qui coûte.* Oblige a man to rise at four in the morning, and it is more than probable he will go willingly to bed at eight in the evening; and, having had eight hours' sleep, he will rise more willingly at four in the morning following. But this sum of ninety-six millions and seventy-five thousand livres is not the whole of what may be saved by my economical project. You may observe that I have calculated upon only one half of the year, and much may be saved in the other, though the days are shorter. Besides, the immense stock of wax and tallow left unconsumed during the summer will probably make candles much cheaper for the ensuing winter, and continue them cheaper as long as the proposed reformation shall be supported.

For the great benefit of this discovery, thus freely communicated and bestowed by me on the public, I demand neither place, pension, exclusive privilege, nor any other reward whatever. I expect only to have the honor of it. And yet I know there are little, envious minds who will, as usual, deny me this, and say that my invention was known to the ancients, and perhaps they may bring passages out of the old books in proof of it. I will not dispute with these people that the ancients knew not that the sun would rise at certain hours; they possibly had, as we have, almanacs that predicted it, but it does not follow thence that they knew *he gave light as soon as he rose.* This is what I claim as my discovery. If the ancients knew it, it might have been long since forgotten; for it certainly was unknown to the moderns, at least to the Parisians, which to prove I need use but one plain simple argument. They are as well instructed, judicious, and prudent a people as exist anywhere in the world, all professing, like myself, to be lovers of economy, and from the many heavy taxes required from them by the necessities of the state, have surely an abundant reason to be economical. I say it is impossible that so sensible a people, under such circumstances, should have lived so long by the smoky, unwholesome, and enormously expensive light of candles, if they had really known that they might have had as much pure light of the sun for nothing. I am, etc.,

A Subscriber.

John Trevor

William A. Paton

Prologue (excerpt)

One night some months ago, after reading about new proposals to bring economic security and contentment to us all by the simple expedient of Federal legislation promising more and bigger handouts, I had an unusually vivid dream, and I'd like to tell you about it. I realize that it's always difficult to describe visits to the dreamworld in words that serve to convey to the listener or reader an impression that corresponds, even faintly, to the experience of the dreamer, but I'll do my best.

I suddenly found myself overlooking a vast plain, the edges of which were lost in a sort of purple fog. In the central area stood an enormous, glass-like vat or tank, open at the top, giving off vapors that strongly suggested hot Irish stew or mulligan. Surrounding this container were a great multitude of creatures, something like human beings but reminding one of recent pictures of imaginary visitors from Mars. Although varying in size and other characteristics a prominent feature of all was the paunch. I also noticed that all or nearly all of these weird creatures were equipped with two long pipes, a pouring-in pipe and a drawing-out pipe. The general practice seemed to be for each to spend considerable time and effort pouring in some ingredient which represented its special contribution to the stew, and from time to time each would lay aside its pouring-in pipe and devote itself to sucking out from the top of the tank, through its other pipe, some of the savory mixture. As I watched this strange scene a change began to develop. More and more individuals began to neglect the pouring-in operation and spend an increasing amount of time at the business end of their drawing-out pipes. At first the change was not very notice-

able and the majority went ahead with the intermittent activities of pouring in and drawing out. But as the number devoting their attention solely to consuming stew increased and the number actively engaged in pouring in dwindled, those who were continuing to pour in finally began to see what was going on. When this stage was reached—realization by the decreasing number of pour-iners that they were being exploited by the increasing number of draw-outers—the process of change moved with startling rapidity to a climax. In what seemed no longer than a matter of seconds the orderly, rhythmic process of contributing and consuming disintegrated before my eyes. Almost with one accord the remaining contributors threw their pouring-in pipes away and frantically grabbed their drawing-out pipes. And as the contents of the tank rapidly declined under this mass attack the creatures set up a horrible howling and pressed toward the tank in a desperate effort to keep the ends of their pipes in contact with the falling level of the life-giving stew. In an instant, as often happens in dreams, what had been no more than interestingly disturbing became a frightening nightmare. In the final mad rush great numbers of the creatures were trampled to the ground around the base of the tank, and those temporarily surviving climbed on the bodies of the dead and dying in their struggle to reach the top and thus get within sucking distance of the fast-diminishing contents. The howling became unbearable, the pleasant odor was replaced by a terrible stench—and I woke up, literally in a cold sweat and with a feeling of nausea.

Usually, after a bad dream, the experience fades rapidly and by the time one is dressed in the morning the whole thing is practically forgotten. In this case, however, my nightmare continued to haunt me, and was undoubtedly the marginal factor—the final prod—in the chain of circumstances that induced me to sit down and write this book.

Evoe (Edmund George Valpy Knox)

Only a Suggestion

I thought as I sat by the shore of the sea
What a wonderful, beautiful thing it would be
If the Briton, the Teuton, the Gaul and the Slav
Should take all the guns and the tanks that they have
And sink them out there in the infinite main,
And then begin building them over again.
For no one, you know, is desirous to fight,
They are only protecting the Truth and the Right,
And nothing but armaments endlessly made
Can stop Unemployment and benefit Trade,
And the Heart of a Nation as never before
Is united when making Munitions of war.
How happy the state of the world when it finds,
What is simple to all mathematical minds,
That you cannot go on making gun after gun,
Because there is nowhere to put them when done,
And the largest of factories, even the Banks,
Would refuse in the end to find storage for tanks.
But a little more trust between nations, I think,
Would allow them to meet every August and sink
In a suitable place they could easily settle
Enormous supplies of explosives and metal,
And a cup would be given—the winner to count
As the one that got rid of the largest amount,
And could soonest return to the Blessings of Peace
Which are instantly doomed should Rearmament cease.

I thought as I sat by the shore of the sea
What a wonderful, beautiful thing this would be

For Commerce and Culture, and Friendship and Cash;
And the children, no doubt, would be pleased by the
  splash.

A Modest Proposal

Recently a small group of policy makers from Washington met with several respected Wall Streeters in order to discuss the problem of how to finance the government in face of the general unpopularity of bonds without either impeding the progress of the recovery or feeding the generally expected inflation.

The professional economists and experts on banking and government finance did not come up with new ideas which met with any general enthusiasm. The meeting seemed destined to run into a dead end when a Mr. X made a startling proposal.

Mr. X attacked the problem from an entirely fresh point of view. He said that, as he was a partner in a large stock-exchange firm, he was closer to the thinking of the public than were the rest of the group. It was only because of this more common touch that he dared to speak up among such an erudite and responsible meeting of fiscal experts. But as securities and their marketing were his business, and as government bonds were securities that had to be sold just like other issues, he felt that he might be able to contribute a plan.

Mr. X pointed out that the public would not buy bonds because of the conviction that the inflation was inexorable and that the holder of bonds was bound to lose out in purchasing power. Besides, almost everybody already had suffered losses in bonds, and it is well known that people are loath to buy securities in which they once lost money. Therefore, anything called a "bond" had become an almost unsalable item unless it contained features so favorable as to be ruinous to the issuer.

With apologies to Jonathan Swift.

On the other hand, the public's eagerness to buy anything which was called a "common stock" seemed limitless, and little discretion was brought to bear in making the decisions of what to buy and how much to pay.

In the circumstances, Mr. X thought that if the government did what any intelligent underwriting house would do, namely, tailor its issues to the desires of the market, there should be good promise of a successful flotation. Obviously the government should attune itself to the times—bonds were passé, stocks were now the thing, and, therefore, the government should bring out a common-stock issue.

Calling a government issue a "stock" rather than a "bond" would in itself assure its acceptance by the public. But Mr. X thought that the success of the issue could be further assured if it capitalized on the investing public's enthusiasms and if it were given a certain aura in the market. As regards the latter, of course, there were limits to the advertising and promotion either printed or spoken. It was important not to run afoul of the S.E.C. or the various state security commissions. However, the market itself was eager to emphasize the favorable aspects of any common-stock issue and, in fact, was prone to imagine favorable factors without any unethical encouragement. Thus, Mr. X pointed out, a common-stock prospectus could be circumspect and straightforward in its statements and still assure the issue a good reception. In fact, in several instances common-stock issues had gone over with a bang merely because his firm had headed the selling group—nobody seemed to care what was in the prospectus.

Mr. X felt that the government was in the position to issue the perfect common stock, which couldn't fail to gain the ultimate in popularity. Investors looked for certain things in common stocks. These were (1) growth, (2) protection against inflation, (3) market popularity, (4) leverage. Contrary to old-fashioned opinion, investors were hardly interested in cash dividends or rate of income return or book values. They even gave little heed to price because of the general conviction that any price paid for a stock today would be proved low in the future—growth, inflation, and market popularity would make any caviling about value superfluous.

Now, the government stock issue could be designed to satisfy all four investor objectives. To this end Mr. X proposed that three percent of all government *expenditures* accrue as earnings for the government's common stock. It was too early to discuss the technical details, but in general each department would have to pay three cents into the common-stock fund for every dollar it spent. (This would not be too hard for the bureaucrats to swallow because sales taxes were already ubiquitous. Besides, it might be a good thing if this three percent tax on government spending served to remind officials of the nuisances and burdens the rest of us bear.)

The prospectus of the issue could carry a table showing the course of government *expenditures*, say, from 1929 to date as well as the corresponding figures for three percent thereof. It would be obvious that the earnings for the common stock would have grown more than twentyfold in the three decades. Few blue chips now outstanding could equal this growth record. The public judges growth by the record of the past and extends that record into the distant future. There is no doubt that, in view of the public's confidence in the future, it would envisage a truly startling earning prospect for the government's common stock. It would probably be considered the premier growth stock in the country.

The stock would also be considered a perfect inflation hedge. Its earnings would be geared exactly to the one factor the public believes determines the extent of inflation—government spending. Furthermore, the stock would represent ownership in a huge amount of material things both above and below ground, to say nothing of things in the air and, perhaps in the near future, on other planets. The real estate in Washington alone is a tremendous inflation hedge. Then, there are millions of acres of public lands, national parks, military installations, etc. The public would not be backward in conjecturing that oil, uranium, or any number of other riches would be found and prove to make the stock even a better inflation hedge. Mr. X reminded his audience that it was not necessary for the investing public to believe that any of these assets would ever be sold at a profit or distributed. Stocks were considered inflation hedges if the public knew or guessed that assets existed even if they were never to be realized on.

Market popularity for the issue was assured by its size and the huge operations of the venture. No other issue could possibly be kept in the public eye so much as the government's common stock. Every day hundreds of items about some aspect of the issuer's operations would be prominently displayed in the press and reported over the air. News about an issuer keeps investors interested in the issuer's stock and the government stock would enjoy the highest amount of advertising. Mr. X said that in this connection there was only one drawback—the management of the venture might not be highly regarded, and there would be some doubts about the enterprise's efficiency. Such reservations, however, would not react too badly on the stock because poor management and inefficiency would increase government expenditures and thus would increase the stock's earning power!

With respect to leverage, the stock would also appeal to the public. It might follow over $280 *billion* of debt and many billions of contingent liabilities. Mr. X felt that probably the stock would at most represent an equity of 40%. This would depend on the issue price, which he discussed later.

As the stock was to be presented as a growth security, it was important to keep the cash dividend extremely low but to raise it consistently by minute amounts. A generous dividend would give the stock the wrong aura for it then would be considered a good income stock suitable for widows and orphans and not a dynamic security. Everybody knows that sound, good income-bearing stocks are not too popular. Present-day investors don't want income but only a capital gain. It would be a great mistake to make the dividend too attractive.

Mr. X made an estimate of the probable price at which the stock could be issued. So ideal an issue should command a price/earnings ratio at least as high as those that have been applied to such stocks as I.B.M., M.M. & M., Polaroid, etc. These have at times sold at about 45 times earnings, and Mr. X said that his firm would surely be willing to issue the government's stock on this basis. Perhaps they might even be willing to exceed this figure. On the basis of government expenditures of $80 billion, the earnings applicable to the stock would be $2.4 billion. Multiplying this figure by 45 would bring the total value of the issue to $108 billion. He suggested a price of $400 a share (around the price of I.B.M.), which means that 270 million shares would be issued—about as many shares as General Motors has outstanding.

Mr. X pointed out that, if it were desirable to issue more stock, increasing the percentage of expenditures reserved for the stock could offset any dilution. He mentioned, also, that warrants to buy the stock—say at 20% above issue price—could be sold to satisfy the most speculatively inclined investors and to bring additional sums into the Treasury. At a later date convertible-bond issues would also be possible.

Mr. X's idea was considered so novel that none of those at the meeting was willing to support him except behind closed doors. However, it was deemed advisable to get the public reaction to the plan and that, therefore, its outlines should be "leaked off the record" as a trial balloon. This is why this was written.

Rubik's Fiscal Policy

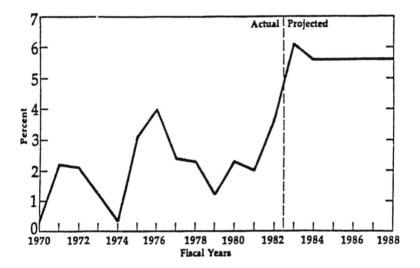

Good morning, class. We're going to start today with a pop quiz. (Groans and moans.)

Here is a chart and a list of multiple-choice questions. You have 10 minutes to complete your answers. (Whispers, buzzes.) And NO talking, please.

1. This chart represents:
   a) Projections of the world oil price used to justify shale oil projects, the Siberian pipeline and loans to Mexico.
   b) The interest rate on Certificates of Deposit of money-center banks.

c) The terms of trade for the Mexican tortilla against the Indian pita.

d) Dolly Parton's voice-o-gram on "Know When to Roll 'Em."

2. Whatever it represents, the likelihood of this chart being true would:
   a) be about the same as the oil price projections used to justify shale oil projects, etc.
   b) get above zero only if the whole government tried to make it come true.
   c) be as hot as jalapeno.
   d) have a probability distribution resembling Dolly Parton's profile.

(Cries and shrieks.) No OUTBURSTS, class.

3. An economist confronting this chart would:
   a) break into tears.
   b) break into giggles.
   c) break out the Scotch.
   d) move to the Brookings Institution.

4. An investor looking at this chart would:
   a) turn "unsettled."
   b) go short on interest rate futures.
   c) go long on the weisswurst.
   d) go back to roulette.

5. A businessperson facing this chart would:
   a) punt.
   b) relocate to Long Beach.
   c) take a banker to lunch.
   d) change accountants.

(Rumbles and thuds.) Class, this is not a zoo. RETURN to your seats. At once!

6. A CEO studying this chart would:
   a) increase inventory.
   b) decrease inventory.
   c) send out for caviar.
   d) change accountants.

7. A Congressperson viewing this chart would:
   a) schedule some personal appearances back home.

b) leave on a fact-finding trip to Mexico.

c) call for an investigation of bratwurst imports.

d) raise taxes.

8. A short essay on this chart would make the following point:

    a) fiscal policy should be cancelled.

    b) fiscal policy is driven by assumptions.

    c) fiscal policy is best made while eating liverwurst.

    d) fiscal policy is not the sport of sissies.

Time's up, class. Pass your answers to the front. Class? Class!

Answer: This is a chart of the "structural deficit," published in the Congressional Budget Office report released Feb. 3. It depicts the Unified Budget Deficit as a percentage of Gross National Product, based on compilations and projections by CBO and the Office of Management and Budget. If you circled all (c)s above, you understand what is currently driving fiscal policy.

Confronting the Cheese Crisis

Mouseville had a new problem. Actually, it wasn't so much new as suddenly more pressing. A sense of urgency had been instilled by the cryptic warning of the village wisemouse. "The chickens are coming home to roost," he said.

The wisemouse, it was well known, was not one to bandy frivolous phrases. And everyone knew that he was not talking about the return of the common, egg-laying variety of chicken. It had to be something else. Just what, exactly, most of the towns-mice did not know. But the feeling that *something* had gone wrong in the community was rather widespread. The older mice could feel it in their bones, like the approach of bad weather.

Trouble had been building up for some time. Mouseville and its residents had been in a generous (some would say profligate) mood for many years. The Mouseville town council had voted large amounts of aid for less fortunate mice in foreign lands. Spending had been heavy, too, for defense systems to protect mice in many countries from bears and dragons. Mouseville busi-nessmice had spent heavily to build overseas factories, and tourists from Mouseville had been scampering around the globe spending in a big way.

Year after year, more of Mouseville's currency—the rallod—had been flowing out of Mouseville than had been flowing in. And the sticky part of the whole business was that the rallods in the hands of foreign mice (unlike those held by Mouseville's own citizens) were a claim against Mouseville's treasure—the wheels of cheese neatly stacked in air-conditioned vaults at Fort Xonk.

What made the problem acute for Mouseville just now was that a Euro-mouse publicly had cast aspersions on the value of

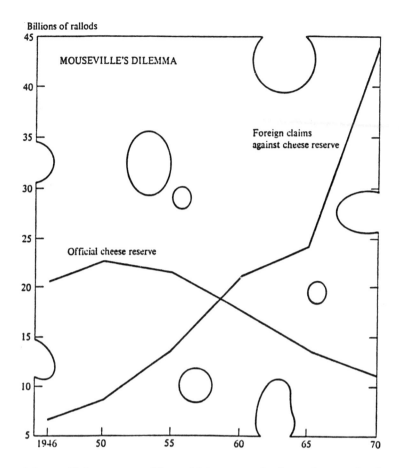

Billions of rallods

MOUSEVILLE'S DILEMMA

Foreign claims against cheese reserve

Official cheese reserve

1946   50   55   60   65   70

Mouseville's currency. The criticism was the latest in a rash of complaints. And the Euro-mice were threatening to exercise their rallod claims against Mouseville's cheese hoard and wipe it out.

Imagine . . . a town without an official cheese reserve! How utterly devastating. A town just had to have a warehouse full of official cheese. Even though official cheese was not available for domestic consumption there was a mystique about cheese. It had a grip on mice that no one had been able to break for thousands of years. You didn't have to be a cheesebug to realize that.

It was against that crisis background that the Mouseville town fathers met in secret session. The chairmouse called for a plan of action. The council members responded, one by one:

"I say let's plead for a little more time. After all, Mouseville's accounts with the rest of the world have been unbalanced for only 15 years. It's not that long ago that everyone was talking about the rallod gap. Why all the impatience?"

"No, that will never do," broke in another council member, his tail twitching in anger. "I say let's let them know that we don't buy their threats. Embargo cheese. No more exchanges of cheese for rallods. Let's dethrone cheese. Cut the rallod's ties to cheese."

Amidst a chorus of yeas and nays, yet another councilor-mouse shouted: "Let's give out all the cheese down to the last nibble and have done with it. It's Mouseville's productive power that counts, not its cheese hoard."

"Exactly right," shouted a Keynesmouse, adding: "I have always considered cheese to be a barbarous relish."

"Huzzah!" joined in a councilormouse, known both for his eloquence and his Bryanesque learnings. With a sweeping flourish of his paw he squeaked: "You are crucifying mousekind on a cross of cheese."

That last comment immediately brought a rejoinder from across the council table: "Not so. We do need a cheese reserve. It's very handy to have cheese when you want to operate in strange lands. No one questions you when you have cheese in your pocket. And besides, that cheese reserve is the only thing we have left to instill a little iron in our spine when it comes to spending. Take the cheese away and the sky's the limit on paper rallods."

The rumble of agreement that followed the speaker's comment convinced the council chairmouse that most of the members did not favor passing out Mouseville's cheese hoard down to the last nibble. He pressed for other suggestions. A council member who had been quiet up to now rose and spoke:

"I recommend that we double the price of cheese from 35 rallods to the nibble, which was set in a rather whimsical way in 1934, to 70 rallods to the nibble. The value of our cheese hoard would double at the stroke of a pen. We could then go on spending more than we are earning for years into the future. It would also encourage new cheese production. And besides, at a price of 70 rallods who would want to pay out that much money for a nibble of cheese? After all, cheese is expensive to store, and everyone knows that cheese doesn't earn any interest."

Mauswagens and Alpsmice

The plea for raising the price of cheese found support. It had a certain amount of surface appeal—an easy way to solve the problem by simply making cheese worth more. Unless other countries made a similar change Mouseville's exporters would get a real break because their prices in foreign markets would decline. On the other hand, merchants making their living selling foreign-made goods in Mouseville would find the going tougher, as was made plain by a councilormouse who did a tidy business in imported mini-chariots:

"Double the price of cheese and Mauswagens would go up from 1,850 rallods to 3,700 rallods. I'd lose my share of the Mouseville market. This sounds like a plot hatched in Detroit."

The meeting was heating up. Several paw fights broke out. The worldly wisemouse tried to calm things down:

"Gentlemice, please! The gains from devaluation are chimerical. In 1934, when the rallod's cheese content was changed, most other currencies were changed by a like amount. Each country saw to it that no one else got a trade advantage by jiggling the value of its currency in relation to cheese."

Opposition to a higher cheese price began to build up. "Why raise the cheese price and give a big windfall to all those Alps-mice," shouted one member, a trifle jingoistically. To which the chairmouse heatedly replied: "That's quite enough. Let's not indulge in gnome-calling." But the opponents were not to be hushed up. One councilormouse, his whiskers bristling, let out a thunderous squeak:

"Raise the cheese price and every town with cheese in its reserves will suddenly think it is richer. Spending worldwide will skyrocket. Inflation—not only in the rallod but also the dnuop, cnarf, kram, and the aril—will get a horrendous boost."

Cheers of support rang out among several members of the council, who already were greatly alarmed at the way inflation had hurt the average workmouse and nestowner. A bankermouse, with whiskers stiffened with just the right amount of wax, exclaimed:

"We don't need all that extra global money through a higher cheese price. After all we have SSRs (Special Slicing Rights) which are paper cheese and are available through the IMF (Internestial Munching Foundation) in Washington."

Mention of the SSRs was a bit technical for most of the councilormice. So was an impassioned discourse on what Mouseville's actions might mean for the "two-tier" cheese price. No one paid much attention to either speaker.

An economouse, the only council member schooled in the dismal science, proposed that the council stress efforts to increase productivity of Mouseville's managers and workers in industry and in government so that Mouseville could earn its way in the world. Spending would need to be trimmed to meet income, he urged. "If you don't do all of those things you can raise the cheese price and, in a very short time, you will be back in the same trap." His comments seemed to make good sense—especially when the economouse assured them that if Mouseville really did mend its ways, mice everywhere in the world would applaud, be patient, and not demand cheese for their rallods. Some might even follow the good example.

Someone called for a vote on a resolution to leave the cheese price alone and, instead, strive to "tackle basic problems." It passed, 9 to 2.

With a sigh the economouse was heard to remark on the way out of the meeting: "Time is running out for Mouseville. The average mouse doesn't realize it, but this is quite serious. We've got to tighten our belts." His companion draped a friendly paw over his shoulder and replied:

"Oh, I guess so. But whatever happens to the cheese price it won't mean the end of the world. The sun will come up the next day. Come on, let's have a nightcap—an interesting Rhine wine and some Strasbourg pâté on delicious little British biscuits. I want to tell you about my next trip abroad."

Martin Gardner

The Laffer Curve

> The Kettle-Griffith-Moynihan Scheme for a New Elec-
> tricity Supply, Traveling in the Olden Times,[4] American Lake
> Poetry, the Strangest Dream that was ever Halfdreamt.[5]
> [4]I've lost the place, where was I?
> [5]Something happened that time I was asleep, torn letters
> or was there snow?
> —James Joyce, *Finnegans Wake*

Economists love to draw curves. In the early decades of modern
capitalism, classical economists were fond of explaining prices by
constructing supply and demand graphs such as the one shown in
Figure 152. If the price of a commodity is on the level indicated by
the broken line *a*, it is easy to see from where this line crosses the
curves that people will buy less of the product. Since the seller will
have an oversupply, he will lower its price to get rid of it. If the
prices are on the lower level of the broken line *b*, increased demand will bid up the product's price and the seller will produce
more.

These up and down forces stabilize the price at *E*, the equilibrium point where the amounts demanded and supplied are
equal. At this point, according to early classical theory, the seller
maximizes profit. If there is a general increase in demand, with
supply constant, the demand curve shifts to the right and *E* rises. If
there is a general increase in supply, with demand constant, the
supply curve shifts to the right and *E* falls. If both curves move to
the left or the right the same distance, *E* stays at the same level.

These curves are still indispensable because supply and demand play basic roles in any economy, even one without free
markets; but these days economists refer to them less, because in a

291

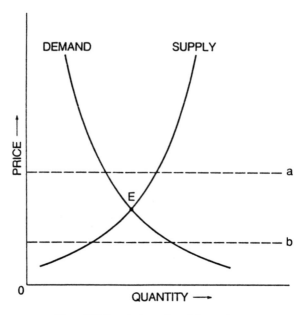

Figure 152 Classical supply and demand curves

mixed economy such as ours hundreds of variables play havoc with the curves. The government, by innumerable stratagems, keeps many prices far above or below what they would be in a free market. Organized labor pushes up wages, and companies pass the increases along to prices, in what Arthur M. Okun of the Brookings Institution calls "the invisible handshake." Oligopolists find subtle ways of getting together to avoid market fluctuations, something they must do to remain efficient.

In the 1960's, when Keynesian economics was still carrying all before it ("We are all Keynesians now," said Richard Nixon), many economists were impressed by the Phillips curve. This curve was first proposed in 1958 by the London economist Alban William Housego Phillips and applied to the U.S. economy in 1960 by neoKeynesians Paul A. Samuelson and Robert M. Solow. As you can see in Figure 153, a typical Phillips curve plots the inverse relation between unemployment and inflation. By taking into account the ability of labor and business to administer prices, the Phillips curve indicates that the double goals of full employment and price stability are not compatible in a mixed economy. Full employment (F) is attainable only at the cost of steady inflation. Stable prices (zero inflation) are impossible without high unemployment (U).

292

Figure 153 The Phillips curve

What to do? The best we can hope for, implies the curve, is to find a reasonable trade-off that does the minimum amount of harm. If prices rise too high, let a recession pull them down. If too many people are out of work, let inflation restore their jobs. With luck a government may find a point on the curve where "normal" unemployment will combine with an acceptable mild inflation of, say, 4 or 5 percent per year.

While economists were arguing about the "cruel dilemma" posed by the Phillips curve—the difficulty of finding a trade-off that would not lead to either a deep recession or a galloping inflation—a funny thing happened. During the late 1950's and early 1960's the economy got itself into the mysterious state of "stagflation" where, contrary to the curve, unemployment and inflation began to rise simultaneously. The Phillips curve started to disintegrate.

Keynesians struggled to rescue the curve. It was soon obvious that there is no such thing as a Phillips curve that is stable in the short run. The curve can be drawn dozens of ways, depending on what variables (including psychological expectations) are taken into account, and it varies widely from time to time and place to place. Is there a Phillips curve that is stable in the long run? Some say yes, some say no. Even if there is, economists disagree on how

293

to apply it. Should the government try somehow to slide up and down the curve, with inflation and unemployment fluctuating like a seesaw? Should it try "looping" around the curve in various risky ways?

According to Keynesians, a force called demand-pull tries to twist the curve into a vertical straight line, while another force called cost-push tries to twist it into a horizontal line. The long-run curve compromises with a steep downward slope. What is needed, of course, is some way of shifting the entire curve back down and to the left to allow trade-offs that will not lead to social chaos. Some economists, for example John Kenneth Galbraith, believe this can be done only by combining fiscal and monetary policies with wage and price controls. Nothing could be worse says Milton Friedman. In Friedman's monetarist view the long-run Phillips curve is a vertical line at the "natural rate" of unemployment, and any tradeoff effort to reduce unemployment below that line will set off an explosive inflation.

The Phillips curve, Daniel Bell wrote in 1980 (summarizing earlier remarks by Solow), "provided more employment for economists . . . than any public-works program since the construction of the Erie Canal." If unemployment is plotted against inflation for the 1960's, the result is a reasonably smooth curve. But if the same chronological plotting is done for the 1970's, as the U.S. economy drifted deeper into stagflation, the result is what the Wonnacotts, in their textbook *Economics,* call a "mess." Today the Phillips curve has become little more than an out-of-focus symbol of the fact that inflation and unemployment are not independent evils but are functionally linked in complex ways that nobody is yet able to understand.

Now, as a result of the upsurge of interest in "supply-side" economics, the curve of the hour is a brand-new one called, with strangely resonant overtones, the Laffer curve. Arthur B. Laffer is a 41-year-old professor of business at the University of Southern California. The curve was named and first publicized by Jude Wanniski, a former writer for *The Wall Street Journal,* in his bible of supply-side theory, confidently titled *The Way the World Works.* Figure 154 shows how Wanniski orients the Laffer curve at the beginning of his Chapter 6.

Is it not a thing of beauty bare? As any child can see from inspecting the curve's lower end, if the government drops its tax rate to nothing it gets nothing. And if it raises its tax rate to 100 percent, it also gets nothing. Why? Because in that case nobody

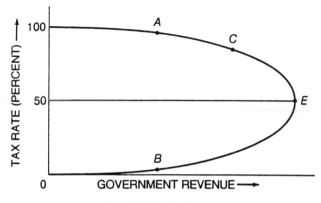
Figure 154 The Laffer curve

will work for wages. If all income went to the state, people would revert to a barter economy in which a painter paints a dentist's house only if the dentist caps one of the painter's teeth.

The Laffer curve gets more interesting when we slide along its arm toward the center. At point A, where taxes are not quite 100 percent, people will find it to their benefit to take some of their income in taxable wages. At point B the economy hums along with unfettered high production, but because tax rates are low the government gets the same small amount it would get if taxes were at A.

Now look at point E at the extreme right of the curve. That is where the tax rate maximizes government revenue. If taxes fall below E, that may stimulate production, but it obviously diminishes government revenue. Because E, by definition, is the point of maximum revenue, the government also must get less if taxes rise above E. The supply-siders stress many reasons for this being so. Some rich people find it unprofitable to work as productively as before. Some escape from excessive tax burdens by finding unproductive "shelters." Some even move to another country where taxes are low. If the government is relying on high taxes for welfare programs, millions of people are encouraged not to work at all. Why work if you can get almost the same income from welfare? Big corporations spend less on research and development. Entrepreneurs, the backbone of dynamic growth, are less willing to take risks. As a result of these factors and others, the economy becomes sluggish and tax revenues decline.

It is important to understand, Wanniski tells us, that E is not necessarily at the 50 percent level, although it could be. The shape of the Laffer curve obviously changes with circumstances. Thus, in time of war, when people and business are persuaded that a sacrificial effort is essential, they are willing to accept a high tax rate while they keep production booming. In peacetime they are less altruistic.

Now, the heart of the supply-side argument is the conviction that our current economy is somewhere near C, far too high on the Laffer curve. Lowering taxes (which some supply-siders believe calls for huge cuts in welfare spending) will give the supply side of the economy such a shot in the arm that the U.S. will slide down the Laffer curve to point E, perhaps not right away but soon. Tax revenues eventually will rise enough to take care of increased funding of the military, stagflation will end, dynamic growth will begin, the budget will be balanced by 1984 and the American dream will regain its luster.

Of course, supply and demand are always intertwined, but the supply-siders call themselves supply-siders in order to emphasize how they differ from neo-Keynesians. John Maynard Keynes stressed the importance of maintaining demand by minimum-wage laws and welfare payments. The Lafferites turn this around and stress the importance of stimulating supply. With the government off the back of business production will soar, new inventions will be made, more people will be employed and real wages will rise. Everyone benefits, particularly the poor, as prosperity trickles down from the heights.

The second book to gild the virtues of Lafferism is George Gilder's *Wealth and Poverty*. The title intentionally plays on the title of Henry George's best seller *Progress and Poverty*, which created a stir late in the 19th century by recommending the abolition of all taxes except a single tax on land. Gilder's book is more impassioned than Wanniski's. "Regressive taxes help the poor!" Gilder exclaims on page 188. William Safire once described capitalism as the "good that can come from greed." Gilder is furious when people talk like that; he finds capitalism motivated by the good that comes from "giving." By this he means that the best way to give the poor what they want, particularly the unemployed young men and women of minority groups, is to leave the free market alone so that the economy will start growing again.

The trouble with the Laffer curve is that, like the Phillips curve, it is too simple to be of any service except as the symbol of a concept. In the case of the Laffer curve the concept is both ancient and trivially true—namely that when taxes are too high they are counterproductive. The problem is how to define "too high." No economist has the foggiest notion of what a Laffer curve really looks like except in the neighborhood of its end points. Even if economists did know, they would not know where to put the economy on it. Neoconservative Irving Kristol, defending supply-side economics in *Commentary,* writes that he cannot say where we are on the Laffer curve, but he is sure we are "too far up." President Reagan's across-the-board tax cuts are, he says, just what we need in order to slide the economy toward point E.

To bring Laffer's curve more into line with the complexities of a mixed economy dominated by what Galbraith likes to call the "technostructure," and also with other variables that distort the curve, I have devised what I call the neo-Laffer (NL) curve. The NL curve is shown in Figure 155. Observe that near its end points this lovely curve closely resembles the old Laffer curve, proving that it was not a totally worthless first approximation. As the curve moves into the complexities of the real world, however, it enters what I call the "technosnarl." In this region I have based the curve on a sophisticated statistical analysis (provided by Persi Diaconis, a statistician at Stanford University) of the best available data for the U.S. economy over the past 50 years. Since the data are represented on the graph by a swarm of densely packed points, the actual shape of the curve is somewhat arbitrary. Nevertheless, it dramatizes a number of significant insights.

Consider any value r on the revenue axis within the segment directly below the technosnarl. A vertical line through r intersects the snarl at multiple points. These points represent values on the tax-rate axis that are most likely to produce revenue r. Note that this also applies to the maximum value of r, producing multiple points E on the technosnarl. In brief, more than one tax rate can maximize government revenue.

Consider any value t on the tax-rate axis within the segment directly to the left of the technosnarl. A horizontal line through t also intersects the snarl at multiple points. These points represent values on the revenue axis that are most likely to result from tax rate t.

Note that at some intersection points lowering taxes from a given tax rate will lower revenue, and that at other points for the same tax rate it will raise revenue. Even if we could determine at which point to put the economy, it is not clear from the snarl just what fiscal and monetary policies would move the economy fastest along the curve to the nearest point E.

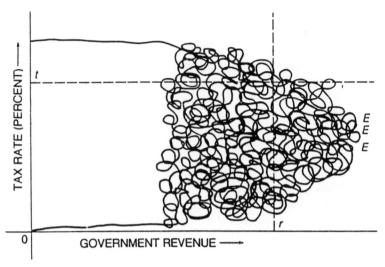

Figure 155 The neo-Laffer (NL) curve

Like the old Laffer curve, the new one is also metaphorical, though clearly a better model of the real world. Since it is a statistical reflection of human behavior, its shape constantly changes, like the Phillips curve, in unpredictable ways. Hence the curve is best represented by a motion picture that captures its protean character. Because it takes so long to gather data and even longer to analyze all the shift parameters, by the time an NL curve is drawn it is out of date and not very useful. I have been told in confidence, however, by one of Jack Anderson's more reliable informants that the Smith Richardson Foundation has secretly funded a multimillion-dollar project at Stanford Research International to study ways of improving the construction of NL curves. It is possible that with better software, using the fast Cray computer at the Lawrence Livermore Laboratory, one will be able to assign current probability values to the multiple intersection points. If one can do so, the NL curve could become a valuable forecasting tool for rational Federal decisions.

The Lafferites combine supreme self-confidence with a supremely low opinion of their detractors. Of the 18 economists who have won Nobel prizes, only two, Milton Friedman and Gunnar Myrdal, appear in the index of *The Way the World Works*. Not even Alan Greenspan, now of the abandoned "old right," gets a mention. You might suppose that, since Friedman and Wanniski are both mentors to conservatives, Wanniski would have a high opinion of Friedman. Not so. Wanniski goes to great lengths in his book to explain why three famous economic models—Marxian, Keynesian and Friedmanian—are all wrong. They cannot even explain why the economy crashed in 1929.

There is now an enormous literature on the many causes of the crash, much of it written by eminent economists. We can throw it all away. Wanniski has figured out the real reason. There would have been nothing wrong with the stock market if Herbert Hoover had just left it alone. Instead he and Congress made a stupid political blunder. Writes Wanniski: "The stock market Crash of 1929 and the Great Depression ensued because of the passage of the Smoot-Hawley Tariff Act of 1930."

How did it happen that the crash occurred in October of the previous year? It is simple. The stock market, says Wanniski, anticipated the dire consequences of the coming restraints on free trade. Not all supply-siders agree. Jack Kemp, the New York congressman who coauthored the Kemp–Roth tax bill (which paved the way for Reagan's fiscal program), is one who does. In Kemp's rousing book *An American Renaissance,* he assures us that Wanniski has "demonstrated beyond any reasonable doubt" the truth of his remarkable discovery.

What do professional economists make of radical supply-side theory? Most of them, including the most conservative, regard it in much the same way as astronomers regard the theories of Immanuel Velikovsky. To Galbraith it is "a relatively sophisticated form of fraud." Walter W. Heller has likened it to laetrile, and Solow terms it "snake oil." Vice-president Bush has called it "voodoo economics." Herbert Stein labeled it "punk economics" (as in "punk rock"), and Martin Feldstein described it as "excess rhetorical baggage." Nevertheless, the books by Wanniski, Gilder and Kemp are said to have much influence in the current Administration.

Lafferites enjoy heaping praise on one another. Laffer, the hero of Wanniski's book, is quoted on the back of the paperbound edition as saying: "In all honesty, I believe it is the best book on economics ever written." Kristol, on the front cover, is more restrained. He thinks it is "the best economic primer since Adam Smith." Gilder asserts Wanniski "has achieved an overnight influence of nearly Keynesian proportions." Gilder has been greeted with similar euphoria. David Stockman, President Reagan's budget director, has hailed *Wealth and Poverty* as "Promethean in its intellectual power and insight. It shatters once and for all the Keynesian and welfare-state illusions that burden the failed conventional wisdom of our era."

How puzzled the President must be by the violent clash between his old friend Friedman and his Lafferite advisers! (The clash is not only over Friedman's monetary views but also over his distaste for the supply-side "gold bugs" who are urging an immediate return to the gold standard.) In the business section of *The New York Times*, Wanniski's attack on Friedman was vitriolic. The burden of it is that although Friedman is "barely five feet tall," he "weighs" so much that he is now an enormous "deadweight burden" on the backs of Menachem Begin, Margaret Thatcher, Ronald Reagan and the U.S. economy.

Will the Lafferism of the Administration succeed, or will it, as many economists fear, eventually plunge the nation into higher inflation and higher unemployment? Economists cannot know. The technosnarl is too snarly. The idle rich might not invest their tax savings, as Lafferites predict, but might spend it on increased conspicuous consumption. The hardworking poor and middle class might decide to work less productively, not more. Big corporations and conglomerates might do little with their tax savings except acquire other companies.

Of course, ideologues of all persuasions think they know exactly how the economy will respond to the Administration's strange mixture of Lafferism and monetarism. Indeed, their self-confidence is so vast, and their ability to rationalize so crafty, that one cannot imagine any scenario for the next few years, that they would regard as falsifying their dogma. The failure of any prediction can always be blamed on quirky political decisions or unforeseen historical events. It is inconceivable, for example, that Friedman would consider the triple-digit inflation in Israel or the recent riots in Britain or high U.S. stagflation in 1983 as suggesting the slightest blemish on his monetarist views even though he enthusiastically supported Begin, Thatcher and Reagan, and all three have in turn been strongly influenced by Friedman's brand of monetarism.

As for the Lafferites, they have all kinds of outs in case Reagan's policies lead to disaster. Some will blame it on Friedman. Others may follow an escape plan mapped out by William F. Buckley. Although the Administration's tax and budget cuts have been called the biggest in American history, Buckley thinks both cuts are not big enough. "The trouble with the Reagan tax cuts," he wrote in *National Review* (July 24), "is (*a*) they are insufficient, and insufficiently targeted; and (*b*) the cuts in the budget are equally insufficient. . . . You cannot make long-range, significant cuts by concentrating on only a single one-third of the budget. It is the equivalent of saying you are going to lose weight by exercising only your right leg."

One can hope that President Reagan will not try to reconcile these conflicting conservative views by resorting to astrology. This possibility is not quite as remote as one might think. In an interview with Angela Fox Dunn the President said he followed the daily advice for his sign in the syndicated horoscope of Carroll Righter. Born on February 6, Reagan is an Aquarian. "I believe you'll find," he told Dunn, "that 80 percent of the people in New York's Hall of Fame are Aquarians."

President Reagan and his wife Nancy have for many years been personal friends of both Righter (who advises Gloria Swanson and other Hollywood figures) and the astrologer Jeane Dixon, who lives in Washington. "I'm not considered one of his advisers," Dixon cryptically told newspaper columnist Warren Hinckle, "but I advise him." Joyce Jillson, who writes a syndicated astrology column for *The Chicago Tribune* and has among her clients several Hollywood studios and multinational corporations, says that in 1980 Reagan aides paid her $1,200 for horoscopes on eight prospective vice-presidential candidates. The White House communications director has, however, called her a liar. Michael Kramer writes in *New York Magazine:* "Ronald Reagan, says Ronald Reagan, is a nice, well-intentioned man who loves his family, likes to consult his horoscope before making major decisions, and cries when he watches *Little House on the Prairie.*"

Will the President seek help from the zodiac in trying to decide whether to follow Friedman or Laffer or someone else? One may never know. As the Yale economist William Nordhaus put it (*The New York Times*, August 9, 1981): "We can only hope that supply-side economics turns out to be laetrile rather than thalidomide."

Edible Workers (excerpt)

The more that one studies human nature, the plainer it seems that the one crying need of civilization is Edible Workers. It is only when toilers are edible that they never grow old. At present the employer has no great financial incentive to keep his men ruddy and plump, and in fresh, sunny workrooms. At present there is suffering when he suddenly discharges his men. How happy a good employer would be with appetizing young workers whom it really paid him well to keep healthy when business was good, and whom he could lay off when he liked without anyone's suffering. In fact, it would be the other way round—there would be public rejoicing, and the employer would become a benefactor when he laid off his labor, and when nice young edible workers were sold at a discount. The unemployment problems of today would be instantly solved. In hard times there would be no more bread lines, but feasting instead.

Joan Beck

Modest Proposals on Health Costs

Washington is awash with schemes to keep rising health-care costs from giving the economy pernicious anemia. But one idea the politicos haven't proposed was sent to me last week by a reader of this column.

Money for big medical bills should be collected on a voluntary and anonymous basis, he suggested, like the pleas the media now make occasionally for a baby who needs a liver transplant or a Third World tot who must be flown here for heart surgery.

A critically ill person who had no friends or supporters would be left to die untreated—and good riddance—according to the reader's plan. Nice people would have their medical costs underwritten by sympathetic contributors and would get well. So everyone would be motivated to be good and kind to others, lest they fall ill and need financial help. And *voilà,* the nation soon would be populated only by the good and the helpful.

So complicated has the financing of health care become that it's hard to tell the bizarre and bogus from what would be called, in any other industry, imaginative marketing. A hospital in Las Vegas, for example, has offered chances on a Caribbean trip to patients who check in on weekends when plenty of empty beds are available.

The state of Florida has put out a "shopper's guide" to gallbladder surgery that lists charges made by hospitals throughout the state for surgical and other expenses. The purpose is to start some price competition, encourage patients to shop around and gradually force prices down.

The Reagan Administration seems to waver between pushing free-market strategies and considering prospective-payment programs, which are essentially bureaucratic price-fixing. But it hasn't even begun to tap either regulatory solutions or free-market strategies that could bring hospital costs down. For example:

- Tobacco companies could be required to include in every pack of cigarets a coupon that could be saved and later cashed in for 20 cents worth of lung-cancer surgery or chemotherapy as needed. That could substantially reduce the taxes and insurance premiums we all pay for extra medical care for smokers.

- Hospitals could be encouraged to develop do-it-yourself options for patients. Patients who are willing to walk instead of ride to the operating room, bring their own brown-bag lunch, make their own beds, and insert their own IVs could get reduced rates.

- Like airlines, hospitals could offer two or three classes of care—an idea already under some discreet discussion. Economy-class hospital patients would have to stand in line to check in, would get narrower-than-usual hospital beds packed elbow-to-elbow together, have to eat airline-type meals, and stow their personal belongings under their beds, but would pay less than those who went first class.

- Like car dealers selling '82 models when '83s are already in stock, hospitals could have end-of-the-model-year closeout sales of discontinued therapies and last year's model sutures, bandages, pacemakers, and antibiotics.

- Discounters could start high-volume, cut-rate hospitals where all treatment and surgery are priced 20 per cent or more below usual. Big-name designer surgeons with unbooked time could sell their surplus surgery at bulk rate to the discounters. By buying appendectomies, heart bypasses, and other operations by the lot, discounters could also pass on savings to patients.

- Like the airlines frequent-flyer programs, patients could accumulate points for minor treatments and surgeries that could be saved and traded in for a free operation of their choice—a face lift, perhaps, or a tummy tuck.

- Like retailers' white sales, hospitals could offer seasonal specials to help even out patient loads and keep empty beds at a minimum. Patients who are willing to be treated for pneumonia in July instead of February, for example, or skiers who break legs in August instead of January would get a break in price. Disease-of-the-month specials would enable hospitals to mass-produce treatments and pass savings on to patients.

- Pharmaceutical houses and hospital-supply companies could provide lower-cost seconds and irregulars. Misshaped pills (provided they contain proper ingredients), lopsided bandages, and hospital gowns in discontinued patterns could give patients substantial savings.

- Twofers, his-and-hers operations, special family rates, free gifts (limo ride to the hospital, your choice of flowering plant, free table setting of china) with every admission and one-day sales extravaganzas to encourage impulse treatment are just a few other successful marketing strategies that could shake up hospital financing and change the way hospitals, as we know them, do business.

Jonathan Swift

A Modest Proposal

For Preventing the Children of Poor People
in Ireland from Being a Burden to Their Parents
or Country, and for Making Them Beneficial
to the Public (excerpt)

It is a melancholy object to those who walk through this great town, or travel in the country, when they see the streets, the roads, and cabin-doors, crowded with beggars of the female sex, followed by three, four, or six children, all in rags, and importuning every passenger for an alms. These mothers, instead of being able to work for their honest livelihood, are forced to employ all their time in strolling to beg sustenance for their helpless infants. . . .

I think it is agreed by all parties, that this prodigious number of children in the arms, or on the backs, or at the heels of their mothers, and frequently of their fathers, is, in the present deplorable state of the kingdom, a very great additional grievance; and therefore whoever could find out a fair, cheap, and easy method of making these children sound, useful members of the commonwealth, would deserve so well of the public, as to have his statue set up for a preserver of the nation.

But my intention is very far from being confined to provide only for the children of professed beggars; it is of a much greater extent, and shall take in the whole number of infants at a certain age, who are born of parents in effect as little able to support them, as those who demand our charity in the streets. . . .

I shall now, therefore, humbly propose my own thoughts, which I hope will not be liable to the least objection.

I have been assured by a very knowing American of my acquaintance in London, that a young healthy child, well nursed, is, at a year old, a most delicious, nourishing, and wholesome food, whether stewed, roasted, baked, or boiled; and I make no doubt that it will equally serve in a fricassee or a ragout.

I do therefore humbly offer it to public consideration, that of the hundred and twenty thousand children . . . computed, twenty thousand may be reserved for breed, . . . the remaining hundred thousand may, at a year old, be offered in sale to the persons of quality and fortune through the kingdom; always advising the mother to let them suck plentifully in the last month, so as to render them plump and fat for a good table. A child will make two dishes at an entertainment for friends; and when the family dines alone, the fore or hind quarter will make a reasonable dish, and, seasoned with a little pepper or salt, will be very good boiled. . . .

I have reckoned, upon a medium, that a child just born will weigh twelve pounds, and in a solar year, if tolerably nursed, will increase to twenty-eight pounds. . . .

Infants' flesh will be in season throughout the year . . . ; the skin . . . , artificially dressed, will make admirable gloves for ladies, and summer boots for fine gentlemen. . . .

I can think of no one objection, that will possibly be raised against this proposal. . . . I have . . . no other motive than the public good of my country, by advancing our trade, providing for infants, relieving the poor, and giving some pleasure to the rich.

Kenneth E. Boulding

The Green Stamp Plan (excerpt)

There are a number of possible methods of population control none of which are particularly acceptable at the moment. What might be called the "Irish solution" involves creating a rather deliberate housing shortage and strict family territoriality, so that a couple cannot marry and begin to have children until the old folks die off and leave them the farm. In the Irish case, those who are unable to find a niche in Irish society tend to emigrate. This, however, is clearly not a solution which can be applied to the world as a whole, even in these days of space travel, as it is very clear that the earth is the only decent piece of real estate in a very long way. Another possible but quite unacceptable solution is infanticide, carried out by government order. One could even invent science fiction variants of this such as the death lottery, in which a big holiday would be held every year to kill off exactly enough people to bring the population back to equilibrium. My own suggestion as given in THE MEANING OF THE TWEN-TIETH CENTURY (Harper & Row, New York, 1964) is some-times called the "Green Stamp Plan." According to this plan every boy and girl at adolescence is given say 110 green stamps, 100 of which entitle them to have one legal child. We then set up a market in these stamps so that the philoprogenitive and the rich can buy them from the phoboprogenitive (those who do not want to have children) and the poor. The price of these green stamps will automatically achieve a population equilibrium. If the whole society is highly philoprogenitive, the price will be high and that will check the birthrate; if the society is on the whole selfishly concerned with its own pleasure and unwilling to raise children, the price will be low and that will encourage births. As an incidental benefit, the rich will have loads of children and become poor, and the poor will have few children and become rich. If the number of illegal children rises, then the number of stamps received at adolescence will be reduced. The penalty for having an illegal child obviously would have to be some form of sterilization. This modest and humane proposal, so much more humane indeed than that of Swift, who proposed that we eat the surplus babies, has been received with so many cries of anguish and horror, that it illustrates the extraordinary difficulty of applying rational principles to processes involving human generation.

My plan illustrates well the use of the market as a regulator of the great aggregates of society which must be regulated by social means but, at the same time, with a minimum of interference with the behavior of individuals by outside coercion. If you contrast my Green Stamp Plan for population control with what seems to be the only real alternative, the legal limitation of all families to two children, with some exceptions in the case of favored and powerful people, the former, which employs the relatively impersonal pressure of the market, seems much to be preferred to the latter, which calls for the direct coercive intervention of the state, for certainly nobody wants a government inspector coming around and telling him how many children he can have. One sees the same problem in the contrast between the use of the market for the allocation of consumer goods and the imposition of direct rationing which creates administrative problems of an almost insoluble nature and is only tolerable under conditions of extreme social stress, as in war or revolution.

Martin S. Feldstein

'Twas a Night in the Sixties

'Twas a night in the sixties
And all through the land
Unemployment was falling
Inflation in hand.

The stock market was rising,
Without any care,
In hopes a Dow thousand
Soon would be there.

The Keynesians were snuggled
Secure in their Chairs,
While visions of multipliers
Allayed all their cares.

Paul with his textbook
And Art with his gap
Had settled their brains
For a long postwar nap.

When out in the land
There arose such a clatter,

This study extends earlier work by C. C. Moore, to whom my debt is obvious. It was presented at the 1980 Harvard Economics Department Student-Faculty Christmas party. Although I am always grateful to the National Science Foundation and National Bureau of Economic Research, neither organization provided any financial support for this project.

A voice that was crying
That money could matter.

Away from their desks
They flew in a flash
To see who was claiming
Such power for cash.

They looked at their models
With equations precise,
That gave semblance of proof
To conclusions so nice.

When what to their wondering
Eyes should appear
But a miniature sleigh
With eight tiny reindeer

With a little old driver
Who was having such fun
They knew in a moment
It must be Milton.

More numerous than eagles
His supporters they came
And he whistled and shouted
And called them by name.

First John Say and then Hume,
Then Marshall and Mill,
Now Brunner and Meltzer
And Anna and Phil.

From the U. of Chicago
To Minneapolis–St. Paul
Then dash away! Dash away!
Dash away all!

As economic theories
With which economists play
When they meet with an obstacle
Assume it away,

So off to the journals,
Their papers they flew,
With monetarist theorems,
Rational expectations too.

And even in Cambridge
Was heard the new truth,
The theorems and lemmas
Of each little proof.

The Keynesian thinkers
Were spinning around
When onto the scene,
Milton came with a bound.

He was dressed all in gold
From his head to his foot
And his ideas were polished
And ready to put.

"Velocity's stable,
$M1$ and $M2$,
Which shows what the Fed
Shouldn't be trying to do."

"That curve by Phillips
It really is straight
And the cost of funds
Is the *real* interest rate."

He wrote many a word,
And with evidence too.
At the NBER
His volumes they grew.

His ideas how simple.
He puts them so well.
It would be no wonder
When he got his Nobel.

A wink of his eye
And a nod of his head

Soon gave Keynesians to know
They had something to dread.

Then he sprang to his sleigh
To his team gave a whistle
And away they all flew
Like the down of a thistle.

But I heard him exclaim
As he drove out of sight,
"Keep freedom for all,
And keep money tight."

Alan S. Blinder

Christmas, Revisited

'Twas the month after Christmas, and all through the
   states
Not a factory was stirring. They'd all closed their gates.
The prime rate was kept by the Fed rather high,
In hopes that inflation would wither and die.
The workers were nestled all snug in bread lines,
While visions of safety nets danced through their minds.

And the House and the Senate, with little remorse,
Had just settled their brains upon staying the course.
When out in the land there arose such a clatter,
They sprang to their polls to see what was the matter.

Away to the White House they flew like wild geese,
Tore open the door and knocked over Ed Meese.
The latest bleak forecast of real GNP
Had shaken their faith in supply-side theory.
Then what should be seen above the high risers,
But a free-market sleigh pulled by pin-striped advisers.
And a tall handsome driver was seated upon.
They knew in a moment it must be St. Ron.

More cheerful than cherubs, his economists came,
And he whistled and shouted, and called them by name:
"Now, Laffer! now, Gilder! now, Stockman and Regan!
On, Feldstein! on, Kudlow! Wanniski and Sprinkel!
From the depths of the trough to the top of the Dow!
Recovery, recovery, recovery now!"

They had so much faith in the virtue of markets,
They invisibly handled their sleigh, and then parked it.
Then up to the rooftop the economists trudged,
To do it with mirrors. But the world hardly budged.
Then, after a while, they saw that recession
Was slowly but surely becoming depression.
They were desperately searching to find a way out.
When in walked St. Ron, showing few signs of doubt.

He came in surrounded by bakers and deavers,
With clothes tailored by all the nation's best weavers.
He carried tight money and huge guided missiles:
The things that had helped still the factory whistles.
His eyes—how they twinkled! He smiled serenely!
His cheeks were like roses. His hair was groomed cleanly.

But yet he was cross and impatient with voodoo.
He looked at them sternly and said, "What would you
    do?"
To a man they replied with a graceful maneuver,
"Let's follow the policies used by Herb Hoover!"
Then his broad friendly face and his trim little belly,
Broke out in a laugh, like a beanful of jelly.

"Reaganomics is working. Is that what you mean?
If they can't afford bread, let them eat jelly beans.
We can't pay them welfare. The rich can't afford it.
Free market initiative. We must reward it."

A wink of his eye and a twist of his head,
Made the congressmen know they had something to dread.
So quickly they scurried right back to the Hill,
Where they couldn't agree on a puny jobs bill.

The President stood there and surveyed the nation.
He smiled as he thought how he'd vanquished inflation.
Then he sprang to his sleigh, to his team gave a whistle,
And rewarded each one with a new MX missile.
And I heard him exclaim, as he mounted his horse:
"Merry Christmas to all, and to all a staid course."

315

Index

Adams, Franklin P., 86, 99
Aesop, 86–87, 101
Afterlife, 89; advantages of funerals, 164–66; choice and scarcity in Heaven, 121; harp-playing or swimming,121; time and the hereafter, 122, 124. *See also* Scarcity; Time
Arbuthnot, John, 87, 130, 164–66
Aristotle, 168, 176, 219
Atkinson, Brooks, 169, 195
Auth, Tony, 40, 72
Automobiles: love of, 128; price of Mauswagens, 289; traffic congestion and options, 147

Balanced budget, 273; amendment defined, 48
Banana. *See* Recession
Barzun, Jacques, 87, 107
Bastiat, Frédéric, 129–30, 153–57, 244
Beck, Joan, 303–5
Bell, John Fred, 37
Belloc, Hilaire, xiv, 217, 220
Benefits and costs of toothbrushing, 180
Bentley, Edmund Clerihew, 2, 13
Bergstrom, T.C., 170, 208–9
Bevington, Helen, 2, 12
Bierce, Ambrose (pseud. G.J.), 70,

86, 100, 168, 172–73, 218, 224–25
Billboard, Interstate-85, 1, 16
Blinder, Alan S., 169, 179–84, 246, 314–15
Blough, Roy, 71
Breeze, Hector, 129, 150–52
Bronfenbrenner, Martin, 2, 17–18
Buchwald, Art, 6, 130, 158–59
Budget: defined, 116; the several-year, 116; like Sisyphus, 223. *See also* Balanced budget
Burke, Edmund, 16
Boulding, Kenneth E., 39, 63–66, 243, 246, 257, 308–9

Carlyle, Thomas, 15, 88
Choice, 96, 173; cost of, 167; and time, 167; of a wife, 205
Clemens, Samuel Langhorne (pseud. Mark Twain), 40, 80–81, 244, 261
Clotfelter, Caroline Postelle, xiii, xv, xvii–xix
Common good, 86, 101; the worst did something for the, 102
Competition: foreign, 129, 155; in the price of health care, 303
Consumers: and automobiles, 144; bargain-minded, 246; not buying in Mouseville, 77;

319

Consumers (*continued*)
defined, 48; importance of,
100; sacrifice of, 153–54
Consumer's surplus, 45
Cost. *See* Opportunity cost
Cow: cash, 218; device for production of milk, 142; endorsed,
228; as hostile container, 141;
negotiable, 218; promissory,
218, 231; similarity to a napkin, 228; tendered in payment
of income tax, 228–29
Currency: and banking schools,
218; cattle as, 226; greenness
of, 241; as international reserve, 241, 287; Mouseville's
rallod, 286–87

Daumier, Honoré-Victorin, 217–
18, 223
Dawn, defined, 172
Day: defined, 172; haggard look
at five o'clock, 196
Day, Clarence, 128, 141–43, 246,
302
Debt: height of, and years to
count, 245; in thousand-dollar
bills, 245
Deficit: is a, a deficit? 245; of the
1980s, 246; the structural, 285
Demand, 100; for artificial light,
156; effective, 254; for gold,
232
Depression, 89; the Great Cat of
the early 1930s, 78. *See also*
Recession
Deregulation: explained, 49; of
the market, 246
Desire: for Bibles, 109; for a fifth,
107; for hay, 108
Dickinson, Emily, 87–88, 110
Diminishing marginal utility: of
guilty and uneasy moments in
bed, 174–75; of prayer, 123
Dismal science, 4, 15, 88. *See also*
Economics

Ecclesiastes (*King James*), 238
Econometrician: budding, 83; like
a farmer, 68

Econometrics, sausages and, 69
Economice. *See* Economists
Economic forecasters: like six
Eskimoes in one bed, 71; compared to soothsayers, 73
Economic humor: book of, not
very long, xiii; costs and benefits of reading a collection of,
xiii; with a grain of salt, xvii; as
mathematical parodies, xiv
Economic policy: irrational expectations, 243; macroeconomic,
243. *See also* Fiscal policy
Economics: of the Afterlife, 121;
like a Brueghel painting, 19; of
brushing teeth, 179; as the dismal science, 4, 15; language of,
37–39; exercise in mathematics, xiv; basic principles of,
xviii; of sleeping, 208; tommyrot, 53
Economics teachers, 37, 262; as
sadists, 42; soporiferous, 42
Economists: agree on many
things, 5; never agree, 5; aversion to plain English, 25; break
out the Scotch, 284; brush their
teeth, 180; more cheerful than
cherubs, 314; clannishness, 3;
employment for, 294; end-to-
end, 1, 5, 38; compared to dentists and internists, 241; failings
of, 2; feeling of superiority, 3;
Hungarian, in large wooden
box, 6; introducing one, 4; lecture by, tax-deductible expense,
4; Math-econ most colorful of
Econ caste, 26, 31; love to
draw curves, 291; at their
mothers' knees, 245; by marriage, xvii; compared to sheep,
6; compared to teaching golf
pro, 7; one-armed, 5; play with
theories, 311
Employment and incomes, 252
End-to-end. *See* Economists
Equilibrium: and effective demand, 254; point, 291; of population, 308
Evoe. *See* Knox, Edmund George

Valpy
Exchange, foreign, as romantic as young love, 8
Externalities, defined, 206–7
Extrapolation, 40; and the shrinking Mississippi, 80; and soothsaying, 75

Fawcett, Millicent, 170, 210
Feldstein, Martin S., 246, 299, 310–14
Fiscal policy, 245, 283; while eating liverwurst, 285; not for sissies, 285. *See also* Economic policy; Macroeconomics
Franklin, Benjamin, 87, 129, 168, 238, 244, 268–72
Frost, Robert, 41, 82, 88, 115

G.J. *See* Bierce, Ambrose
Galbraith, John Kenneth, 3, 15, 38–39, 46–47, 70, 294, 297, 299
Gardner, Martin, 245, 291–301
Goldberg, Rube, 128, 140
Gordon, Scott, 88, 121
Government: into and out of the bedroom, 215; deficit finance and effective demand, 243, 253; finance, 278; fiscal deficits, 217–18; handouts, 150–51, 274; advantages of inefficiency on government's common stock issue, 279–81; -sponsored private profit (South Sea bubble), 127; -sponsored sex, the pill, and the pimp, 214–15, 256; and taxes, 244–45, 252

Hart, Johnny (John Lewis), 87, 106
Health care, 246; rising costs of, 303; closeout sales, do-it-yourself patient options, and disease-of-the-month, 304–5
Herbert, A.P., 218, 227–31, 244, 262–65
Holmes, Oliver Wendell, 39, 61, 85, 96
Huff, Darrell, 40, 75

Human capital theory, 180–81
Humorous writing about economics, xiv

Income: and the price of pins, 252; tax on, evaded, not avoided, 264; and toothbrushing, 181
Inflation, 257, 278, 280, 310, 314–15; and the price of bananas, 317; in the rallod, dnuop, cnarf, kram, aril, 289; cost of Aspen ski ticket as leading indicator of, 133; underlying rate explained, 50
Invention, 141; of the cow, 141; of the hen, 142; and monopoly of sunbeams, 160–61
Invisible hand, 126; defined, 85; and handshake, 292; the Priests of the Cult of the, 253; in the sexual marketplace, 211

Johnson, Larry, 246, 316

Kafoglis, Madelyn L., 170, 204–7
Kelly, Walt, 243–44, 258
Keynes, John Maynard, 49, 124, 241, 243, 288, 296
Keynesian, 246, 248–49, 292–93, 299–300, 310, 312–13; defined, 49; demand-pull and cost-push, 294; multiplier, 217; as a pejorative, 39
Knox, Edmund George Valpy (pseud. Evoe), 245, 276–77

Labor: division of, 91; new type of, 143
Laffer Curve, 245; explained, 294–96
Language of economics, 2, 25, 37–39, 42, 44, 291; compared to ambiguity and archaic construction of Bible, 46
Leacock, Stephen B., xiii, 16, 38–39, 44–45, 53–60, 88–89, 124–26, 217, 221–22, 244, 266–67
Leamer, Edward E., 40, 68–69
Leijonhufvud, Axel, 3, 24–35

Levine, Arthur S., 171, 211–15
Light, Christopher U., 243, 252–56
Linear programming, 66; marriage as a vector, 65
Lunch, no free, 168
Luxury: employment of the poor, 102; growth of, 100; life of, 101; marriage a taxable, 265

Machlup, Fritz, 70
Macroeconomics, xviii; defined, xviii; Macro-modl, 30; policy, 243. *See also* Economic policy
Macroeconomists, and choleric economy, 241
Mad Magazine, 37, 42
Malthus, Thomas, xiii–xiv, 5, 86, 88, 119–20, 245
Management: benefits of poor, and inefficiency on government equity, 281; Office of, and Budget, 285
Manchester, Harland, 129, 147–49
Mandeville, Bernard de, 87, 102–4
Marginal utility, 87. *See also* Diminishing marginal utility
Market(s): for green stamps, 309; for health care, 246; strategies to bring down health costs, 304; for textbooks, 145; virtue of free, 314–15; micro and macro perspectives, xviii
Market price, 110. *See also* Price
Market value: of a physicist, 204; of a wife's services, 207. *See also* Value
Marshall, Alfred, 39, 52, 145, 219, 311
Martial, Alfred, Unemployed, 219, 239–41
Mathematical economics: gets rid of readers, 39; a racket, 60; techniques of, with ridicule, 92
Mathematical economists: glossolalia of Math-Econ, 32
Maugham, W. Somerset, 238
Mencken, H.L., xiv, 1–2, 8–11

Microeconomics defined, xviii
Model(s): bad taste in mouth, 179; changes, cost of, 144; couple, 262; earnings and whiteness of teeth, 181; with equations, 311; modl-making in Econ tribe, 29; mother told me so, 179; 189 toothless exclusions from, 184; of toothbrushing, 181; woman's place in home, 204; working, 273
Monetarism defined, 49
Monetarist, 246, 248, 311–13, 315; view of long-run Phillips curve, 294
Money, 113, 125; biological analogues for, 239–41; greenness of, 241; and fathers, 237; invention of, 141; is, is not, a million or three, 236; lent, 234; sound of, 219; spent, 115, 133; voted, 237. *See also* Currency
Monopoly of sunbeams, 162; petition against, 162
Morgan Guaranty Trust Company, 40, 76–79, 245, 286–90
Musgrove, Philip, 169, 190–94

Nash, Ogden, 218–19, 234–35
National income, imaginary, 220
National Lampoon, 43
New Statesman. See *Statesman, New*
Nonperson, study of, xviii
North, Gary, 170, 201–6

Oliphant, Pat, 247, 317
Opportunity cost: of decision to work, 168; increasing, defined, 89; of listening, 37; of marriage to educated wife, 201–2

Parkinson, C. Northcote, 169, 185–89
Paton, William A., 244, 274–75
Payments, Balance of: the rallod gap, 287
Pennsylvania Gazette, 178
Petition: of Candlemakers, et al,

155; of Colliers and Cooks, et al, 160; of upholders (morticians), 164

Political Economy. *See* Economics

Pope, Alexander, 87, 105, 127, 132, 218, 232–33

Population control, 88, 246, 308

Poverty: and laziness, 176; of the Math-Econ, 31; not for the rich, 99; and surplus babies, 246

Powell, Dwane, 2, 14

Price: of cheese at thirty-five rallods to the nibble, 288; and the energy crisis, 158; every man's, 111, 114; of green stamps, 308; of legal children, 246; of pins, 252; of the sun, 156; two-tier cheese, 289

Profit: government sponsorship of private, 127; in owner's head, 116; and red ink, 116; South Sea scheme, 127; with an observant wife, 118

Protectionism, 154; against sun, 155

Punch, 218, 226

Quincey, Thomas de, 87, 108

Quinn, Jane Bryant, 70

Rational expectations, 312; defined, 50

Recession: banana, 50; the Great Cat of the early 1930s, 78; defined, 50; and depression, 315. *See also* Depression

Resources, distribution of sexual, 212–23

Robertson, Dennis H., 40, 67

Rogers, Will, 15

Ruff, Larry E., 124

Samuelson, Paul A., 39–40, 73, 145, 292, 310

Savings in book publishing, 145–46

Scarcity, 88; in Heaven, 89, 121–22; from plenty, 119; of sexual resources, 212

Schorr, Bill, 243, 248

Self-interest, xiv, 85, 125; of butcher, brewer, baker, 131

Sharpe, Myron E., 2, 19

Shaw, George Bernard, xiv, 3, 5, 16, 21–23, 39, 62, 86, 217

Siegfried, John J., 41, 83–84

Sloth, 105, 141; the golden-haired ground-, 141–42; compared to rust, 176

Smith, Adam, xiii–xiv, 8, 11, 45, 85–87, 89–91, 125, 127, 131, 239, 299

Soporifics, first law of, 209

Southern, Terry, 88, 111

South Sea Company, speculation in stock, 127

Spending, advantages of wasteful, to trade, 87

Statesman, New, 15

Stearns, Linhart, 245, 278–82

Stein, Gertrude, 219, 236–37, 245

Stein, Herbert, xiii–xv, 1, 4–7, 39, 48–51, 243, 249–51, 299

Stigler, George J., xiii, 85, 92, 124, 128, 144–46

Stock market, 74, 127–28, 133, 139–40, 279, 310; "Red-White-and-Blue Chip" government equity, 245; South Sea scheme, 127, 132

Stoopnagle, Colonel. *See* Taylor, Frederick Chase

Sun, 129, 161, 197, 269, 272

Supply, 100; and demand, 291–92

Supply-side economics, 246, 294, 314; defined, 50; as laetrile, 301

Swift, Jonathan, 86–87, 129–30, 160–63, 244, 246, 259–60, 306–7, 309

Tastes, simple, 98, 111

Tax: and axe, 225; on capital gains, 136; collectors, 224; death and, 224; income, 263; on marriage and virtue, 265; on somebody else, 267; on sun-

Tax (*continued*)
  beams in catoptrical cookery,
  162; system simplified, 244; on
  shuttered windows, 244, 270;
  on vices and folly, 259
Taxation: grievous, 244; eternally
  lively, 8
Taxes: house rent and, 261;
  litmus test, 250; NIMBY, 88;
  "read my lips," 250
Taxpayers, desire of, for lower
  taxes, more services, 129
Taylor, Frederick Chase (pseud.
  Colonel Stoopnagle), 88, 116–8
Theory of Moral Sentiments, The,
  85
Time: choice, 167; constraints on,
  and the value of e, 190; dimensions of, in Heaven, 88, 121–
  22; spent in bed, sleeping, 176,
  209
Timothy (*King James*), 238
Trade: balance of, in impressions,
  221; the oldest profession, 210;
  for the public good, 131; the
  very wheel, 87, 102, 125
Trever, John, 244, 273
Twain, Mark. *See* Clemens, Samuel Langhorne
Turgot, Anne-Robert-Jacques, 16,
  38, 70

Unemployment, 245, 310;
  defined, 258; rates of, during
depression of 1930s, 245–46;
stagflation, 255; stopped by armaments, 276

Value: basis of, 125; of boredom,
  168; of Mouseville's cheese reserve, 288–89; "diamond-
  raisin" paradox of, explained,
  106; parody of paradox of, 87
Veblen, Thorstein, 3, 20
Vice: the poor, the wheel, and the
  trade, 102–3; taxed, 259
Viner, Jacob, 16, 38
Virtue, 104–5, 265

Wall Street Journal, The, 74,
  283–85
Wants, 96, 105. *See also* Desire
Wealth, 105, 176
Wealth of Nations, The, 8, 85,
  127, 145
Wicksteed, Philip H., 3, 21–22,
  87, 89, 109, 123, 168, 174–75
Wisconsin Securities Company,
  128, 133–39
Wordsworth, William, 88, 120
Work: defined, 168; elastic in de-
  mands on time, 185; night,
  195; Pinmakers out of, 254
Workers, 125; edible, 302; Fede-
  rated Grizzlies, 143

Yardeni, Edward E., 71

324